I t is a poor and weak society, indeed, that is not prepared to have its values and premises challenged. Indeed progress can only come where people have the ability to challenge the conventional way of doing things. This applies to planning more than to most aspects, since planning at once brings together the power of the local community in its democratic form; and the wishes, hopes and fears of individuals who may be affected. This is what makes planning such an explosive issue.

Nevertheless, planning conventions must be open to challenge as well, even on an overcrowded island such as ours. Firm planning regulations are necessary to stop over-development in unacceptable ways which damage our natural and human environment. But it is also absolutely vital that we never get ourselves caught in an inflexible planning structure which excludes human beings and their hopes and beliefs from the planning process.

I have been fascinated by the Tinker's Bubble experiment. It is "in my backyard". It has generated considerable and powerful feelings, including in my own village. But my judgment is, that after two or three years of this experiment, the outcome has been to add, not diminish the quality of life in our village as we have had to cope with different life-styles and different ways of looking at our world. It is for this reason that I have always supported the Tinker's Bubble experiment, even though it clearly falls outside the accepted planning regulations.

Simon Fairlie's book, which clearly incorporates, but is not exclusively built around, the Tinker's Bubble experiment, provides an alternative way of looking at things. I think many of the ideas that are contained in this book are harbingers of a new way of thinking about our world and ought to be influential in the future. I wish him and it well!

Paddy Ashdown MP

About the author

Simon Fairlie turned eighteen in 1968, then worked for twenty years as an agricultural labourer, building worker and stonemason before being ensnared by the computer and joining the editorial team at the *Ecologist* in 1990. *Low Impact Development*, originally published in 1996, was inspired by difficulties he experienced obtaining planning permission for Tinkers Bubble, a community smallholding in Somerset where he lived for ten years. He now works as the founding director of Chapter Seven and editor of *The Land* magazine, but makes his living by selling and teaching the use of Austrian scythes.

Low Impact Development

Planning and people in a sustainable countryside

Simon Fairlie

A report and guide prepared in association with
The Land is Ours

Second enlarged edition

JON CARPENTER

First edition published in 1996 by

Jon Carpenter Publishing, Alder House, Market Street, Charlbury OX7 3PH

Reprinted with minor revisions 1997

Second edition 2009

ISBN 978 1 906067 07 6

Printed in England by CPI Antony Rowe, Chippenham

I will arise and go now, and go to Innisfree
And a small cabin build there, of clay and wattles made:
Nine bean rows will I have there, a hive for the honey-bee
And live alone in the bee-loud glade.

W. B. YEATS

(From *The Lake Isle of Innisfree*, reprinted with permission from *T h e Collected Poems of W B Yeats.*)

What sort of law is this — what monstrous "law"
That makes a man demolish the house he built
With love on his own land?
The robin and the wren, the skylark too
Have leave to build, and love, and rear their young
In any trees, on ground, or where they will
Without the by-your-leave of chartered fools.
But you my son, and dear Maria too,
Albert and Rose, who love your little house
Must raze, pull down and totally destroy
The little house you built on your land:
Destroy the lares et penantes of a home.
This home of yours, my Dai, that must be razed
Will raise itself a cry that shall be heard
Across our land! Your home will be destroyed
To satisfy the whims of city fools,
The motor'd hordes that spew across our land.
The razing of your home will raze, my boy,
The wicked laws that caused it to be razed
For we shall do some razing of our own.
We'll raze these rules — and sack these men
And get a true law passed to save our land
From second-homers, speculators — those
Who look upon the sacred soul of Wales
As something to cash in on, to defile,
And give the right to any honest man
To build his own house on the land he owns.

JOHN SEYMOUR

(*You Snivelling Clerks – Lines to my Son on Hearing that he has been Told to Destroy his House.*)

ACKNOWLEDGEMENTS

The work has been carried out in co-operation with The Land is Ours — an organization calling for greater access to the land for all social classes — and has been funded by a number of groups and individuals. Submissions have been invited and received from a wide variety of organizations (listed in Appendix G) and from individuals too numerous to mention. The way I have used these submissions, and the conclusions I have drawn from them, are entirely my own responsibility.

My sincere thanks are due to the funders, to all contributors, and to those who have assisted in the preparation of this work by supplying information or photographs, by according interviews, by commenting on the text, or by contacting the author with their own individual planning story. I would like to extend personal thanks to Penny Ross, who provided me with a power point for my — alas! — mains-powered computer; Mike Zair, who fed the horses while I was plugged in; Emma Must, who gave me my first sentence; Chris Black, for his generosity and vision; the people of Tinker's Bubble; and the staff of Yeovil Public Library.

This book is dedicated to Jade.

CONTENTS

Introduction

PLANNING IS BORING. That, at any rate, is a view shared by many members of the public — even the planning magazines make jokes about the perceived dullness of the profession. Of course, planners themselves do not find it boring and can rabbit on for hours about 'material considerations' or 'Grampian conditions'. They sense that they are regarded as a race apart by more normal mortals: a queer grey-suited clique, living in its own world, something of a cross between between policemen and trainspotters.

This boringness — perceived or actual — may help to explain why the environmental movement in Britain has paid scant attention to the planning system over the last 20 years. Planners are the principal strategists, decision makers and enforcement officers of the Department of the Environment (DoE); it is they, more than anyone, who decide what our environment will look like, where people, animals and plants will live, how we use our land and how much concrete will be poured over it every year. And yet in all the vast literature that has emerged from the environmental movement in recent years there is barely one book that concentrates upon the nuts and bolts of the planning process from a green perspective.[1] Friends of the Earth, Britain's main multi-issue green lobbying organization, does not have a planning or land-use officer. Advocates of direct action are better known for their battles with the Department of Transport (DoT) than for chaining themselves to planning department doors or attempts to enliven public inquiries into local plans. It is hardly surprising then that planners, who like to see themselves as protectors of the environment, are often out of touch with the green movement and green ideas.

All those lengthy local authority notices in small print, tucked away amongst the small ads in the local paper, which most of us do not read, are descriptions of how our local environment is going to change. If, having passed them over, we find out too late that a line of trees is to be chopped down for an access road, or an Edwardian mansion is to be demolished to make way for a gaggle of bungalows, then who is to blame? The public do not have the time to examine every small-print proposal or make representations every week to the planning committee. Local planners on the other hand — who often shoulder the blame — are trying to balance different interests within the community as fairly as they can within the guidelines laid down by the DoE. They tend to get knocked from all sides — greens, developers and the DoE; as one senior planning officer put it to me, the profession is 'punch drunk'.

Small wonder then that planners tend to retreat into their bureaucratic carapace and rarely make a move which cannot be justified by lengthy jargon-ridden citations from national, regional and local policy documents. And small wonder, in turn, that many people find the planning process intransigent and unimaginative. If the environmental movement wishes to influence the development of our green and pleasant land before the point is reached when the only option left is to squat trees, then it needs to take a much more searching and inspired look at the way the system operates and press for changes which may not have to be enormous to achieve a significant effect. And if planners want to understand why their best efforts to protect the environment are so unappreciated, they should pay more attention to what the green movement — and Agenda 21, which is the outcome of 25 years of green lobbying — is saying.

The author of this report, like most other members of the public who do find planning fascinating, became interested in the planning system through fighting it. For nine years I lived in France in a self-built wooden shack on a smallholding, earning my living from agricultural work and building. When I returned to England, I found that I wasn't allowed to live in this way. Most rural residences were bought up by people who didn't work (and sometimes didn't even live) in the country, and planning permission to build a cabin on a piece of land was virtually unobtainable. When, with friends, I rented a house with a sizable garden on a country estate, we were thrown out after three years to make way for a golf course. I lived in a van for two years, and eventually, with some other people, bought a bare-land smallholding. To accommodate ourselves we pitched tents on our land.

In the two years since we moved onto our land, we have been through almost the entire gamut of planning procedure: committee decision, enforcement order, stop notice, Article 4 application, Section 106 agreement, appeal, call in by the Secretary of State and statutory review in the High Court. All this for seven tents! Insofar as I have any expertise in planning it derives from this experience. I have to declare an interest, and pursuing that interest has forced me to look at the way the planning process operates and realize that it is, in fact, rather interesting. My understanding of the complexities of the planning system is not, therefore, based upon years of professional experience. I am writing from the viewpoint, not of a planner, but of one of the planned. I trust that planners will view whatever misconceptions I may have about the planning system with the same weary, condescending tolerance that they habitually show towards lay ignorance when working in their professional capacity.

If one is faced with eviction, on environmental grounds, from a small tent on one's own smallholding, a stone's throw away from a new and empty 30 foot high concrete block barn erected with the blessing of the planning system, and from a cottage occupied by a man who commutes to the nearby town, one's initial reaction may, like mine, be that the regulations are daft. However as one learns how the rural planning system operates, one appreciates that there is a logic in it; and that if that logic is twisted, it is more by history than by the planners. Britain's rural economy has been moulded by a singular set of historical circumstances: enclosure and industrialization have led to a countryside which supports less than a third as many rural workers as in France. Those who wish to find out more about this historical background may read the works of Jesse Collings, George Bourne, J.M. Neeson and Marion Shoard, among others.2 My concern is to pick up this story where these authors have left off.

Part One of this book describes how over the last fifty years the 1947 Town and Country Planning Act and its successors have tried to deal with the environmental and social problems that were the legacy of enclosure and industrialization by excluding still more people from the countryside; and how in many ways this has helped to exacerbate the problems. The countryside has been degraded by industrial agriculture and colonized by urban incomers; its partition between these two forces is turning it into a cross between a factory and a drive-in museum.

Part Two proposes a way in which, without radical changes to the planning system, apparently insoluble social and environmental problems can be combined to provide a democratic solution: a way in which the people presently excluded from the rural scene can participate in its revival. If permission to build or live in the countryside were to be allocated, not just to those who can afford artificially inflated land prices, but to anyone who could demonstrate a willingness and an ability to contribute to a thriving local environment and economy, then a very different kind of rural society would emerge. Low impact development is a social contract, whereby people are given the opportunity to live in the country in return for providing environmental benefits. Planners will recognize this as a form of what they call 'planning gain'. The mechanisms to strike such a bargain are for the most part already written into the English planning system and there is thus no need for any major structural changes. It is to the credit of the 1947 Act that the English and Welsh planning system is flexible enough to allow this.

There are many areas of planning that are barely touched upon in this book. It does not cover the important question of how to make cities greener and more sustainable, and thereby ease pressure on the countryside; it side steps the heated debate as to whether future development should take place in new settlements or on the edge of existing towns and villages; and it only touches upon the question of how to create 'sustainable settlements'. There are many much better qualified than myself performing these tasks.

Instead this book looks at the problem from the bottom up: it considers the scope for small scale, environmentally sound residences and workplaces in the countryside, outside the prescribed development zone, or village 'envelope'. In no way should this be taken to imply that low impact development is preferable outside villages; in many circumstances it is not. The book concentrates on the open countryside for two reasons. Firstly, changes in agricultural priorities, the introduction of set-aside, and a trend towards the fragmentation of farmland raise important questions about the countryside: What is it for? Who is it for? And how can the rural economy be made sustainable? Secondly, there are simply not the opportunities within villages for the kind of projects under discussion, partly because of lack of space, partly because of price. Where a low impact project can feasibly and affordably be carried out within the prescribed development zone, then it is right to question the need for siting it outside.

The concept of low impact development is not my own. It has emerged out of the efforts of a wide variety of interests — ranging from local planning authorities and those working in sustainable technologies, to permaculturalists and travellers' organizations — to find solutions to these problems.

However the term is not totally satisfactory. While it accurately describes those forms of development that only have a minimal adverse effect upon the environment, it does not adequately cover any forms of development that might be felt to have a positive or beneficial effect. This a particular problem in situations where the environment is so dire that almost anything would be an improvement. Jim Paton, of the Advisory Service for Squatters comments: 'A while back I was in the habit of talking about 'urban low impact housing' but I have stopped using this term now ... Our urban aims should be high impact. We want to make a substantial change for the better to a degraded environment'. Some people concerned with the rural environment also have their doubts about the expression. 'Low impact' does sound apologetic, doesn't it?' writes Sue Clifford of Common Ground, 'We need more positive words ... but I haven't thought of any'.

Neither have I. One correspondent suggested 'Earthcare' (a term used by permaculturist Bill Mollison), which is accurate, but sounds like a brand name for an ecologically sound garden product; the prospects of this expression making headway in the planning system are slim. The word 'sustainable' has been considered; but 'sustainable development', as defined at the Rio Earth Summit, has a social content which distinguishes it in meaning from the term 'low impact development', which relates more strictly to environmental matters — though the two concepts are profoundly linked. Moreover there is some confusion between 'sustainable development' as envisaged at Rio, and 'a sustainable development', which in planning parlance might signify, for example, a solvent farming enterprise. I have therefore stuck with an expression which at least has the virtue of having a familiar and fairly precise meaning for planners: 'low impact'.

The attraction of this term to planners is not a coincidence. Its apologetic nature is in deep accord with certain assumptions that underlie modern rural planning policy. These assumptions are linked to what the US landscape theorist Robert Thayer has called 'landscape guilt' — a deep seated feeling that modern development is intrinsically at odds with the environment, resulting in a corresponding need to mitigate, to zone, to hide or to disguise it.3 The question of landscape guilt will crop up repeatedly in this book. But here we need only note that planners are professional practitioners of landscape guilt — and consequently terms such as 'minimal impact' and 'low impact' are ones with which they feel instinctively comfortable.

One other factor commends the use of the apologetic term. While it is not easy to define 'low impact', the concept is initially easy to understand. To an extent (but only to an extent) it is a quantitative term, which presupposes a continuum of degree. It is clear for example, to most people, that a six-by-eight-foot shed has a lower environmental impact than a sixty-by-eighty-foot warehouse; or that a single lane track has a lower impact than a motorway. When it comes to a more qualitative term such as 'positive impact', however, we enter at once into a minefield of subjectivity. An imposing stone clad villa that some people (including presumably the architect and the buyer) may view as a positive asset to its surroundings, others may experience as a pretentious monstrosity or a blot on the landscape. No system for regulating human impact can afford to provide so welcoming a harbour for every conceivable architectural prejudice.

This is not to say that the term 'low impact' does not have its own difficulties. What of a planning proposal for a small cottage that involved planting a large belt of native trees in a flat and heavily deforested area? Such a scheme could be said to have a high impact upon its degraded surroundings, and one which most people would agree was positive. However insofar as a proposal can be said to have a high positive environmental impact, it can equally be said to have a low negative environmental impact. And here is the crux of the matter. As long as we remember that 'low impact' is shorthand for 'low adverse environmental impact', then we will not get into semantic difficulties: the cottage and its trees can safely be so defined. In other words a low impact development is not necessarily one that is unobtrusive in its surroundings or that does not alter the existing landscape; **a low impact development is one that, through its low negative environmental impact, either enhances or does not significantly diminish environmental quality**.

This then is the definition of low impact for the purposes of this book. I apologize to those who may have found the above discussion pedantic; but if the movement for low impact development is to make any impression upon the planning system, then sooner or later the term may have to stand up to scrutiny in the law courts. And I apologize to those who may feel that 'low impact' is a misnomer; I can only point to the large number of concepts and movements that have flourished under a terminologically inaccurate banner — for example, the Conservative Party.

This book is an attempt to distil the ideas and suggestions that have arisen around the concept of low impact development into a coherent and politically acceptable policy, and to explain it in terms sufficiently robust and rigorous to be acceptable to planners, but comprehensible to the general public. It starts with a historical overview of the effect of the planning system on the rural economy; it ends with specific recommendations for adjusting the nuts and bolts of rural planning procedure. I hope it will let some refreshing air into a debate that after seventy years has grown stale. I hope also it will serve as an aid to people who wish to make a low impact planning application, and to the planners who must respond to these applications.

Simon Fairlie
Tinker's Bubble and Yeovil, 1996

Foreword to the Second Edition

*L*OW IMPACT DEVELOPMENT sold 2500 copies between 1996 and 2004, when it went out of print. It was not reprinted, largely because the computer file on which it was stored had become corrupted. Since then I have received a number of requests for it to be reissued, and the exorbitant price asked for secondhand editions on Amazon and E-bay has convinced me that it is worth republishing.

Many of the photos have proved impossible to relocate, and have been scanned from the book, probably with some loss of quality. The text has been left as it was in the original, although there are many things I would change if I allowed myself to tinker with it. The original recommendations, and the appendices have been replaced by a chapter updating the book to 2008.

There are also a few matters in the book which need addressing.

(i) I have adjusted my definition of low impact development (a concept which has acquired the acronym LID). In the introduction, I defined a low impact development as one that 'through its low negative environmental impact either enhances or does not significantly diminish environmental quality'. This definition gets bandied around all over the place (most recently in a Welsh Assembly consultation paper on affordable housing); but I now favour the following:

> 'LID is development which, by virtue of its low or benign environmental impact, may be allowed in locations where conventional development is not permitted.'

I prefer this revised definition because wrapped up in it is the main argument: that low impact development need not be bound by the restrictions necessary to protect the countryside from 'conventional' high impact development; and that as a consequence, LID is affordable, because it can use land whose price has not been artificially inflated by being allocated for conventional development. Low impact development is therefore, almost by definition, low cost.

Development which 'enhances or does not significantly diminish environmental quality', but which for some other reason can only be allowed in locations allocated for conventional development, does not meet this definition of low impact development.

(ii) One weakness of the book is the insufficient attention paid to the plotland movement. When I was doing my research, the otherwise excellent interlibrary loan service failed to locate for me a copy of Dennis Hardy and Colin Ward's *Arcadia for All*, then out of print. I foolishly contented myself with articles by Colin Ward covering the same subject, not realizing that I was neglecting the best book ever written about the UK planning system. As a result I failed to appreciate fully the panic that the plotland movement sowed amongst those sections of the middle classes responsible for introducing the 1947 Planning Act, or the extent to which the Act was an explicit means of keeping plebs out of the countryside. To redress this deficiency, I have included in this edition an article originally published in *Chapter 7 News* in Summer 2001, summarizing *Arcadia for All*.

(iii) The other main weakness of *Low Impact Development* is its failure to address issues that might arise from the spread of what I have termed 'ecoburbia'. Fully half of the demand for low impact development comes from people looking for a plot of one to five acres on which to build a house and attain 'self-sufficiency', though in practice the level of self-sufficiency sought is usually dwarfed by an outside income. With just one acre available for each person in the UK, the prospect of large numbers of people pursuing a quasi-subsistence lifestyle on excessive areas of land is unsustainable — and it is probable that many such plots would degenerate into nothing more than very large gardens, resulting in car dependent, low impact sprawl.

The potential for this scenario emerging from ill-formulated low impact policies poses a problem, but it is not fatal to the underlying theory of low impact development. The aspirations of these down-sizers are commendable, and ought to be encouraged and provided for by any planning system that aims to meet the needs of the population. This kind of eco friendly lifestyle can, I consider, best be served by co-housing projects near existing settlements, where the amount of land attached to each house is no bigger than a decent sized garden, but the project as a whole provides agricultural land for those of its residents who wish to pursue subsistence land-based activities — in effect a common, serving much the same purpose as the commons of pre-enclosure days. Collective projects of this kind can also reduce car-dependency far better than a rash of individual plots, by providing car-share schemes and other transport benefits.

Low Impact Development was interesting to write because it was pitched at two audiences, the low impact developers themselves, and the people whose job it is to regulate them — the planners and the planned. I have, I dare say, had some success at explaining to those who are attracted by low impact lifestyles why the planning system erects barriers, and at suggesting how to address them. The reception from planners has been much frostier.

At the end of the original introduction to this book I wrote; 'I hope it will let some refreshing air into a debate that after seventy years has gone stale.' Unfortunately, it has done little of the sort, and, the debate is as sterile as it ever was, at least in England. Of the few planners who have countenanced low impact development, either as a result of reading this book, or because they have had to deal with a low impact application, most view it as little more than special pleading for oddballs.

Very few have grasped that LID represents an entirely different dynamic for organizing development control.

The theory of LID expounded in this book is not that difficult to understand or to summarize. The current system, dating back to 1947, operates as follows: a restricted amount of land is allocated for residential or other uses, resulting in a scarcity of development land, monopoly control by corporations who buy options on land likely to be allocated, an escalation in its price, a lack of affordable housing, massive indebtedness of a large proportion of the population, and a host of other repercussions, including the overheating of the UK economy and the 2007-2008 'credit crunch'. The state has confiscated the right of its citizens to build a dwelling and house themselves, turned it into a speculative commodity, and encouraged its use as collateral for financial adventures that have well-nigh bankrupted the country.

LID, on the other hand allows people to build anywhere (or at least on any land within a wide circumscription), but only if they conform to agreed environmental criteria. This criteria-based method of development control eliminates the artificial prices attached to allocated land, and the monopoly control of such land in a capitalist economy. It creates an incentive for developers to compete with each other, not by outbidding each other for scarce development sites, but by drawing up projects that will be judged to be more sustainable than those of their rivals. It allows the individual to compete for living space on equal terms with the developer.

Perhaps I didn't make this as explicit as it could have been, partly because some of these ideas were not fully formulated in my own head. That is why Chapter 4 is only five pages long. In an article published in the August 2003 issue of *Town and Country Planning*, I pursued the theory of LID further, proposing a transitory two tier system with low impact, car-free opportunities operating in areas in the countryside, in tandem with established allocation policies around towns and settlements. Planning authorities, I suggested, could calibrate the extent of LID they found acceptable by weakening or strengthening the criteria, as required. I got almost no feedback to these proposals from the established planning profession, .

I might have been led to conclude that I was out on a limb were it not for the fact that a wave of similar criticism of the existing planning system is emerging, not, from planning theorists in universities or environmental NGOs, but from the cornucopian right — people like Mark Pennington of the Institute of Economic Affairs, Mischa Balen of the Adam Smith Institute and James Woudhuysen and other architects associated with the group Audacity.

I do not agree with these neoliberals who, to a greater or lesser degree, advocate that people should be allowed to build where they want with few if any environmental constraints, and so favour suburban sprawl rather than low impact development. But at least they are blessed with the ability to think critically, and recognize the harm that the monopoly of artificially scarce development land inflicts upon the population. The planning establishment, particularly its professional organization the Royal Town Planning Institute, still appears to be incapable of envisaging any alternative to the current sixty-year-old system, even when it is now so heavily implicated in the country's economic downfall.

I ought really to rewrite the whole book, and what I produce here — a reprint together with an update of developments over the last twelve years — is the lazy option, from one who has grown weary of struggle. After twelve years I can confirm that planning is indeed boring, not because the issues are intrinsically dull — far from it — but because such is the dead weight of English planning bureaucracy that you have to produce a mountain of verbiage to change the position of a single comma.

Peter Mandelson once remarked that only when you are bored of what you are saying will the public start to hear you. I am therefore republishing *Low Impact Development* it in the hope that the ideas within it it will be picked up by somebody more eloquent or influential than I, and better qualified to work within the corridors of established power, who will awaken the dulled intellects of our planning theorists and bureaucrats.

Simon Fairlie, Flaxdrayton, January 2009

PART ONE

Chapter 1

Fifty Years of Rural Planning: Protecting the Environment

'The planning system … reconciles the needs of development and conservation'.
White Paper, *Rural England*.

'Planning may be an attempt to reconcile the irreconcilable'. M. J. Elson.

Before the Industrial Revolution, Town and Country Planning as we know it did not exist, nor did planning permission. When, in the seventeenth century, Richard Maddocks took his barn to pieces and 'sett it up for a dwelling house at the foot of Myddle Hill … and there he sold ale',[1] there was no army of planning policy managers and development control officers to inform him that he had moved it to an area of open countryside inappropriate for residential and retail development. 'Landowners were free to use their land in any way they wished, subject only to any grant under which they held it, and to obligations placed upon them at common law'.[2] Life before industrialization may have been nasty, brutish and short; but nobody had to waste time filling out forms in order to build on their land.

Before planning

In the countryside, there was no planning because it wasn't needed: the built environment was not felt to be in conflict with the natural environment. When, in the 1790s, residents of Stoke sub Hamdon demolished hovels set up by squatters on Ham Hill, it was probably because they feared that the incomers might claim poor relief from the village — not because the structures were erected without planning permission in an area now designated as a Country Park. When purists over the centuries decried vulgar decoration on church buildings, they deemed it to be an offence to God, rather than to Nature or architectural tradition. Building may have presented a threat to the social order or to the spiritual order, but it was rarely seen as a threat to the environment.

Part of the landscape: a cottage painted by an unknown 18th century artist. From The Dyce Collection, courtesy of the Victoria and Albert Museum.

To an extent the harmony between the built environment and nature can be attributed to the relatively small population. With only five million or so people living in pre-industrial Britain, there was little danger of the countryside being swamped by development. Settlements were small and isolated, connected by muddy lanes running through belts of farmland and across uncivilized (though not necessarily uninhabited) tracts of heath and forest. Nature was kept at bay through a cycle of ploughing, grazing and coppicing, which if it were not maintained would permit the weeds, the scrub and eventually the forest to reclaim its own. If there was competition between the built environment and the natural environment, it was of no account, because the forces of architectural development were far too dispersed ever to achieve a convincing victory over the forces of nature.

But this is not the whole story. Can we assume that if medieval Britain had been able to sustain a rural population of some 20 million, the impact of so many cottages upon the rural environment would have engendered a raft of Tudor planning laws? The answer is almost certainly no. There are areas in the world — Kerala in South India, for example — which house a rural population as dense as that of modern England, with far less impact upon the environment and no significant planning constraints. It is most unlikely that a quadrupling of the number of thatched half-timbered cottages in Tudor England would have raised many eyebrows — and nowadays, it would be regarded as a positive boon, especially by estate agents.

Today, it is widely felt that pre-industrial development and building methods were intrinsically more in harmony with the environment than modern buildings are. 'It has become almost a commonplace' wrote Harry Batsford and Charles Fry in 1938, 'to comment on the quiet fitness of these old cottages to their surroundings and to the purpose for which they were built'.[3] This may be nothing more than a subjective judgment. But its widespread acceptance is reflected in the demand for old rural cottages that has raised their price well above that of modern houses in similar condition. And — subjective or not — it is a view held by the planning profession, which dictates that, in rural situations, modern residences should maintain elements of the local vernacular style.

Why is it, then, that so many people prefer old houses and cottages to modern rural dwellings? It is hard to find any serious study of this perplexing question. As town planner Thomas Sharp wrote in the 1930s: 'The house must harmonize with the landscape. That is the golden rule upon which everybody is agreed. It is easy to formulate it, because it is so obviously true; but it is difficult logically to analyse it. Wherever does this harmony lie?'[4] Most design guides produced by planning departments are content to offer tips about 'good design', 'appropriate siting', 'good and bad practice' and so on, without any attempt to tackle this fundamental question.

In fact Sharp did tentatively identify two qualities particular to pre-industrial buildings which provide a logical explanation why so many people find old cottages — and old barns, mills and warehouses — more fitting to the countryside than their modern counterparts.

The first of these qualities is rootedness. 'That [old cottages] should have become part and parcel of the landscape is not surprising ' remark Harry Batsford and Charles Fry, 'for their materials are largely those of the countryside to which they belong'.[5] Before the arrival of railways, builders were limited to local materials within a day's cart journey, and all but the most prestigious buildings were constructed from whatever was close to hand: local stone or clay, timber, thatch, wattle and daub or mud. Most buildings were essentially bits of the local environment gathered and stacked up so as to form a weatherproof structure. It is hardly surprising that such constructions should appear to be part of the landscape, for that, in fact, is what they are.

A modern house, by contrast, may well have nothing in its fabric which derives from the locality. Typically its slates will hail from Spain, its timber from Norway or Indonesia, its bricks will be made from clay mined a hundred miles away, its aluminium window frames from bauxite mined in Asia or refined in the USA, its gutters from oil extracted from the North Sea or the Middle East. There is no reason to expect that such a Babel of materials should fit into the local setting, and any attempt to make it appear so is likely to come across as pretentious or dishonest.

The second quality of pre-industrial buildings is one which, for want of a better word, may be called irrectitude — a lack of straightness. Nature abhors a straight line: there is nothing in the classic English landscape straighter than the straightest tree. Before the nineteenth century, creating a flat surface by hand from the gnarled fruits of the natural world was prohibitively expensive. Peasants who wished to see edges as precise as those that delineate the modern brick-built semi, would have had to view the painstakingly chiselled ashlar walls of the local mansion; if they wished to wipe anything as smooth as a formica table top, they would have had to seek out polished marble columns in some nearby cathedral. The builders of the more humble cottages, barns and mills, like builders everywhere, aspired to straightness and symmetry and, given the limitations, they often did a good job. Yet by modern standards the lines of their buildings are soft, blurred, gently inclined or wavering; they are distinct from the landscape, yet remain at home within their setting of rolling hills or burgeoning foliage.

Since the industrial revolution, however, the straight line has come to predominate. What is hardest for the hand is easiest for the machine. Perfect edges and identical units are what mass production prefers, and it produces them by the million. Over the last 150 years the nature of building materials has radically changed: stone sawn dead square, cloned bricks and tiles, immaculately planed wood, rolled steel joists. Lay any of these a few millimetres out of line and it won't forgive, nor will the architect. Craftsman with modern materials have no choice but to build straight and true; they have traded the limitations of geology and geography for the tyranny of mechanical accuracy. The modern brick-built villa, whatever stylistic concessions it may make to the local vernacular, imposes an artificial geometry upon the landscape. Its rigid outline, its mechanical tiling, its machined window frames, its telephone wires and TV aerial, its manicured lawn, and its tarmac access road trimmed with lamp posts and road signs all speak of another world. Distinctiveness has turned to intrusion, aspiration has become arrogance, and Nature has been relegated to the status of backdrop — a 'view'.

These qualities of rootedness and irrectitude go some way towards explaining the attraction that old rural buildings hold for us. They are highlighted here, not because they provide an easy formula for sympathetic development in the countryside — they do not, and this book does not advocate a slavish imitation of traditional styles. They serve simply as a reminder that architecture and nature are not irrevocably opposed, that it is possible to build in ways that have a low impact upon the countryside, and that for centuries people in Britain and around the world managed to do this, without even trying.

Over the last seventy years, unprecedented development in the countryside has given rise to an assumption that all building is intrinsically harmful to the rural environment. Britain's surviving cottages remind us that this does not have to be so. However the response of the planning system to this onslaught has been to circumscribe the permitted extent of high impact development, rather than to ascertain qualities that make low impact building in the countryside acceptable.

The urban octopus

England and the Octopus was the title of a polemic published in 1928, attacking the 'tentacle growth' of urban sprawl. It was written by Clough Williams-Ellis, the man

Urban inroads into the countryside: the same road before widening (in 1928) and after (in 1931). Photos: K Reitz and Son, from *Town and Countryside*, Thomas Sharp, Oxford 1932.

behind one of the few examples of alternative rural architecture in Britain, Portmeirion village in Wales. The book's argument was summed up in one damning sentence:

> Having made our towns with such careless incompetence, those of us who have the means to be choosers are calmly declining to live in them and are now proceeding with the same recklessness to disperse ourselves over the countryside, destroying and dishonouring it with our shoddy but all-too-permanent encampments.[6]

Williams-Ellis was identifying a social movement which continues to this day, and which provides the main, perhaps the only, justification for rural planning. Nowadays this exodus from the cities is known by the less edifying title of 'counter-urbanization', although the zoological image is more accurate than ever: one only has to look at a road map of London, a cephalous M25 with blue tentacles stretching sixty miles or more into the hinterland, to see that the octopus is still growing. As G.K. Chesterton commented in a review of Williams-Ellis' book in *Architects Journal*: 'The struggle to save the country ... from the modern anarchy of machinery run mad, is very rightly expressed as the struggle between a man and a monster'.[7]

Chesterton went on in his review to propose that a firm line should be drawn between the rural domain and the urban: 'It is necessary to assert again most fixedly and emphatically ... that town and country are two completely different things: that each should have its totally different dignity'.

England and the Octopus contained an epilogue by the man who was to become the most distinguished town planner of the mid twentieth century, Sir Patrick Abercrombie. Abercrombie was then Secretary of the newly formed Council for the Preservation [now Protection] of Rural England (CPRE), a lobbying group of influential gentry concerned at the rapid suburbanization of rural England at the hands of developers — although this did not prevent him later becoming author of the Greater London Plan. He also wrote the standard planning text book of the inter war years in which he agreed with Chesterton that town and country should remain distinct: 'The essence of the aesthetic of town and country planning consists in the frank recognition of these two elements, town and country, as representing opposite but complementary poles of influence ... the town should indeed be frankly artificial; the country natural, rural'.[8]

This dualism was lifted to an almost mystical plane by another planner, Thomas Sharp, in 1932: 'The strong, masculine virility of the town; the softer beauty, the richness, the fruitfulness of that mother of men, the countryside, will be debased into one sterile, hermaphroditic beastliness ...The town is town; the country is country: black and white: male and female'.[9] Sharp was prophetic about the crucial role played by motor transport. With the growing use of the car, he wrote '*all* the land in the country can be regarded as building land and consequently *all* the land in the country is being laid out as a gigantic building estate'.

Within a few years the body of opinion represented by Abercrombie, Williams-Ellis, Sharp and the CPRE — together with the Garden City movement associated

A 1930s view of the octopus in Lakeland. Courtesy of the Rural History Centre, Reading University.

with the Town and Country Planning Association — succeeded in shifting the entire focus of planning from town to country; even the name of the discipline changed from Town Planning to Town and Country Planning. The profession of town planner had originated in the nineteenth century as a response to the public health problems involved in accommodating rapidly increasing numbers of people in burgeoning industrial cities. The 1909 Housing and Town Planning Act had as its primary objective 'to secure, the home healthy, the house beautiful, the town pleasant, the city dignified and the suburb salubrious'.[10] The 1932 Town and Country Planning Act and the 1935 Restriction of Ribbon Development Act, on the other hand, reflected a growing suspicion that qualities such as dignity and beauty were beyond the understanding of the architects of the inter-war suburban housing boom — and that the unlimited access provided by the motor car meant that building in the countryside had to be restricted to certain areas. Rural planning had arrived and its primary aim was to keep the town out of the country. British society had entered into a Faustian pact: the right to build anywhere was to be sacrificed for the right to drive anywhere.

It was the Second World War which brought to a head these embryonic attempts to deal with the land use problems arising from apparently inexorable suburban expansion. By 1945, much of the urban infrastructure had been bombed, and a visionary Labour government had been given an electoral mandate to build a new Britain. Rural planning policy was dominated by two concerns: to preserve the countryside from urban sprawl and to maintain a healthy supply of agricultural land as a strategic and economic asset. The impetus for rural preservation came from the CPRE and its friends: Abercrombie sat on the 1940 Barlow Report, which set the stage for post-war planning. The agricultural interest was articulated in the 1942 Scott Report on Land Utilization in Rural Areas, which, whilst emphasising the need for establishing national parks and nature reserves, maintained that elsewhere agricultural land should be protected at all cost.

These two concerns — agriculture and the environment —were viewed as mutually self supporting and were conveniently rolled into one. After all, the British countryside, give or take a few areas of semi wilderness that could be designated nature reserves, was agriculture. It was agriculture that had created the patchwork of hedged fields, the downland, the belts of protective woodland and the dry stone walls that were now under threat. As the Scott Report put it: 'The cheapest and indeed the only way of preserving the countryside in anything like its traditional aspect would be to farm it'.[11]

The Town and Country Planning Act 1947 therefore proceeded on the assumption that all forms of development, except agriculture, were an urban threat to the countryside, and needed to be strictly controlled. The framework by which this was to be achieved was as follows: local authorities were required to draw up a development plan which would delineate zones showing, for example, 'the direction in which a city will expand; the area to be preserved as an agricultural green belt, and the area to be allocated to industry and to housing'.[12] However these plans did not give automatic permission for certain kinds of development within a zone or automatically prohibit other kinds. Instead, every significant proposal was to be judged, on its merits, against the background of the plan. In other words, for most kinds of development, site-specific planning permission was necessary. The only exception was agriculture: any farmer could build more or less what he or she wanted.

The 1947 Act gave statutory sanction to Chesterton's and Abercrombie's vision of town and country as two distinct worlds. It revived the original Roman meaning of urbs as a walled city, although now the walls consisted of blue lines on the planners' map with a green belt beyond. The Act envisaged rural Britain as constellations of discrete industrial and residential settlements set in a matrix of open countryside where any form of development other than farming was frowned upon. Fifty years later that is still, in theory, what we have got.

The 1947 Act remains to this day the basic reference point for all subsequent planning law. It is regarded with almost biblical reverence by many planners who claim, for example, that: 'It is impossible to exaggerate the importance of the 1947 Act for it provided the most comprehensive and radical framework for the control of land use in the world ... This machinery for planning administration and policy implementation has, despite its shortcomings, been the envy of the world'.[13]

A cynic might suggest that this machinery is the envy, not of the world, but of the world's planning profession, for it involves a formidable amount of work. The task of drafting and ratifying a rolling programme of local, county and regional development plans which are not binding, and which therefore require the adjudication of some 600,000 or so individual planning applications and appeals every year, is a wonderful sinecure for bureaucracy.

Nonetheless, the system does have a measure of flexibility and an appeals mechanism for giving a hearing to projects that cut across the grain. The right of appeal offers citizens the opportunity to explain why their own particular project should be regarded as an exception to the plan. Admittedly, this flexibility is more accessible to those who understand the process, or to those who can afford to pay lawyers who understand it. Legal aid is not available to people lodging or objecting to a planning application, and there is a widespread and largely accurate perception that the flexibility of the English planning system is only accessible to those who can afford it.

Yet this flexibility does exist and it is what has ensured the post-war planning system's durability. Over a period of nearly half a century, during which the systems for administering education, health, local government, local taxation and numerous other sectors of society have been subject to momentous upheavals and reversals, the planning system has remained stable. It has provided the vehicle for a number of popular measures, such as the Green Belt legislation introduced by Duncan Sandys in 1955. It has proved able to absorb shifts in government policy as they filter down from DoE Circulars and Planning Policy Guidances through the hierarchy of development plans to influence local planning authority decisions. It has been considerably quicker to recognize the need for a change in transport policy than has the Department of Transport. And above all it has managed, through its flexibility, to retain the allegiance of both developers and the countryside lobby and, as a juggling act, that is no mean feat. Whether it has retained the allegiance of the common or garden rural public is another matter.

Reconciling the irreconcilable

How successful has the post-war planning system been in stemming the growth of the urban octopus? How has it fared in its mission to 'reconcile the irreconcilable' needs of development and the environment? Has it, in words taken from the recent Government White Paper, Rural England, (though an identical sentiment can be found in any one of a hundred different reports) been able to 'make adequate provision for development to sustain the economy' whilst ensuring that it 'conserves the rural environment'?[14]

For the most part, the planning system has adopted a strategy not so much of reconciliation as of separation. The urban onslaught against the countryside has been more or less contained within development zones specified in local plans, the two worlds separated by a no man's land of green belt. The deep countryside remains relatively inviolate, except where it is chosen for the route of a major road scheme or the site of a new tourist development or dormitory settlement; large areas of the English countryside do remain fundamentally rural, largely thanks to planning restrictions, and for this we should be grateful. The rate at which rural land has been swallowed up by the urban development has declined since the 1930s. If the planning system had been less robust over the last 50 years, Britain would undoubtedly have lost even more of its natural and architectural heritage.

But the octopus is still spreading, albeit at a slower rate. According to detailed research by the CPRE, some 11,000 hectares of rural land are lost to urban development every year.[15] The bounds of urban development, regularly redrawn in the rolling programme of county structure plans and local plans, are edging steadily outward. The DoE, in its Regional Planning Guidances, decides the number of new houses that will be required in each county, and these targets form the basis for the county structure plans. For example, in the South East, nearly 200,000 new housing plots are required over a five year period.[16] Overall, the Government estimates that 4.4 million new homes will have to be built in the next twenty years, increasing the housing stock by almost 20 per cent. According to the Government these estimates reflect demand, not from population growth (which is minimal), but from the fragmentation of families — a curious prediction from a Government ostensibly committed to preserving family life. But there is a growing suspicion, from the CPRE and other commentators, that just as the building of roads generates more traffic, so the building of houses generates the formation of more households, and the government's household projections may be 'self-fulfilling prophecies'.[17] Certainly the Government has done little to stem the demand for new housing, for example by encouraging the formation of shared households by young adults.

Around existing settlements, in particular, there is a feeling that urban encroachment has merely been delayed. Sooner or later there will be a further round of development plans that will impose another tranche of housing or sanction a bypass that will stretch the envelope further into the surrounding countryside. It is for this reason that so many green belts are 'sterile' areas, where land bought in anticipation of future development (for its 'hope value') awaits release for development in a state of suspended animation. The stifling of confident long term rural investment in such areas, because of the spectre of development, is in effect a form of 'blight'.

The frontier between town and country has thus become the battle line in a war of attrition between the forces of urban development and the countryside lobby. Although this is a conflict in which only the developers stand to make any gains, both sides accept the rules of combat as laid down in the 1947 Act. Developers clamour for additional releases of land or a relaxation of restrictions, but they are happy to abide by a system which prescribes a steadily expanding area for development. Conservation bodies voice their alarm at the erosion of the countryside, but see no option other than to advocate a strengthening of the planning system which sanctions this erosion.[18] Even more cavalier conservationists, such as Clive Aslet of *Country Life* magazine, whose *Countryblast* is a tart update of *England and the Octopus*, envisage no radical alternative.[19] Aslet revives the questions which 'formed the passionate debate in the 1930s, when ... tentacles of ribbon development had wrapped themselves around the arms legs and chest of England'; he fulminates against the ravages perpetrated by developers, road builders, tourists, commuters, barn converters, British Telecom and other urban colonists of the countryside; but all he proposes is stronger enforcement of the planning system.

So widespread is this faith in the planning system, that at times the sceptic may wonder whether there is not a tacit alliance between the forces of development and the forces of conservation. Sir Jonathan Dimbleby, president of the CPRE, vaunts the fact that 'when CPRE was campaigning in support of Structure Plans in the 1980s, we had ranged alongside us some of the key land users in the economy — notably the house builders and the minerals industry. They knew full well the advantages of being able to predict the pattern of future land use several years ahead'.[20] More radical environmentalists may wonder whose side the CPRE is on. It is sometimes difficult to dispel the feeling that the countryside lobby is collaborating with the development industry in carving Britain into two: an urban zone within which almost any kind of development is permitted somewhere, and a rural zone where (in theory) nobody but large scale farmers are allowed to do anything. The conflicts over the frontier between the two are faintly reminiscent of the permanent state of phoney war described by Orwell in *1984*: 'a warfare of limited aims between combatants ... who are not divided by any genuine ideological difference.' Neither camp seriously confronts the question that lies at the root of the whole problem: what is it that makes modern development so unbearable and destructive that we are placed in the impossible position of wishing to flee our cities and yet having to fence off our countryside?

The focus on these border wars has also, at least until recently, served to obscure the fact that the main threat to the countryside has not come from urban encroachment, but from quite another source. While urban development in the countryside has tailed off since the Second World War, the destruction of the English landscape has dramatically accelerated since 1947. The primary culprit has been the very sector of the economy that the 1947 Act blithely entrusted with protection of the countryside — agriculture.

The source of this mistake can be traced to a fundamental flaw in post-war planning policy, encapsulated in Chesterton's, Abercrombie's and Sharp's distinction between the two opposing poles of 'town and country', 'urban and rural'. This analysis has proved disastrously wrong. The threat to the countryside has come not just from urban development (which has been contained) but from industrial development. Industry — 'machinery run mad', as Chesterton put it — is by no means a uniquely urban phenomenon. The kind of farming encouraged after the war 'in the national interest' has been nothing if not industrial, has had no interest in maintaining the fabric of the countryside intact, and has not been contained.

Exemption from planning permission has allowed the industrialization of agriculture to proceed at full throttle. As we now belatedly realize, hedgerows have been ripped out, wetlands drained, downland and meadows ploughed up, woodlands cleared and the countryside peppered with monstrous asbestos and concrete hangars that are the very antithesis of sensitive architecture. In 1940, the German

An example of the effects of industrial agriculture. Anthony and Sheila Stocker 'made a good living' and reared four children between 1961 and 1980 on their 83 acre Suffolk farm (see photo above).
However, when they sold up, the farm became part of the much larger unit of a neighbouring farmer, who made radical changes to increase grain output (see photo below).
Photos: Anthony Stocker and Marion Shoard. First published in *This Land is Our Land*, Marion Shoard, Grafton Books, 1987.

Luftwaffe made an aerial survey of much of Britain, especially the east and the south. 'These magnificent photographs', wrote Oliver Rackham in 1986, 'record every tree, hedge, bush, pingo and pond in several counties'. They show that 'except for town expansion, almost every hedge, wood, heath, fen etc. on the Ordnance Survey map of 1870 is still there on the air photographs of 1940. The seventy eventful years between, and even World War II itself, were less destructive than any five years since'. The commonest cause of this post-war orgy of vandalism, Rackham concludes, 'has been destruction by modern agriculture; the second, destruction by modern forestry. Urban development comes a long way behind'.[21]

For some years now bodies such as the CPRE, politicians such as Gerald Kauffman and writers such as Marion Shoard[22] have been advocating that farmers, like anyone else, should have to apply for planning permission not only to construct buildings, but also for major changes in the use or condition of their land — for example if they wish to uproot a hedge or divert a stream. So far planning policy has hardly budged. This is not a solution favoured either by the Country Landowners Association or by the Conservative Government. The 1995 White Paper, *Rural England*, prepared by MAFF and the Department of the Environment with avuncular assistance from the Country Landowners Association, states only that the Government will 'take additional steps to prevent the abuse of agricultural permitted development rights, while ensuring that unnecessary burdens are not placed on genuine farmers'.[23]

So far the government has only imposed planning restrictions on smallholders with less than five hectares, though there are moves to double the threshold to ten hectares. As far as 'genuine' (i.e. larger scale) farmers are concerned, the Government prefers a voluntary approach whereby funds are directed to landowners and farmers — 'land managers' as they are now called — to 'provide environmental benefits' through the EU, the Environmental Land Management Scheme (ELMS) and the Countryside Stewardship scheme. This is tantamount to paying the foxes to watch the chickens, and how effective it will be remains to be seen. The destruction of hedgerows, woodland and so on has abated, partly because the subsidized industrialization of agriculture has been reined in to prevent the creation of unmanageable surpluses (although a recent rise in global wheat prices may turn the tide once again). As long as the orgy of destruction remains unprofitable, the foxes will doubtless be only too happy to be paid for guarding what chickens remain.

Agenda 21

Until recently the word 'environment', as far as the planning system was concerned, signified such matters as landscape, amenity and nuisance; in rural areas, 'protecting the environment' was more or less synonymous with 'protecting the countryside'. But since the 1992 Earth Summit in Rio, the term has taken on a far broader meaning: environmental concern has become inextricably linked with the concept of 'sustainability'. The planning profession, which comes under the wing of the Department of the Environment, now has to face challenges of an altogether different order.

Sustainable development is frequently defined as 'development which meets the needs of the present without compromising the ability of future generations to meet their own needs'.24 Regrettably, this has often been interpreted to mean environmental protection in a narrow sense. But the underlying objective of meeting people's needs requires not only the protection of environmental assets, but also their equitable distribution. Thus the three key objectives of the Rio Summit's Agenda 21 are:

• 'To reduce our use of energy and raw materials and production of pollution and wastes;

• 'To protect fragile ecosystems;

• 'To share wealth, opportunities and responsibilities more fairly between North and South, between countries, and between different social groups within each country, with special emphasis on the needs and rights of the poor and disadvantaged'.[25]

Agenda 21 notes that 'because so many of the problems and solutions being addressed by Agenda 21 have their roots in local activities, the participation and co-operation of local authorities will be a determining factor in fulfilling its objectives,' and recommends that 'by 1996, local authorities in each country should have undertaken a consultative process with their populations and achieved a consensus on "a local Agenda 21" for the community'. [26]

In the UK, to assist local councils in this undertaking, the Local Agenda 21 Steering Group, which represents all local authority Associations, commissioned the Local Government Management Board (LGMB) to publish guidelines. Their first publication, *Local Agenda 21 Principles and Process: A Step by Step Guide*, provides a check list of relevant policy areas for local authorities. Among those which concern planners are the need to:

• Promote development which reduces the need to travel;

• Take access to amenities rather than mobility in itself as the overall aim;

• Encourage a shift away from car use towards less environmentally damaging modes;

• Provide better public transport for disadvantaged people;

• Encourage energy efficient and environmentally benign building practices;

• Tackle fuel poverty through improving the energy efficiency of low income housing;

• Encourage resource- and energy-efficient patterns of development;

• Favour sustainability-enhancing developments such as wind farms;

• Protect habitats — not only rare and 'critical' ones;

• Constrain development within natural 'carrying capacity' limits.[27]

Though incomplete, this is a daunting list and it is hardly surprising that some local planning authorities should have taken an ostrich-like approach to the chal-

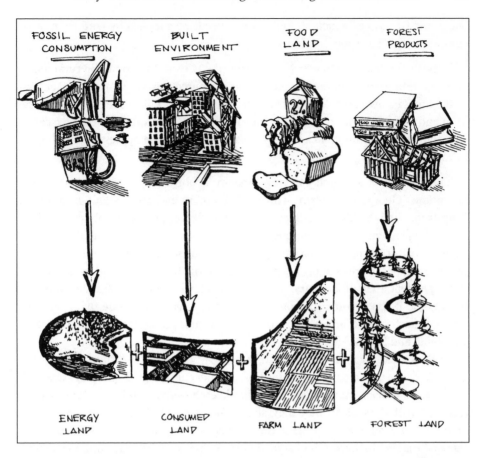

FOSSIL ENERGY CONSUMPTION   BUILT ENVIRONMENT   FOOD LAND   FOREST PRODUCTS

ENERGY LAND   CONSUMED LAND   FARM LAND   FOREST LAND

Converting consumption into land area. All goods and services use various types of finite natural resources, and these can be converted into land-area equivalents. The total area of land needed for all the categories of consumption and waste disposal generated by a given community is known as its 'ecological footprint'. If a community's ecological footprint is larger than its physical land area, then the difference is known as 'acquired carrying capacity' – or 'ghost acres'. Illustration by Phil Testemale from *Our Ecological Footprint*, Mathis Wackernagel and William Rees, New Society Publishers, 1995.

lenge, or remained content to wait and see what emerges in revised Planning Policy Guidances from the Department of the Environment. On the other hand, other authorities have made serious attempts to confront the issues raised by the LGMB.

Devon County Council, for example, are joint authors of a report entitled *Developing Sustainable Communities*, which takes on the thorny question of 'carrying capacity', or assessing the 'global or ecological footprint of [the] community'.[28] This involves drawing up a balance sheet of all the goods produced, consumed, imported and exported by the community; these sums are calculated, not as would normally be the case in financial terms, but in the amount of acres required to produce these goods. Any community that required more acres to supply its needs than it actually possessed would be in a state of 'deficit': this shortfall, which the Devon report calls

'Acquired Carrying Capacity' (ACC), must needs be supplied by land from other communities. The report continues:

> Provisional data for Greater Manchester (the City and surrounding rural areas) suggests this large community requires an Acquired Carrying Capacity of at least ten times its own area. Much of a community's ACC will be overseas and consequently out of sight and out of mind. Methods of production used overseas to resource the community can be both eco-destructive and oppressive, but largely invisible.

The concept of acquired carrying capacity is borrowed from the work of US agronomist George Borgstrom, who used the more evocative term 'ghost acres'. Borgstrom cited the UK, Germany, Japan, the Netherlands and Italy as countries heavily dependent upon ghost acres, maintaining that the UK 'farmed' two ghost acres abroad for every acre of agricultural land in Britain itself.[29] The concept of ghost acres does not only apply to agriculture. Britain has so neglected its forests that it is dependent upon timber harvested unsustainably in Indonesia, Canada and elsewhere; and it has become so protective about its own countryside that it imports minerals such as iron and coal from open cast mines in countries such as Brazil, Colombia and South Africa.

As the Devon document points out, 'it is an early priority for sustainable communities to reduce the demand for acquisition of other communities' carrying capacity'. This does not mean, that communities should eschew trade and strive for self-sufficiency; but it does mean that they should not depend upon a disproportionate amount of the world's resources at the expense of other communities on the other side of the globe. In the words of Agenda 21: 'A change in the consumption patterns, particularly in industrialized countries, towards those which can be attained by all within the bounds of the ecologically possible has to be a central component in the drive for sustainable development'.[30]

This in turn means using local resources wisely. For example, urban councils will no longer be able to sanction the construction of retail outlets with a life expectancy of only 15 years. Rural communities will no longer be able to squander abundant supplies of manure, whilst employing chemical fertilizers derived from a dwindling supply of fossil fuels; the wisdom of consigning large acreages of valuable grassland to recreational horse use will come under question; Ministry of Agriculture regulations restricting the feeding of food wastes to pigs may need to be reviewed. Above all, a sustainable lifestyle will require something close to the abolition of the private car. This may sound unduly alarmist; but at present the number of households in the world without access to an automobile is rising faster than the number with access to one.[31] It is difficult to imagine how, under these circumstances, equitable private car ownership for all the world's peoples can ever become an ecological possibility.

The pursuit of sustainability involves a searching reappraisal of our way of life that goes way beyond the wildlife monitoring and community mapping projects (admirable though they may be) that have become the hallmark of some councils' initial response to Local Agenda 21. It will involve radical changes in consumption patterns, production processes and — what is more relevant to planners — land use priorities. Sustainability is becoming an increasingly important consideration in planning appeals. There can be little doubt that as we enter the next century, sustainability will become the dominant criteria for making decisions about land use, and planners will have to become well versed in these complex matters.

Nearly all local authorities now have an environmental co-ordinator whose job it is to see that the question of sustainability is given due consideration in all policy areas. Nearly one quarter of these co-ordinators are located in the planning department. They have been described as 'among the most motivated and best qualified individuals in local government'[32] — an encouraging verdict, because they certainly need to be.

Chapter 2

Fifty Years of Rural Planning: Meeting People's Needs

'It is not for the government to determine who should live where, but ... '
White Paper, *Rural England*

'MEETING PEOPLE'S NEEDS' — the underlying objective of Agenda 21 — has never been a priority of the planning system, which is geared instead towards protecting the environment and enhancing the economy. The people who live and work in the country — the Phil Archers and the Clarrie Grundys — have their individual economic and environmental priorities, which may not necessarily accord with the more abstract demands of 'the environment' and 'the economy'; these human concerns have been affected by planning legislation quite as much as the landscape and the Gross Domestic Product. Indeed it could be argued that the social effects of the post-war planning system — whether by accident or design — have been more far reaching than its environmental effects.

Betterment: the skeleton in the cupboard

The 1947 Act changed the lives of country folk, not so much through what it set out to achieve as through what it failed to enact. There was one important and contentious component of the Act that was never properly implemented and after a number of abortive attempts was quietly dropped — the so-called 'financial provisions', which can be summed up under the heading 'betterment'. Today this legislation is no more than a skeleton in the dusty files of Marsham Street, but its ghostly presence still looms over the planning profession as a reminder that there is unfinished business. Given that betterment involves the redistribution of staggering sums of money, it is astonishing that few people today except planners have even heard of the term.

Betterment means the increase in value of a plot of land that derives from it being accorded planning permission which other similar sites are refused. The 1947 Act recognized that while many landowners would lose land use potential through the introduction of planning restrictions, owners retaining or acquiring planning permission would benefit 'by the imposition of restrictions on the other land'. In other words, the right to develop acquired a scarcity value, and this value, in the absence of compensatory mechanisms, accrued to the owner of the land to which these rights were attached.

The Labour Government hoped to divert this unearned increase in value to the State. The 1947 Act contained a 100 per cent 'development charge' which was to levy from the developer the difference between the original use value of the land and its new development value. But this levy was abolished by the Conservatives in 1954. In a 1965 White Paper,[1] another Labour Government wrote: 'It is wrong that planning decisions about land use should so often result in the realizing of unearned increment by the owners of the land to which they apply', and the 1967 Land Commission introduced a new betterment levy, though this time of only 40 per cent. This too was abolished by the Conservatives, in 1971.

Labour's attempts to limit the profits made by landowners were never particularly popular, perhaps because the profits were absorbed invisibly into the State's coffers, perhaps because the measures were associated with draconian Compulsory Purchase Order powers and a move towards the nationalization of land. However the problem that they attempted unsuccessfully to redress still exists and in fact has been exacerbated. The prices for development land have risen considerably over the last 45 years (though in fits and starts), while the price of agricultural land has risen much slower. According to a study of three regions undertaken by the Joseph Rowntree Foundation, 'the gap between housing and agricultural land prices was far greater in 1991 than in 1981 ... At their peak in South Cambridgeshire, housing land prices were about 150 times those for agricultural land and in North Hertfordshire over 200 times'. After the boom of 1989, land prices fell back but remained well above their 1981 levels.[2]

The fifty- or one-hundred-fold increase in value that takes place when agricultural land becomes development land inevitably benefits somebody, and has to be paid for by somebody else. The critical questions are, 'Who benefits?' and 'Who pays?'

The beneficiaries of this transfer of wealth are relatively easy to identify: landowners who have sold agricultural land with prospects for planning permission at above agricultural prices; developers who have acquired planning permission for land bought at agricultural prices; the banks, building societies and other investors who have lent money on that basis; and other parties such as estate agents and insurers whose income is related to the value of property. They are raking in what one district council Director of Planning has called 'obscenely huge' profits.[3]

Who then pays for these profits? At a purely financial level, betterment is paid for by the person who buys or rents the property. In the case of dwelling houses this means ordinary members of the public, such as you or I. In many cases the value of the development rights will equal or nearly equal the value of the house plus the agricultural value of the land. In some situations, home buyers may have enough capital to pay for the building and land costs, but be forced into obtaining a mortgage to pay off the development rights costs, and this will further increase their total payments by adding a burden of interest that they would not otherwise require. The house buyer or tenant is in effect paying for 'the right to be somewhere', a right that was taken for granted before the advent of planning permission — and he or she is paying very dearly. Bereft of their 'financial provisions', the planning acts have become a licence for developers to make money. In Howard Newby's words 'local plans become speculators' guides and the increase in value becomes in effect, a highly regressive form of indirect taxation on home owners and others who eventually use the land after it has been developed'.[4]

The exact amount of this transfer of wealth can only be guessed at but it is extremely large. If the 2.2 million houses that the Government anticipates will be built outside urban areas in the next 20 years involve an average increase in land value of £ 25,000 per house,[5] the total profit from betterment will be £55 billion. To this sum can be added any increase in land value occasioned by the building of another anticipated 2.2 million new homes in urban areas; and the increase occasioned by the construction of commercial buildings on green field sites. All this is betterment arising from future development. On top of it should be added all the interest being paid by mortgage holders on the artificially high land value of their existing homes, be they first- or second-hand.

What makes the question of betterment more disquieting is that it represents a drain of wealth from the countryside to the city. When rural land, usually on the edge of villages or towns, is urbanized, then some at least of the eventual users of the land will be local people who because of the restrictive planning laws have no option but to seek accommodation in a built-up area— residential tenants, home buyers, small businesses and so on. The beneficiaries of betterment however are largely urban based developers and financial institutions, except for rural landowners who make a windfall sale and who are perhaps less than likely to be members of the rural community. When the rural economy sells land for development which it subsequently needs, it often ends up buying back expensively from the city what was originally sold cheap.

But from another point of view, and one frequently held by planners, it is the community that pays for betterment. The increase in land value that a developer accrues by acquiring planning permission, say, for an estate of 50 houses on the edge of a village is gained at the expense of those who already live there and whose intimacy with the surrounding countryside may be disturbed, whose roads will be filled with unwanted traffic and whose community will be overwhelmed by a sudden influx of newcomers. These are the 'externalities' of development, the costs inflicted upon the community and the environment by a new development.

Many planners would like to see the money that is presently going into developers' pockets redirected towards the community to offset these costs. This would mean that tenants, home buyers and other occupants would still have to pay for 'the right to be somewhere' — but at least their money would be going into the community in which they and their neighbours lived. James Redwood, Director of Planning and Technical Services for Lewes District Council, faced with local villagers irate that they are to be swamped with new housing, puts the arguments thus:

Putting a system of betterment in place would act on the planning process in a number of complementary ways. In the first place, communities would be essentially less antagonistic to development, as the motivation for development would be less market-driven. Secondly the value of any development would go back into the community to enable it to plan positively for itself.[6]

Redwood here articulates what has always remained a sore point with planners. The original 1947 Act envisaged that the money accruing to the State from betterment would be used to acquire land for projects that would benefit a new Britain. Planning would be 'positive' in the sense that planners would initiate projects that were deemed to be socially beneficial. Instead the planning system is reactive, its role merely to assess and control whatever speculators and developers propose.

Positive planning is a top-down concept of the kind favoured by Labour Governments and by officials who have faith in the ability of bureaucracies to decide what is beneficial for the community. It is easy to see why the betterment levy was so fiercely fought off by Conservative governments. Even today a heated battle is being waged over the extent to which local authorities may extract what they consider to be community benefits through 'planning gain' — for example by making a developer pay for a new road or community centre. The Government remains adamant that 'it is not acceptable for local planning authorities to seek to secure a percentage of enhanced land value'.[7]

The determination of the dominant party in UK politics to ensure that the profits of development are not returned to the community has had a radical effect upon British culture. As one planning textbook observes:

> The abandonment of attempts to solve 'the betterment problem' ... is more than a matter of land taxation or even equity. The so-called 'financial provisions' of the 1947 Act underpinned the whole system and made positive planning a real possibility ... This change, made some forty years ago, is far more fundamental than the high-profile changes made under the Thatcher regime.[8]

In fact, some degree of positive planning is still possible through the use of planning gain, and as we shall see, it is by tackling the question of betterment in this way that many of the social and environmental problems raised in this book can be resolved. But the questions of land taxation and equity should not be passed over: they play a significant role in the rapid growth of industrial agriculture and the consequent acceleration of counter-urbanization.

Preserved in aspic

In 1946 there were 976,000 full-time and part-time agricultural workers in England and Wales; by 1989 there were 285,000.[9] This is not the first time that an industry has lost nearly three-quarters of its work force in less than half a century, nor the last. But given that in 1947 farmworkers comprised a significant proportion of the nation's work force, and that for centuries the economy and culture of the greater part of the country revolved around the farming community, this loss of jobs has been nothing short of tragic.

The causes of the rapid industrialization of agriculture are manifold: technological advance, competition, entry into the EU, globalization of markets, the power of the supermarkets — all these and others may be cited as reasons for the post-war movement to tear up the fabric of the countryside in the interests of agricultural efficiency.[10] In the face of such forces, it is easy to argue that the planning system is complicit only by default; by failing to control agricultural development.

This is not entirely the case. Because urban development has been constrained, while agriculture has not, the price of building land has risen in relationship to the price of agricultural land. This has meant that goods produced in facilities on developed property have become proportionately more expensive in comparison to goods produced from agricultural land. Relatively cheap land means relatively cheap food; relatively expensive development land means relatively expensive manufactured goods. The rise in the difference between agricultural and development land prices is one of several reasons why household expenditure on food has nearly halved over the last 35 years while household expenditure on housing has nearly doubled.[11]

This in turn has meant that farmers have to produce more, and use more land to buy farm inputs and other goods that derive from the high-land-price economy. According to Richard Body, a British dairy farmer in the 1950s could earn a living with 15 dairy cows, whereas by the 1980s a farmer needed 75 cows to maintain the same income in real terms.[12] The situation is one of declining terms of trade, analogous to that experienced by Third World countries which find that a given quantity of cocoa, for example, will only buy half as many tractors as it did a decade previously. The result of this increasing pressure to sell cheap and buy expensive has been that the successful farms have borrowed, expanded and increased production, while the smaller farms have been squeezed out.

It is perhaps dangerous to implicate the issue of land prices too heavily in the scenario of post-war farm concentration (though Chapter 4 will describe how the structure of land prices makes it exceedingly difficult for a small farmer to set up). Whatever the reasons, farms have been disappearing at the rate of about two per cent every year,[13] and with them the number of farmworkers. Even by 1976 there were more tractors than farmworkers on British farms.[14] The Rural Development Commission estimates that between 60,000 and 100,000 workers will leave agriculture and related industries during the 1990s.[15]

The effect of a steep decline in the numbers of jobs in the agricultural sector, combined with stringent planning restrictions in rural areas on anything that is not agricultural, should not have been hard to predict, and is now self evident. The countryside has lost most of its workers. In their place have come people who don't work in the countryside but earn their income in the town (and not infrequently in the development industry) — commuters, owners of second homes, retired people. The incomers' arrival has been facilitated by the increase in mobility that has arisen from the construction of motorways and the rise in car ownership; but they have been able

Demolition of houses erected without planning permission is uncommon, but it does happen. This photograph shows the demolition of a stone cottage by Charnwood District Council in Leicestershire in October 1995. The cottage was restored by the Pickavant family (who have been horsemen for three generations) as part of an equine livery centre – a form of agriculture that is not accepted as *bona fide* agriculture. Photo: Echo Press (1983) Ltd.

to seize the opportunity because over two-thirds of rural workers have lost their source of income through a combination of unregulated agricultural rationalization and draconian planning restrictions on anything else that might offer an alternative. High fliers in an urban population which can get planning permission to do more or less anything somewhere in the conurbation, have access to far more money than rural people, who are not allowed to do anything other than try to hang on in an industry that is shedding most of its workers — or else move to the nearest town.

These incomers have bought up virtually all of the more desirable old buildings in villages and have snapped up farmhouses and farm cottages when these have been sold separately from the land previously attached to them. They have even moved in to buy newer houses that were constructed for the indigenous population, for example through the intermediary of housing associations.[16] Their car-borne mobility has taken custom away from local shops, post offices and public services.[17] Indeed according to a study cited by the CPRE in their submission to the White Paper: 'Instead of countering depopulation, counter-urbanization may actually cause it. Thus, although migrants have moved into the countryside, they retain their spending links with the town. To the extent that they replace people who had more local linkages, the demand for services falls, reducing local employment opportunities, and increasing the incentive for local people to leave'.[18] In other words, the youngster who once might have worked behind the counter in the village grocery is now more likely to find a job as a till operator in a supermarket in the nearest town.

They have also changed the face of the countryside in other ways. For example, many among the incoming population have participated enthusiastically in a new form of land use for fields which have been marginalized by industrial agriculture. Horseyculture, as the keeping of horses as pets is sometimes known, occupies about 15 per cent of lowland grassland, much of this in the counties around London. The price of pony paddock — small areas of redundant pasture — is often two or three times the price of ordinary agricultural land. There are now over half as many horses in this country as in the days when they pulled carts on the farm, though nowadays they are ridden primarily for the purpose of keeping them fit — when they are not being carted around in horseboxes pulled by Range Rovers.[19]

But ironically, horseyculture is not regarded as an agricultural activity and hence is subject to planning permission. Small farmers who want to diversify by turning unprofitable arable or pasture land into a potentially profitable equiculture and livery centre are likely to encounter planning problems, particularly if they should need to erect a dwelling to provide 24 hour surveillance. Horseyculture is an acceptable pastime for those who can afford to spend a quarter of a million pounds on a farmhouse and paddock, or £5,000 on a present for their daughter; but it is not regarded as a *bona fide* livelihood for those who wish to make a living from agricultural land.

In the run up to the Government's recent White Paper on Rural England, there was considerable concern that the countryside was becoming 'a museum' or was 'being preserved in aspic'. The President of the Country Landowners' Association (CLA) concluded his foreword to the CLA's submission with the comment: 'The countryside is not a museum or a playground. It is a place where people live and work'.[20] Another submission, from Herefordshire CPRE quoted eight statements, from the likes of William Waldegrave, John Gummer, the Duke of Westminster and Lord Shuttleworth, making the same point — no less than three of them referring to the proverbial aspic.[21]

There is a genuine concern from all strata of society (not just the consumers of aspic) that the countryside has lost its *raison d'être*, and is being rapidly colonized by urban interests which have no understanding of what it is that makes a living countryside, let alone any interest in making it live — a process of gentrified rural dereliction. Yet many of the worthy voices contributing to the White Paper are, simultaneously, ebullient about the dynamism of the rural economy, which they claim 'has outperformed urban areas'.[22] 'The growth of small firms is higher than in urban areas', states the Rural White Paper, 'and levels of rural unemployment are generally lower than the national average'.[23]

However nobody doubts that this performance is due primarily to the migration of urban jobs to the periphery of relatively attractive and salubrious villages — in fact it is not rural at all but proto-urban. 'In many respects life in the countryside has become similar to life in the towns,' states the Rural Development Commission in its submission;[24] and the White Paper concludes that: 'Rural activity is … much more like that of urban areas'.[25] Even the CPRE acknowledges, apparently without regret, that 'the broad economic and occupational differences between rural and urban areas appear to be diminishing … In economic terms, the question arises as to how much longer it will remain useful to distinguish between rural and urban areas.'[26]

This is, on the face of it, an astonishing statement from an organization committed to the Protection of Rural England and a far cry from the advice of the CPRE's founder, Patrick Abercrombie, sixty years ago that 'the town should indeed be frankly artificial; the country natural'. Yet it is perhaps not so surprising as all that, for it is the planning policy elaborated under Abercrombie's influence that has done much to contrive this urban dominance. The unrestrained growth of industrial agriculture and stringent planning restraints on other rural activities and dwellings have emasculated the traditional rural economy and shepherded the majority of the working rural population into residential and industrial estates on the edge of small towns and suburbanescent villages; the remaining countryside has been bequeathed to the combine harvester and the Range Rover.

The urbanization of rural culture is now scheduled to spread deeper into the countryside with the current enthusiasm for 'diversification'. Commenting on the White Paper, *Rural England*, George Monbiot observes:

> Curiously, nearly all the proposals for revitalizing the rural economy discuss only the urban economy, and how to move it into the countryside. There have been numerous calls for a relaxation of planning constraints in order to facilitate tele-cottaging or the movement of insurance and software companies from towns to villages. While these initiatives may be welcomed in many rural areas, and afford people otherwise condemned to commuting a more sustainable pattern of life, they fail to reflect the special characteristics of the place itself. This interaction is essential if rural areas are to be locations in their own right, rather than simply nodes on the Internet. If life in the countryside is to be distinguishable from life everywhere else — and if opportunities are to be provided for people whose skills are best employed outdoors — then the rural economy must be allowed to thrive alongside the transposed urban economy. A rural economy is necessarily land-based: reflective and responsive to an area's resources.[27]

Lost livelihoods

There is an assumption among planners (most of whom, it should not be forgotten, are townies) that a land-based, agricultural economy consists uniquely of farmers and their farmhands.

This view is inaccurate. Since the Black Death in 1348, and probably since long before then, the countryside has supported a large number of landless poor whose livelihood has depended upon a combination of casual work backed up by subsistence production. Until the nineteenth century this way of life was based largely upon access to common land. The progressive enclosure — or privatization — of common land over the centuries has caused this way of life to decline, but it is by no means dead. J.M. Neeson observes that the landless poor of the past 'escape the view of historians looking only at manorial papers ... the rights of the landless are better documented where they resisted the loss of commons at enclosure'.28 It is for similar reasons, perhaps, that the situation of today's landless poor escapes the view of the forgers of modern rural policy.

For many centuries, the countryside found space for those who did not fit readily into the more formal economy of landowner and tied labourer. In the reign of Elizabeth I for example, squatters could set up and secure a cottage on a common provided they could prove that they had resided there 40 days.[29] The Tudor monarchs actively encouraged such measures to defuse the problems caused by a class of landless peasants, displaced by a wave of enclosure of common land for sheep farming. Without access to land and a home, these refugees had little alternative other than to form themselves into bands of brigands or beggars, roaming the country, terrorizing gentlefolk. As a result of concessions towards squatters, in the seventeenth and eighteenth centuries 'landless commoners were often almost, rather than absolutely, landless. They were land poor ... Some had gardens, pightles (small plots) of meadow or small assarts (clearings), and yards with stalls or sheds suitable for pigs and poultry, or in some cases a couple of sheep or a horse'.[30]

These people could earn cash, through working for landed farmers, or through collecting marketable goods from the commons — firewood, bark, furze, bracken, reeds, sand, hazel rods, hazel nuts, berries, mushrooms, herbs, briar stocks for grafting, fishing bait, lizards, song birds ... to name but a few. But they also needed and possessed a subsistence basis to fall back on when work was unavailable or out of season. Some families had a small plot of land of their own to cultivate; most relied on the commons for a wide range of subsistence products including food, grazing and fuel. The value of this subsistence production was by no means negligible: a poor cow turned out on the commons would bring in the equivalent of half a low paid labourer's annual wage.[31] These two elements of the rural economy — cash and subsistence — were complementary: cash acquired the commodities that could not be produced domestically, while subsistence production provided security — or to borrow a modern phrase, 'income support'.

At the end of the eighteenth and the beginning of the nineteenth century there was a second and far more devastating wave of enclosures which effectively did away with the commons. About 7,000,000 acres of common land were privatized through Acts of Parliament, and 'it is probable that the same area was enclosed without application to Parliament'.[32] Though it sparked off numerous protests and riots, the disappearance of this subsistence basis for the rural poor did not generate a class of wandering beggars and brigands. There now was an alternative for the dispossessed: displaced rural labourers could find employment in factories in the cities, the very cities that a century later were to stretch their tentacles back into the countryside.

But for the landless independent peasant who preferred to remain in the country,

A Gypsy woman in her bender, circa 1910. Benders have been used for centuries by the rural poor: 11,000 were recorded in the 1880 census. Photo from *Romany Life*, Frank Cuttriss, Mills and Boon, London 1915.

times were hard. Concentration of land ownership was high, agricultural wages were low and the cost of living was rising. Moreover, by the turn of the century, in areas within the reach of London, the tentacles of the octopus were beginning to be felt. In 1912, George Bourne described the economic, cultural and moral disintegration of the Surrey village where he lived for more than twenty years, a village populated mainly by landless peasants descended (Bourne surmised) from eighteenth century squatters. Although the local commons had been enclosed in 1861, patches of them remained for some years informally accessible to the local people and continued to serve as a subsistence base. But around the turn of the century these former commons were progressively bought up by 'speculating architects and builders' and sold off to 'the leisured classes', quadrupling the population of the village. Bourne concludes: 'It is the recent building boom that has caused enclosure to take its full effect... To the enclosure of the common more than to any other cause may be traced all the changes that have subsequently passed over the village. It was like knocking the keystone out of an arch. The keystone is not the arch; but once it is gone all sorts of forces, previously resisted, begin to operate towards ruin, and grad-ually the whole structure crumbles down'.[33]

As the human costs of rural dereliction became apparent, at the end of the nine-teenth century an influential body of opinion, championed by Liberal MP Jesse Collings, began calling for a measure of land reform that would give England's peasant class a basis for subsistence.[34] 'Three acres and a cow' was Collings' battle cry. Collings' efforts finally bore fruit in the 1920s and 1930s when the Smallholding and Allotment Acts were introduced empowering councils to provide land for the needy; and the Government's Land Resettlement Scheme — an expedient solution to the problem of the unemployed — was initiated in England and Scotland, with varying degrees of success.[35]

Today, the Land Resettlement Schemes have been abandoned, while the remaining 5,000 county smallholdings are now often larger than the average sized farm in any other country in Europe.[36] Typically they are advertised as 'Farm Business Tenancies' and instead of three acres and a cow, they offer '100 acres with approximately 360,000 litres of milk quota' to those with 5 years agricultural experience and who also have 'available to them, without borrowing, a large proportion of the capital requirement for the holding'.[37] The Government wants to see these farms sold off at a potential profit of £350 million.[38] Collings' vision of a subsistence base for the poor has fallen by the wayside.

But it is the post-war planning system that delivered the final *coup de grâce* to the class of land-poor labourers, by making it impossible for them to acquire planning permission. Government planning policy dictates that the only valid grounds for the erection of an agricultural dwelling are that a farm requires an additional agricultural worker — either the farmer himself or an employee — and can provide him a minimum agricultural wage. Casual workers, subsistence farmers and all the other independent characters on the rural scene are simply not allowed to build in the countryside. Of course, those who were still installed in 1947 when planning permission became obligatory, could stay on; but since the cottages in which they lived have proved attractive to urban incomers, as the old folk have died off there has been no way in which this reservoir of semi-subsistent seasonal workers can be replenished. Post-war planning policy has in effect acted as another form of enclosure. Deprived in earlier centuries of the land which provided a basis for subsistence, the poor but independent members of the rural community now find themselves deprived of the right to build a home.

Most casual workers in the informal rural economy now tend to be housed in council or 'affordable' housing on the edge of key villages and have bills to meet and rent to pay. In hard times, security is supplied, not by a pig and a cow, but by the receipt of income support and housing benefit. Unlike livestock, these cease to yield when the recipient is re-employed, creating a poverty trap, from which the only convenient escape is a well paid permanent job. And since permanent jobs in land based industries are declining, it is within the urban economy that former casual rural workers, or their children, are most likely to find employment.

This ignominious absorption of the rural landless into the urban economy might be justifiable if it could be shown that they were economically redundant. Yet perversely, the prospects for earning casual wages in the rural economy have, if anything, improved in recent years . Lizard catching, furze gathering and so on have long disappeared, and jobs which can be easily mechanized, such as fruit picking and hay making have declined, though they are still available. But contract work such as tractor operation, sheep shearing or scanning for animal pregnancies is flourishing; traditional activities such as firewood collection, coppice work, charcoal burning, horse work, farriery, harvesting thatching straw, cider making, dry stone walling, hedging laying, gathering wild medicinal herbs, collecting Christmas decorations, and so on are experiencing a revival; and a variety of new opportunities have arisen, including conservation work, tourism, the recycling of scrap and the salvage of agricultural byegones.

The resurgence of casual and seasonal work is no quirk or coincidence. In part it is in response to the need for what the Government calls a 'flexible workforce' able to weather rapid changes in the economic climate. In part it is a symptom of counterurbanization: more and more people are becoming disillusioned with a shoddy industrial environment and demanding surroundings and products which they view as authentically rural. A well maintained rural environment needs people working in it: to maintain walls, hedges and ditches, to thin and coppice woods, to keep back invasive plants, to cut reed beds, to repair towpaths, to control rabbits and squirrels, to maintain water meadows, and so on — and to market the byproducts of such operations. There is an enormous amount of work that used to be done, that needs to be done and that is once again being undertaken.

However, irregular labour intensive employment of this kind is not well paid. It needs to be underwritten by a home base which provides security rather than generates debt. The inhabitants of Kings Hill, a group of over twenty people living on their own land in bender tents in Somerset, earn money from activities such as fruit picking, charcoal burning, footpath restoration and festival site preparation. They observe that 'as is normal in rural areas, much of this work is small scale, temporary and low paid; but our low cost life style ... enables us to take on employment which is not viable or attractive for people with higher personal expenses or transport costs'.[39] The basis of the bender dwellers' low cost life style is their access to land bought at a price which does not include the costs of development rights. The right to build their own dwelling is the mainstay of their rural livelihood.

This is not to say that other traditional subsistence activities are no longer economic. A poor cow (nowadays more likely to be called a rare breed) kept on a couple of acres, giving only 500 gallons of milk a year, will supply milk and dairy produce worth over £1,500 in the shops. Access to fuelwood can replace heating bills of about £450; access to clean water, bills of up to £300. The Tinker's Bubble Trust, a settlement of six adults and four children on a 40 acre holding, estimates that through subsistence production of dairy products, vegetables, fuel and so on it can obtain goods worth up to £1,000 per adult per year — equivalent to a third of their required personal income.[40]

In both these cases, the settlers' right to live on their land is contested by the local planning authority. The stranglehold exerted by the planning laws upon this type of lifestyle has become more apparent in recent years because access to land has considerably improved. In the 1980s, Marion Shoard described the plight of one frustrated would-be smallholder:

In May 1981, unemployed, thirty-two-year-old Dave Batty walked from Hull to the Houses of Parliament to deliver a note to the Prime Minister, drawing attention to the plight of the unemployed. Mr. Batty, an ex-farmworker and ex-lorry driver had called at every Jobcentre along the way, but none had been able to offer work. As he waited in the Commons Central Lobby, he said: 'My idea of heaven would be ten acres of land. If I had that, I'd happily go away and not bother anyone about work again'. The chances of Mr. Batty getting his hands on ten acres of Britain are virtually nil. In 1981 that amount of land would have cost him about £17,000... Even if he were in work, on a farmworker's wages, he would have had little hope of saving the sum he would need.[41]

Fifteen years later Mr. Batty's chances of getting some land have improved. Although in the intervening years wages have doubled, large areas of agricultural land have been 'set aside' and the price of all but prime arable land has stagnated. Mr. Batty could still find a ten acre plot for £17,000; if he shared a larger holding with others in the same position, he could obtain workable agricultural land for not much more than £1,000 per acre, or the equivalent of a packet of cigarettes a day for fifteen months. His main problem now would be planning permission.

Moreover, as unemployment has risen, the number of people sharing Mr. Batty's idea of heaven has almost certainly increased. It is impossible to gauge the numbers of people who, if the opportunity were available to them, would seek to establish a home and a livelihood in the countryside, but one particular social phenomenon, unique to Britain, suggests that it is by no means negligible. The so-called new age travellers took over where Mr. Batty left off. Instead of walking to parliament, they bought vans and drove out into the country, creating a minor social cataclysm in the process. Douglas Hurd memorably referred to them as 'mediaeval brigands' and his words were perhaps closer to the truth than he intended, for the root cause of today's traveller problem is the same as in Tudor times: lack of access to land. The only difference is that lack of access nowadays results, less from enclosure of common lands, than from enclosure of development rights. The number of travellers may not be large by comparison to the general population, but there is every reason to believe that they represent the tip of an iceberg of suppressed demand. For every unemployed adventurer that takes to the road, there are a dozen or more who have not glimpsed any way out of a dead end predicament. For many of these people the answer will lie in a more imaginative 'do-it-yourself' approach to urban renewal; but some at least would thrive in a rural setting were they given access to a pightle of land.

Over the last three years the Government has been advising Gypsies and nomads to buy land and apply for planning permission,[42] and this is precisely what a considerable number of travellers have done. So far, planning authorities have proved reluctant to grant approval. But the problem will not go away and the ball is still in the planners' court. Some solution to this complex and longstanding problem of how to accommodate poor people in the countryside, other than herding them, at great public expense, into social housing on the edge of suburbanescent villages, has to be found.

Chapter 3

Tales of the Dispossessed

'Peasant farmers can't buy land with a house. We've been gazumped'.
Sussex smallholder.
' Nor will [active citizenship] be possible unless we use the advent of
newcomers to the countryside as an advantage and a resource, rather than a
problem and a burden'.
White Paper, *Rural England*, p.13.

IN 1991, when Jill Delaney applied for permission to put up a shed for her free range chickens at Steeple Langford, she was refused permission by Salisbury District Council on landscape grounds because the site was on a flood plain 'very visible from the A36'. A new A36 dual carriageway between Steeple Langford and Salisbury was (and still is) due to be bulldozed, with the council's blessing, right across this very flood plain, so one may question the depth of the council's concern for the environment. In fact one member of the planning committee, Councillor David Parker, came out with a completely different set of objections: 'We must put a stop to these quasi-agricultural activities which are springing up all over the country,' he said and went on to explain: 'What I mean by "quasi-agricultural" is a mess of peasant farming, or subsistence farming, which already prevents the Common Agricultural Policy from working in Europe ... hobby farming is a thing of the past in the UK'.[1]

One of Ms. Delaney's problems is that she does not have more than 5 hectares and therefore does not benefit from the right to build agricultural buildings enjoyed by larger farmers.[2] The same is true of Mr. Harker (not his real name),[3] who calls himself a 'hobby farmer' and who, with his wife and brother, keeps 20 pigs and 12 sheep on their three acre field in Hertfordshire. They have spent nearly £1,000 trying, without success, to obtain planning permission for a shelter to house their sheep when lambing and to store feed and machinery. 'The local parish council', say the Harkers, 'are on our side and want to see the land used for more animals, but it's the district council who just keep refusing us ... In our innocence we did actually believe land was here for animals and not for people who move into the country and take over, these seem to be the ones who object most...'

One of these objectors is the owner of the non-working farm — 'the yuppie farm' as Mr. Harker calls it — which backs onto their field. Besides objecting, this farm owner has also, through a solicitor, made an offer to buy the field, although he states that he has no immediate use for it. The Harker family, at the time of writing, were in the process of making their fourth application for planning permission. 'I'm afraid the expense of coming up against yuppie land owners may prove too much for us', says Mrs Harker. 'The land cost us £13,000 and we can't do anything with it'.

In Europe, as Councillor Parker acknowledges, hobby, subsistence and peasant farmers have been given some protection from the monopolistic tendencies of industrial agriculture. Part-time farming keeps small areas of land cultivated, supplies specialist markets, and ensures that in France, for example, over three times as many people are employed on the land as in Britain. The policy in this country has not only been to stack the economic cards against part-time farmers, but sometimes also to prevent them farming by refusing permission for their small sheds and barns.

It is not only part-timers with a few acres that have problems. Imagine a couple, Jack and Jill, who wish to buy a smallholding with the £35,000 they have obtained from the sale of their flat in Swindon. They scan the property pages of local newspapers and find notices such as this one:

> Demand for Second Homes. Michael Chandler of Fox and Sons Country House Department reports an increased demand for country homes by purchasers who will retain their flat or smaller dwelling in London or some other centre in which they work. Consequently, he is expecting a lot of interest in The Cottage, although this name does not clearly demonstrate the fact that the house has with it about 26 acres, thereby being, one could say, a small farm. The property, in the village of Cann, just outside Shaftesbury, has four bedrooms and up to three reception rooms and is on the market at £248,500.[4]

An accompanying photo reveals that this 'cottage' is well endowed with rooms because the adjacent barn has been converted.

Jack and Jill are not dismayed. They know full well that even a cheap bungalow with 26 acres will be beyond their reach, but that doesn't matter because Jack knows a bit about building, and he has always wanted to build his own house.

Eventually the couple find an ideal property. It consists of 18 acres, has water, and includes potentially arable land, pasture and a copse from which they can obtain fuelwood and building materials. There is a small derelict stone structure on the site, which could quickly be roofed to provide shelter. The price is £27,000 which leaves a sum for capital investment. The couple resolve to buy the holding — the only remaining hurdle is planning permission.

Jack and Jill consult their local planning officer, and he arranges an interview with the planning authority's land agent. They show him plans for fencing the pasture, managing the woodland and building up a horticultural business that will supply domestic needs and provide cash crops; they plan in the first few years to supplement their income with part-time teaching and building work. The land agent, however, is not impressed: he advises them that in the present agro-economic climate there is no prospect of them making a viable living from the land. On the basis of the land agent's decision the planning officer informs Jack and Jill that the council will oppose any application for planning permission for a dwelling, either for restoration of the stone shack or for a new building. It is no concern of his that the copse urgently needs management, that the pasture has been degraded by years of haphazard grazing, and that the stone structure will tumble if not attended to, nor is he interested in the fact that Jack and Jill are full of enthusiasm to look after these neglected assets. His concern is to stop unwarranted development in the countryside, as defined by Annex E of Planning Policy Guidance No. 7.

Jack and Jill's problem is that they do not pass the *functional* and *financial* tests prescribed in that document. As regards function they cannot, in the planners' view, provide a convincing reason 'to be on hand day and night in case animals or agricultural processes require essential care at short notice', or 'to deal quickly with emergencies'.5 As regards the financial test, they cannot prove that their holding is 'financially sound', a standard which has never been fixed at any statutory level, but which is proverbially supposed to be the equivalent of the income derived from 50 dairy cows. Since the Agricultural Holdings (Units of Production) Order 1994 calculates the net annual income from an average cow to be £292, this suggests an annual income of £14,960 before fixed costs such as rent, depreciation and so on are taken into account. In practice, planning authorities and Inspectors may be inclined to look sympathetically upon a sum that falls short of this figure. But Jack and Jill are aiming for an income of about £7,000 per year, supplemented by their own produce, and for the first few years part of that will be derived from activities unconnected to the land.

The planning official politely points out to them that Annex E states that 'normally it will be as convenient for farm and forestry workers to live in nearby towns or villages as it will be for them to live where they work. This may have domestic and social advantages as well as avoiding potentially intrusive development in the countryside'.

Jack and Jill do not despair, but resolve to locate premises nearby where they can live whilst they build up the holding to a level that is considered sufficiently viable by the planners to warrant planning permission. They find a small house to rent in a village five miles from their holding, at a price of £350 per month. However, when they have done their sums they estimate that the cost of renting the house, paying the bills and providing transport comes to over £6,000 per year — approximately the sum they hoped to be earning off their holding after several years hard work. They might (if they got rid of their savings) be able to reclaim at least some of the rent in the form of housing benefit. But this would place them in the uncomfortable position of having to prove a low income to receive housing benefit whilst having to establish a high income to have a chance of receiving planning permission — a classic poverty trap.

What do Jack and Jill do? In this fictional case, they take a holiday in the South of France to mull it over. There they discover that rural houses have not all been bought up by urban incomers; that with extensive common lands at their disposal it is possible to build up a viable herd of sheep, goats or cows within three years; and that planning control is, in practice, exercised largely at the discretion of the mayor

A settler's house built out of recycled materials on a smallholding in the south of France. Though technically such buildings require planning permission, village mayors will often allow them to remain if they are discreet and provide accommodation for people who bring life to the rural community.

of the local village, who, in the place where they have alighted, is only too glad to see young people taking an interest in the neglected assets of the village. It does not take long for Jack and Jill to make their decision: they emigrate.

The case of Jack and Jill is fictional, but it is typical, and will ring a bell with many people who have tried to establish themselves in the countryside. What follows are testimonies from some of those who have attempted a similar project. This issue is dealt with at some length, because the voices of people in this situation are rarely heard.

> We feel so frustrated that we are unable to live a simple, sustainable low-impact life-style in England. Janet and I would like to be able to buy a few acres of land on which we could live as a family unit, using environmentally sound sustainable agriculture. We would like to build a house and outbuildings for animals and crop storage using local renewable materials; making sure, also, to use the natural lie of the land and trees (planting more if necessary) to screen the buildings and so prevent a visual eyesore as some farms have become. This is impossible in England as we would not be able to obtain planning permission, even though we owned the land.
>
> Some people have managed this by showing they are making their income from their land, producing a crop that needs protection, e.g. strawberries/poultry, and so need to be on site 24 hours a day. This would not be applicable to us as we would be producing food to be consumed on our smallholding by humans and animals with a small surplus to sell, so we

would not be able to show our income in money terms. Our only hope would be that a planning authority would evaluate us on our sustainability rather than our moneyed income. But this seems a desperate hope, especially as a smallholding would take several years of setting up to become as self-sustainable as possible, during which time we would have to have some outside income to sustain us.

You can see our frustration as there are other countries we can go to to live this lifestyle. But we want to stay in England as we feel at home here and have good friends and family here too. (Philip L.)

We own five acres of south facing sloping land in Worcestershire. Our intention is to build a timber building with compost toilets, grey water system etc. When we visited our planning department to discuss our permaculture development plans and our intention to grow organic exchange or retail surpluses, the 'man' just glazed over and read the book about 'outside the normal prescribed development zone, agricultural wage, 50 dairy cows'.

I came away feeling very downhearted. That was weeks ago, and since then ADAS (to whom I was referred) have really been no help: 'Oh no, you can't make a living on 5 acres, and more skilled people have tried and failed'. ... What is an agricultural wage, how can we overcome this hurdle? (Roberta C.)

'We are a collective of people working on a plot of 28 acres in Cornwall, converting it to a horticultural operation based with a high element of perennials such as soft fruit. In 1988 when we bought the land we put a mobile home and a prefabricated shed on the land to live in, but after an unsuccessful appeal we were forced to leave the land and live two miles away in rented accommodation. We need to commute in a car in order to carry things back and forth between our dwellings and the land. To make matters worse, an Article 4 Direction was placed upon our land withdrawing our permitted agricultural development rights. At the moment we are applying for permission to erect polytunnels and to lay gravel for a car park to accommodate the people who wish to come and view our achievements. The Parish Council have objected on transport grounds. The planners don't take into account the fact that we have planted 12,000 trees upon the land and some two miles of hedges. (Plants for the Future.)

James K., a pig and bee farmer who saved many years to buy his 60 acres in East Sussex, reports that he commutes 30 miles a day to and from his holding and pays £450 per month rent on a cottage, which means he has to hold down a job in a tyre works. All the farm buildings once attached to his land his land were sold off and are now used as non-agricultural residences or workshops. Mr. K comments: 'Peasant farmers can't buy land with a house. We've been gazumped ... What I object to is having to show the planners a certain income. It should be sufficient to show that the land is being work'. (James K.)

It is not only prospective smallholders who experience such problems — established farmers can find themselves in a similar predicament:

David Venables' family has farmed Holly Tree Farm in Cheshire for three generations, but he was refused planning permission for a home on the farm. 'I spent my childhood here and wanted to stay here. We looked at a cottage but the asking price was £100,000 and it needed a lot of work'. For five years Mr. Venables commuted seven miles to his farm from a cheaper house in Macclesfield, getting up at 4 a.m. to milk his Guernsey herd, and not returning to see his children until after evening milking at 6 p.m. Eventually Macclesfield District Council relented and allowed him to build a new house on the farm.[6]

Even where the land has supported a dwelling in the recent past, there is no guarantee that it will be deemed sufficient to do so in the present. Mr. and Mrs. C. wrote to planning consultant and journalist, Gordon Holt:

We own a smallholding in Wales at the moment and very quickly have come to the point where we realize we have not got enough land. We have found a parcel of land of 195 acres. The man that owns it bought the farm three years ago when it had 262 acres and two houses on it. He then sold off the house with a few acres leaving the 195 acres. The council do not seem to like this man. If we purchased the land could the council refuse to grant planning permission, given that we would use the land fully for sheep and cattle?

Holt, in his reply, was careful not to raise their hopes:

The business where a farm is sub-divided together with associated dwellings is quite common. Not surprisingly, local authorities do not like it because they feel that the perpetrator has stripped the assets of a farm for his own profit and has manufactured a situation whereby they may be forced to grant planning permission for a further house in the countryside ... Do expect [the local planning department] to be querulous, not only because of the background to the case, but because local authorities are always cautious about granting permission for new 'agricultural dwellings'. You must accept that at best you will obtain permission for a caravan or mobile home.[7]

For a new smallholding, planning permission for a house, however small or discreet, is almost always out of the question. If a planning authority or committee is sympathetic to a planning application it will almost invariably grant temporary planning permission for a mobile home or caravan on the site, usually for a period of three or five years. Mike F., an organic grower in Hampshire, describes his and his partner's successful application:

We have a 12 acre organic holding growing one acre of potatoes, up to three acres field vegetables, a polytunnel and packing-room/workshop. We've been operating for three years and presently live in the nearby village, three miles away.

We made two planning applications in January 1995, one for four more tunnels, a glasshouse and a barn, and the other for an agricultural dwelling. The application was supported by documents outlining the need for each development and a comprehensive business plan showing a profit (ie. wages for my partner and myself) of £6,000 in the first year and £9,000 in the second year. As we don't have any livestock, we used tunnel and glasshouse management to meet the need to be living on site. We expected to go to appeal, but got the offer of a temporary mobile home at first attempt.

The house was a Segal design [self-build, timber-frame] with slate roof (common on nineteenth century cottages in this area), but the planners indicated that if we proceeded with our application for a house, it would be turned down on design grounds, suggesting we 'redesign to a conventional aesthetic, utilizing brick and plain tile roof', so that will be the next battle to fight in a couple of years time.

Even when temporary planning permission for a mobile home is granted it can involve years of difficulty and uncertainty, with the possibility of refusal when planning permission comes up for renewal.

In 1978 the Chaplins bought a nine acre holding in Wales with a derelict cottage upon it, which until the 1920s had been a viable unit. The farm had a long history of planning refusals, although telephone poles and electricity pylons had been allowed. The Chaplins were refused planning permission to repair the cottage on appeal at the first attempt because they hadn't made any allowance for 'notional rent' in their accounts. On a second appeal, they were given three years temporary planning permission for a mobile home.

When the time came for renewal of the planning permission, Mr. Chaplin wrote to the planning committee stating their case for the right to repair the cottage:

'We have lived in a caravan on the site for six-and-a-half years ... We have worked hard under extreme conditions, a family of four now (two older sons being forced to leave home prematurely, because of the long delay), my wife and myself, a daughter now 23 and a son of 15, living in a sub-standard unit of accommodation ... We have built up a profitable business in pigs/pork and eggs, but have not been allowed to develop the land fully because of the uncertainty of our security of tenure.

If after six-and-a-half years we are forced to leave the land, it will mean even greater hardship to myself and my family. The animals will have to be sold, and without them my livelihood would go. We would have to try to sell the land, which, with its history [of planning refusals] will not be easy. I have no wish to be a burden on the housing department or to become another statistic on the unemployment register ... We are already considerably out of pocket. Our household effects have rotted away in the barn due to the extraordinarily long time they have been stored in unsatisfactory conditions. All we desire is to be allowed to carry on with our business with a proper base essential to good farm management, and to live in peace'.

Once again the local planning authority recommended against renewal; but eventually, following a site visit, they had a change of heart. After a seven year battle, the Chaplin's were finally granted planning permission to rebuild the cottage.[8]

Brian H. who runs a four acre organic holding with a mobile home and farm shop in Yorkshire, writes that the ploys and prevarication employed by the council to prevent him from setting up his business have left him 'speechless'. The council has refused consistently to reply to his letters, objected to him replacing uprooted hedgerows and providing screening for his four polytunnels, and tried to impose a condition forbidding him to sell his produce directly to the public. His application for a small bungalow, to the council's design, was turned down at committee stage because (like the Chaplins') his financial projections do not take account of 'notional rent', even though he has no rent or mortgage to pay, low inputs and grosses between £13,000 and £19,000. According to Mr. H. there are another four or five smallholders in the same district who have encountered similar problems: 'The council', he says, 'do not want us'.

Eric Y. and his wife — middle aged divorcees from the Midlands seeking a new start — bought seven acres of land in Somerset. The property came with a mobile home which had first been given temporary planning permission ten years previously, for a livery operation. However the couple decided that a free-range chicken business and egg round would be more appropriate and obtained permission for poultry houses. When the time came for renewal of planning permission for the mobile home, it was refused on the grounds that it was given for a livery operation. Mr. and Mrs. Y. are afraid that, in an appeal, their egg business will not be viewed as viable, even though Mr. Y. states: 'On our land we can live quite happily on about £50 per week'.

The temporary mobile home scenario can also cause great anxiety if the situation changes through illness, divorce or a some other event that makes it difficult to achieve the agricultural targets upon which temporary permission was granted.

Mr. and Mrs. W. acquired 35 acres of woodland and pasture in the West Country in 1990. They went through the familiar round of refusals for planning permission — on the grounds that their 40 breeding sows would not be sufficient to give them a viable income — but finally received five years temporary planning permission for a mobile home in 1992. After a couple of years they found that they could make a better income and share the work load better if Mr. W. pursued the timber and firewood business, while his wife kept free range hens and ran a roadside stall.

However, in 1995 the couple split up and Mrs. W. was left alone on the holding. She still runs the egg and roadside stall business but relies on outside labour to cut the firewood that she sells at her stall. She pays for the labour with money earned from her paintings of local landscapes, an activity which would not be regarded by the planners as agricultural. She knows that in two years time, when the planning permission comes up for renewal, the council could, if they were minded, refuse to allow her to continue living in her home if the agricultural objective is not met.

The cases quoted above are not isolated examples of a marginal problem, but have been repeated across the country — there can be few rural district councils in England that have not had their share of similar applications. The planning journalist, Gordon Holt, writes:

I receive more letters on the subject of gaining planning permission for dwellings or caravans at embryo smallholdings than on any other subject. The situation has not altered for many years and it is still just as difficult, if not more so, to show to a planning authority's satisfaction that a holding is genuinely viable.[9]

To smallholders, the planners' objections seem brutally unfair and full of anomalies. Why, they ask, is the planning system so fanatically determined to make life difficult for people trying to start up a small farming enterprise? What justice is there in a system which allows wealthy city dwellers with no agricultural income whatsoever to buy up farmhouses, and yet denies smallholders the right to live on their land? What sort of ethic of countryside protection permits pylons to be erected on a farm, but refuses to allow its farmhouse to be restored? And what kind of respect can one have for the architectural judgments of a planning authority that readily allows concrete barns to be erected and tolerates the emplacement of an aluminium mobile home, but rejects a timber frame building on the same land, because it does not conform with the 'conventional aesthetic'? While the planners make decisions such as these, however genuine their reasons, many people in the country will continue to believe that the main purpose of the planning system is not to preserve the countryside but to reserve it for urban incomers.

The planners' view

From the planners' point of view, however, there are good reasons for placing as many obstacles as they can find in the way of applications for agricultural and other rural dwellings. In many of the cases outlined above, the planning officers concerned will have their own story to tell. Their mission is to protect the countryside from urban development. Every new house creates a precedent which is an invitation for applications for bogus agricultural dwellings. Having allowed one house, a planning authority may find it more difficult to argue in an appeal against the construction of a second; and if it is not careful it may acquire a reputation as being a soft touch for developers. The problem is exacerbated — if not entirely created — by the very restrictions on building that are designed to protect the countryside: the artificially high price of development land (in the absence of a betterment levy) generates the profits which attract the developers. Market mechanisms can run amok when supply is artificially restricted by command and control.

Planners are wary because the method by which 'agricultural need' for a dwelling is assessed at the moment is susceptible to abuse. Mike Fletcher, a planning specialist with a firm of chartered surveyors in Cirencester, explained in the Financial Times how many high earning city dwellers have built luxury homes in open countryside 'by claiming to be earning a living from worm farming or growing mushrooms'.[10] Ashley Brown, a district planning officer, agrees that this form of abuse is becoming more prevalent: 'How many times have we seen the livestock disappear after consent has been granted?' This form of abuse, he maintains, is carried out 'usually by people who are not genuine farmers and are prepared to take a few risks. The genuine farmer is being tarred with the same brush. When the latter sees the former getting away with it, the planning system is discredited, and local people become cynical'.[11]

Even when the farmer is genuine, there is no guarantee that he or she will succeed. The farmer may go bankrupt or simply die, and whoever acquires or inherits the property may not be remotely agriculturally inclined. The council can impose conditions or obligations tying the house to an agricultural occupation. But these can be circumvented by the city dwelling 'worm and mushroom farmers' of the kind cited above; or they can be overturned if, as PPG 7 puts it, 'changes in the scale and character of farming and forestry in response to market forces' mean that the occupancy conditions 'have outlived their usefulness'[12] — which presumably means if the farm goes bankrupt. The situation is quite legally exploited by a firm of planning consultants which specializes in getting agricultural ties removed from existing dwellings and in obtaining planning permission for new agricultural dwellings. In effect, the firm is restricting supply with one hand and increasing it with the other. The company claims never to take on a case which it cannot win — and to have direct links to people in the Department of the Environment responsible for drafting PPG 7.[13]

In such a context, planners are frequently faced with invidious decisions, and they can hardly be blamed for playing safe and refusing permission, usually on the grounds that the application does not meet the functional or financial requirements outlined in PPG 7. In practice, since functional need is relatively difficult to define and easy to fabricate, this often boils down to the question: 'Is the applicant going to make enough money?' This may be a convenient way of assessing the genuineness of an application, but it stretches the meaning of the word genuine in a rather sinister direction, and there is room for doubt as to whether it is a sensible yardstick by which to measure who should and who shouldn't live in a sustainable countryside.

The deficiencies of the current approach are exemplified in a recent Department of the Environment research report called Planning Control over Agricultural and Forestry Development and Rural Building Conversions, by a number of planning consultants, including a firm called Land Use Consultants (LUC).[14] This report bears looking at in some detail, since its conclusions are likely to find favour not only with the government, but also with sections of the environmental lobby.

The report is alarmed at what it calls the 'fragmentation' of farmland in England and Wales. Redundant farmland is not necessarily being amalgamated into bigger farms; much of it is instead being sold off in small lots to people without land. This fragmentation, the report continues, 'may result in considerable pressure for new

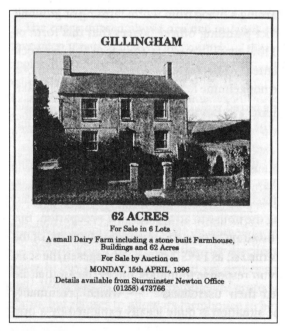

GILLINGHAM

62 ACRES
For Sale in 6 Lots
A small Dairy Farm including a stone built Farmhouse,
Buildings and 62 Acres
For Sale by Auction on
MONDAY, 15th APRIL, 1996
Details available from Sturminster Newton Office
(01258) 473766

buildings and can have a profound effect on landscape character'. While the original farmhouse, and possibly the outbuildings as well, are acquired by urban commuters or weekenders, the bare-land plots tend to be bought up by prospective smallholders who install barns, cowsheds, stables, pig arks, caravans, lorry containers and what have you — 'shackery' as the report calls it — and then sometimes apply for planning permission for a further agricultural dwelling to accommodate themselves. Thus in the Brecon Beacons

National Park, for example, over the last 13 years, 80 planning permissions have been granted for new agricultural dwellings, whilst the agricultural population of the Park has fallen by 10 per cent over the same period.[15]

It is easy to understand why the authors of the report are concerned. Most people would rather not see post-urban shackery, horseyculture development and new agricultural bungalows sprouting willy-nilly over the English or Welsh countryside, particularly when there are traditional farm buildings built to fulfil the same purposes. But the report is short on ideas for preventing the haemorrhage of farmhouses to the commuter economy. Although they do make one constructive proposal to strengthen existing agricultural occupancy ties,[16] the authors shy away from much more robust measures such as tying farm dwellings to agricultural land; such legislation, they suggest, would cause 'hardship' to existing farmers, partly because 'banks may not lend money' on the security of farm buildings which can no longer be sold to a commuter for several hundred thousand pounds. Apparently, the existing farm economy is financially dependent upon the demand for scarce rural dwellings.[17]

Instead, the report advocates making life more difficult for the (usually debt free) pioneers who cannot afford a farmhouse and attempt to set up on the relatively cheap bare-land plots. In particular they recommend the following measures:

• a nationally defined pass mark for the financial test of at least the minimum agricultural wage, plus allowance for any overtime, plus a reasonable return on capital investment (suggesting a total income in the region of £14,000 per annum);

• withdrawal of permitted development rights for anyone with less than ten hectares (the present threshold is five);

• simplifying Article 4 directions, which withdraw permitted development rights, and removing the requirement for compensation;

• tripling the cost of notifying the council of the erection of a permitted agricultural building;

• that 'PPG 7 should note that there are likely to be few situations where a new forestry dwelling is justified'.[18]

These proposals may, if they can be enforced, succeed in diminishing the amount of undesirable 'shackery'. But they will do so by discriminating against smaller landowners (in effect, targeting the victim) — by tackling the problem at its shoots, rather than at its roots. There is no attempt in the report to take a strategic approach to the process of fragmentation. 'It might be questioned whether this fragmentation matters', the report announces in a moment of hesitation in the final chapter,19 but there is no proper discussion of this primordial question, no acknowledgement that many might consider the redistribution of land to less wealthy people to be a good thing. Nor is there any inkling of what activity will be allowed on these redundant bare-land plots if small scale and part-time agriculture is restricted.

In fact the blinkered outlook of the report — and one suspects that the blinkers are imposed by the DoE — almost beggars belief. It does not take into account the view of the Rural Development Commission that the smallest farms may well find themselves quite favourably placed as a result of recent Common Agricultural Policy Reforms: 'A growing proportion are operated as part-time businesses and are buttressed by other sources of family income. This fact and their relatively low indebtedness mean that they can operate with very low returns'.[20] It does not refer to the fact that small labour intensive farms are consistently found by agro-economists to be more productive per acre and per unit of energy used than large ones.[21] Nor does it examine the entirely reasonable suggestion that, since the amalgamation of farmland for industrial agriculture has been responsible for much environmental degradation, fragmentation might be potentially conducive to environmental improvement. After the token seven line paragraph on 'sustainability' at the beginning of the report, the concept is only mentioned once more, in the penultimate chapter, where it is taken as being synonymous with traffic reduction.[22]

The report also passes over, in one paragraph, an entirely different and more imaginative approach to the problem of shackery adopted by two of the 23 district councils in the study sample. This is to allow planning permission for an agricultural dwelling or change of use of an agricultural building, subject to a legal agreement limiting or forbidding the use of temporary structures such as lorry containers.[23] 'Yes', say these authorities, 'you can live there, provided you agree not to make too much of a mess'. Planning deals such as these give people the opportunity to live or work in the countryside on the condition that they respect environmental constraints; the second part of this book will suggest that this kind of approach to rural development is more equitable and more environmentally productive.

Despite all these deficiencies in the report's analysis, its recommendations are likely to be viewed favourably by CPRE, the Countryside Commission and similar organizations, who (the report tells us) see them as a 'step in the right direction' towards comprehensive regulation of agricultural development.[24] They are also likely to be heeded by the Government, which in its Rural White Paper announced 'additional steps to prevent the abuse of agricultural permitted development rights'.[25]

However, if they are introduced, they will be greeted with resentment by many people who live or work in the countryside. Victoria Wood once observed that there would never be a revolution in this country unless they outlawed car boot sales. The right of countrydwellers to rear a few animals on a plot of land is cherished in much the same way. Although the piecemeal erosion of this right is hardly likely to inspire the kind of protest seen in the Welsh firebombing campaign against second homes in the 1980s, one wonders whether the authors and supporters of this report have not underestimated the degree of resistance their proposed measures might meet; or the possibility that widespread non-compliance might make them unenforceable.

In search of a livelihood

Besides smallholders and farmers who wish to live on their holdings, there is a further and wider constituency of people who claim the right to live on their land, without any special reference to an agricultural need.

In November 1995, Ashley Brown, District Planning Officer for Wealden District Council, wrote an article calling for increased powers of enforcement against those who attempted to secure a dwelling in the countryside surreptitiously:

> Over the past couple of years we have had a spate of enforcement cases where somebody has been 'hiding' in the woods in a caravan, shed or in some cases in a haystack, underneath which were living quarters — all in an attempt to emerge after four years to claim lawful residential use and seek permission for a dwelling on the site.[26]

Mr. Brown refers to the ruling (in the Planning and Compensation Act 1991), which states that if a change of use of a building goes unnoticed for four years, then that use becomes lawful.[27] He advocates extension of the time period because 'four years is not that long in enforcement time scales'.

Brown's characterization of these activities as 'ruses and wheezes' is a little unfair. Hiding in a shed or under a haystack for four years is not the kind of scam that would appeal to the serious property speculator: as one couple hiding in a Kent chestnut coppice explains, it means 'black-out blinds at night and a fear that every microlight overhead is from "The Planning Hit Squad"'.[28] Any implication that at the end of the period the smiling culprit can emerge from the haystack with straw in their hair and automatically claim planning permission for a three-bedroomed bungalow with conservatory and garage is wide of the mark. There are opportunities for prestigious barn conversions here; but most of these stowaways are people in need.

Brown's approach to the problem is typical of those planners who consider their only role to be the enforcement of DoE policy and to reporting back when the mechanism is not working. He does not consider the reasons why so many people are defying the planning system in this way, nor does he suggest any positive planning policy which might help to accommodate this demand.

There has been no study of those who, either openly or surreptitiously, pursue a 'do-it-yourself' rural existence in defiance of the planning laws (though there is considerable material on the experience and attitudes of Gypsies and travellers). This chapter cannot provide a comprehensive account of this phenomenon, but it will hopefully go some way towards supplying the answers to three basic questions: Who are they? What do they seek? And how do they justify their right to live in the countryside?

Who are they?

Aside from prospective farmers and smallholders, people setting up dwellings without planning permission can be classed under the following categories. These cases occur predominately, but not exclusively, in the open countryside:

- People repairing ruined cottages or outhouses (often bought in ignorance of the fact that they required planning permission).
- Light industrial or craft workers living in their workshop.
- People living in caravans, sheds or tents on a small plot of land where they

are gardening or keeping animals as a sideline.

• Coppice and forestry workers living in benders or caravans in their woods.

• People building underground houses on their own land.

• People living in sheds on allotments. This may be more widespread than is generally appreciated. Cases have been recorded in North East England, in Southampton and in Somerset.[29]

• A few people are performing a service; for example, in 1995, one Somerset man, living in a small shed, had been lent it in return for checking that Christmas trees on a plantation were not stolen.

• Settlements of benders or tipis, for example Tipi Valley in Wales, Yoke Farm in Herefordshire, and Kings Hill in Somerset.

• Gypsies and travellers who (in accordance with recent Government recommendations) have bought land upon which to settle.

• Nomadic people who stop on land temporarily.

What do they seek?

Clearly, all these categories of people are seeking a secure and affordable place to live. Travellers, in particular, emphasise the need for somewhere 'safe', especially if they have children. An alarming number have had their vans or caravans attacked or fire-bombed by vigilantes and in several cases dogs have been burned or bludgeoned to death. Here is a small number of cases from the list compiled by Friends, Families and Travellers' Support Group, all of them taking place in the month of April 1994:

Somerset: Small well established site attacked by vigilantes firing lead weights. Windows broken only a few feet from sleeping children.

Cirencester: A group of horse drawn travellers have the spokes hammered out of their wheels; girl on site hit round head with iron bar by masked people with balaclavas.

Cornwall: Single parent faces angry farmers with guns in their vehicles who threaten to 'take her out' if she does not leave. In the previous year, the same woman had the grass around her bus set alight by a similar group.

Lincolnshire: Travellers who drive over a mound of earth to regain access to an established site are arrested for damage to a pile of earth. Their children are sent to relations. While in custody, their vehicles are seen being 'ridden around like dodgems' — several are damaged and one is written off.[30]

This kind of victimization is taking place all over England, and is largely unreported in the press. It is one reason why considerable numbers of travellers have emigrated to countries such as Ireland or Spain.

Besides the need for a secure home, individuals cite a number of reasons why they actively choose to live what many would view as an uncomfortable existence on a scrap of land in defiance of the planning system:

Two designs for low impact building, one (above) by a traveller living in a van and the other (below) by a settler living in a tent.

• The need to live near their work. This particularly applies to coppice and woodland workers.

• The desire for a place to keep a few animals and tend a garden on a part-time or subsistence basis.

• The preference for an outdoor life, and in some cases a feeling that living between four brick walls is claustrophobic. 'We want to live in a green environment, and we are prepared to sacrifice the so-called benefits of modern housing to be able to do so'.[31]

• The desire to build one's own house, often in an experimental style. The experimental low impact rural architecture that has flourished in countries such as the US and France (see pictures, pp 34, 60 and 103) is virtually outlawed in the UK.

• The desire to establish a more independent life style, as opposed to being 'spoon fed' by the state.

• The desire for a low consumption sustainable life style; or as one tipi dweller put it, adherence to Gandhian ideals of simplicity which are 'nearly impossible to live by in the context of a society which is geared to maximize consumption at every turn'.[32]

• In the case of Gypsies and travellers, the desire to retain some of the traditional aspects of Gypsy culture in a settled situation.[33]

• The absence of any alternative: 'anyone whose only toehold on the property ladder is £200 worth of canvas and a few wooden poles has a very limited range of alternative options'.[34]

Many of these aims are summed up in a statement sent to the author by Francine I. and Steve P., two semi-itinerant craft workers:

We are a couple living and working together in our chosen lifestyle. We are 29 and 31 years old respectively. We are both professional craft workers specializing in two traditional fields of work: feltmaking and green woodworking. We established the business, four years ago, as a mobile craft workshop to support our travelling lifestyle. Our choice of work was guided by the desire to be able to set up and work anywhere, without being dependent upon mains electricity and high impact resources. We work with manual tools and techniques and use native renewable resources: British wool and wood.

We also build and sell traditional wooden framed tents known as yurts, suitable for temporary low impact accommodation or workspace all the year round. We live in two yurts joined together, using one as a studio. We want to live like we do to lessen the impact which we have on the environment. Living where we work, close to our source of materials, specifically coppiced deciduous woodland, we would be lessening our impact by removing the need to travel.

We want to buy some land with woods, on which we can live and work. Our real desire is to design and construct a solid timber framed building using the yurt structure as its inspiration. The materials for this would ideally come from on-site coppiced woodland. We would want to use renewable energy systems and passive biological systems to cater

This English-built yurt is equipped with a telephone, solar powered electric lighting, and a wood burning stove made out of an old gas bottle. Photo: Sara Hannant.

for wastes. With a detailed management plan, we would actually benefit the environment by creating a broader habitat for flora and fauna.

We want to be allowed to live and maintain this sustainable lifestyle. We do not want to be marginalized or victimized for desiring to live this type of life style. We aim to support ourselves rather than be dependent upon the State. If allowed we would be able to provide low impact housing for ourselves, instead of becoming an addition to another housing list'.

How do they justify their right to live on the land?

Many of these settlers find it inconceivable that they should not be allowed to live on their land. This conviction does not in most cases derive from a sentiment that 'everyone should have the right to do what they want on their own land'. Rather it stems from the observation that 'everyone has got to be somewhere' — a truism that the planning system has found rather difficult to come to terms with. Since the price of development land is way out of reach of these people's pockets, they do not see any option other than to install themselves on land not assigned for development.

A typical example is Mike H., who in 1994 was evicted from eleven acres of marginal land in Galloway, where he was living in a van. 'There doesn't seem to be any place for people to fulfil themselves outside the system. To grow a bit of food and live cheaply. I don't want to get a house and a mortgage where you have to earn £100 a week before you can even breathe … You get out of the rat race and you find yourself in another rat race [i.e the planning laws]. You can't expect everyone to leap into the sea like lemmings'.

They also argue that they are doing no harm. People living in tents, caravans, underground houses and other temporary dwellings not unnaturally point to the green field developments of fifty or more large houses, complete with garages, access roads and street lighting, and ask: 'If they are allowed to do all that in the country-side, why are we not allowed to live in our humble dwellings?' The four year rule cited by Ashley Brown is generally viewed not as a 'wheeze' but as a sensible (and cheap) test of low impact: if nobody notices the dwelling for four years, then it cannot be doing any great harm to anyone.

Finally, aside from smallholders and forestry workers, the majority of settlers do not claim an agricultural need to live on the land. The post-1947 view that devel-opment in the countryside should be restricted to the agricultural industry is neither understood nor appreciated. What many settlers are looking for is a base where they can build up a livelihood, relying, more often that not, on a variety of economic pursuits, backed up by a measure of subsistence production. Some are reticent about citing their contribution to the local economy as a justification for their presence, because at the time they are reliant upon income support; people in this situation tend to emphasise that by providing their own shelter, they are relieving the commu-nity of the need to provide housing or housing benefit. However, well established settlements are usually confident of their contribution to society. The Kings Hill collective, a settlement of ex-travellers, states in its appeal submission: 'As we have become established here, local people have come to know and trust us and we have been able to find an increasing amount of work in this and adjoining parishes ... We believe that our presence here makes a positive contribution to the economic and cultural vitality of the parish and many local residents share this view'.[35]

In summary, settlers justify their presence in the countryside on three main grounds: equity, low impact and livelihood. Since planning policy states that 'the guiding principle in the wider economy is that development should benefit the rural economy and maintain or enhance the environment,'[36] these are strong arguments for the introduction of some measure of low impact development into the country-side, at least on an experimental basis.

The extent of the demand for a low impact life style of this kind should not be exaggerated. Most people do not want to live in benders, caravans or rustic chalets, and the number of people actively attempting to do so at the moment is probably only in the order of tens of thousands. Numerically this does not present a threat to the status quo, and planners would do well to view the existence of this highly envi-ronmentally aware minority as an opportunity, rather than a curse.

PART TWO

Chapter 4

Low Impact Development: Creating a New Land Use

'Sustainable development challenges us all to accommodate development in ways that enhance or protect the environment'.   White Paper, *Rural England*, p.129.

AFTER FIFTY YEARS of relatively smooth passage, rural planners have suddenly ridden into a storm of difficulties. Over the next decade they will have, somehow, to help curb the excesses of industrial farming; to find a role for the large acreages of agricultural land being taken out of production; to identify forms of development that will prevent the countryside becoming a 'museum' and yet will protect or enhance the environment; to cope with an increasing demand for a rural life style, from everybody from commuters to New Age travellers; to help find ways of reducing Britain's dependence on a disproportionate quantity of the world's limited resources; and to establish criteria for sustainable development in accordance with Agenda 21.

These are knotty problems indeed. But a tangled ball of knots will, on examination, often be found to consist of a single length of string. It is by no means easy to unravel the thread that connects all of the above issues. Indeed it would appear that there are several: betterment, industrial agriculture, the global market, non-renewable energy, to name but a few. But in the last few years a growing number of people concentrating on one or other of these single issues have been coming up with similar solutions. There are grounds for believing that current rural planning policy, to borrow a phrase from Wendell Berry, has taken a single solution and divided it up so as to create a number of apparently separate problems.

The term 'low impact development' — together with a hierarchy of lesser categories such as low impact architecture, building, accommodation, dwelling, etc. — is cropping up with increasing frequency in a number of different contexts. It has been used by architects specializing in landscape-sensitive design, by organizations advocating better access to land for travellers, by planners who perceive a need to site a project in open countryside. One draft local plan — for South Somerset — has an entire policy dedicated to 'low impact dwellings' associated with agricultural use.[1]

In most cases the suggestion, or implication, is that there may be a justification for allowing the erection of a building with a low environmental impact on a site where a building of higher impact could not be allowed. More adventurously, it is being mooted that the level of environmental impact of a development provides a better standard by which to judge its acceptability, than the use to which it will be put and the zone in which it will be sited. What, for example, is the logic in refusing permission for a small discreet cottage along a country lane when a farmer can erect a 120 foot long concrete monstrosity in the field opposite without even applying for permission? If the reason for planning restrictions in the countryside is to protect the rural environment, would it not be better to proscribe buildings that have a high and undesirable impact on the environment, rather than, as at present, buildings that are unconnected with a viable agricultural enterprise?

Before addressing this question, it is important to recall that the impact of a building is felt not only in its immediate surroundings but over a wide radius, through the materials that are used in its construction, the energy it consumes, the traffic and waste that it generates and the use to which it is put. An average village semi-detached house has its own ecological footprint: it may derive raw materials from 10,000 miles away, or from an oil well in the ocean; it may draw its water from Wales and deposit its effluents in the North Sea; and it may generate an increase in regular traffic along an already congested corridor by siting a domicile far from suitable sources of employment.

The comprehensive scope of the term 'environmental impact' was emphasised in the proof of evidence of the Kings Hill Collective at their appeal for planning permission for a bender site on their land in Somerset:

> It seems that the Council, in their continuing preoccupation with 'visual amenity', have misinterpreted the term 'low impact' as referring exclusively to visual impact. While we do indeed contend that the benders are of low visual impact, the central concept is that of low environmental impact, due to their temporary nature, and, crucially, their very low resource consumption, both in construction and in use, in comparison with more conventional forms of housing. It is this, coupled with the ecologically sensitive management of the site, which leads us to describe the benders as low impact dwellings, and the project as a whole as an experimental sustainable living system. We would reiterate that we consider this to be precisely the sort of endeavour which local authorities are encouraged to support under Agenda 21.[2]

At present, the issues of environmental impact and sustainability raised by the Kings Hill Collective are regarded as 'material considerations' in the planning process; that is to say, they are to be taken into account when a planning proposal is assessed 'on its merits'. However they are not the over-riding consideration. That remains the siting of the proposal within the zones laid down in the development plan. If an application for a residence, for example, or a workshop, lies within the designated zone for residential or industrial development, then there will be a 'planning presumption' in its favour; if, on the other hand, the site applied for lies outside the designated zone, then there will be a planning presumption against granting permission. In this case the applicant will have to demonstrate sufficient need to qualify as a 'warranted exception'. Occasionally the fact that a proposal has a low visual impact upon the immediate environment may help to swing the case in the applicant's favour. But in most cases, planning permission is granted, not according to what one wishes to build, but according to where one wishes to build it.

Proponents of low impact development argue that there should be a planning presumption in favour of buildings which either enhance the local and global environment, or, at least have a very low environmental impact. Concentrating ugly, resource-hungry houses in dense settlements on the edge of key villages does not make them any more beautiful or any more sustainable — it is largely a manifestation of landscape guilt, an attempt to find the least obtrusive place to put them. Such settlements still extract resources from other 'ghost acres' in the British countryside or elsewhere in the world; and they continue to eat away at the countryside as long as there remains profit in pushing what Laurie Lee once described as the 'crocodile-skin of new houses' further up the valleys. If we are serious about protecting the local countryside and the global environment, common sense dictates that we need to build houses, farms and factories that do just that — buildings that have a low impact on the local and global environment.

If planning authorities were to make it relatively easy to obtain planning permission for low impact sustainable buildings, and correspondingly difficult to obtain permission for high impact unsustainable ones, then it is clear that within a decade or so they would go a long way towards meeting the environmental obligations laid down in Agenda 21. However such a policy would generate more than simple environmental improvement; it would also have a profound effect upon the social and economic structure of the country. It is here that we can begin to unravel the single thread that runs through all of the issues cited at the beginning of this chapter — and at one end of this thread is the question of betterment.

Development land prices are high because building land is restricted to certain zones and hence scarce. The scarcity creates the profits which attract the developers. Any move which allowed a significant measure of low impact building outside these zones would reduce the scarcity and lower the price of building land. The incentive for speculation would thus be considerably reduced. The challenge for the prospective builder or developer would no longer be to find and acquire (preferably at a bargain price) a site with planning potential, but to satisfy the local planning authority or the Department of the Environment that the development was of low environmental impact. A widespread relaxation of planning restrictions for low impact developments would dissolve the problem of betterment — or put another way, the betterment would now pertain to the community in the form of environmental improvement.

In 1994, Tony Wrench outlined a vision of a new category of low impact land use which he called 'Permaculture (PC) Land':

The essence of PC Land would be that there is a contractual relationship between the owner and the local/national authorities. This states, basically:

'I will buy and live on just this plot of land. I will not buy several plots and speculate. I will not let it out. I will conserve energy and nature. I will plant over 20 trees per acre. I will co-operate with my neighbours over transport, infrastructure, power generation, waste disposal, water harvesting and supply, and common land. In return for the freedom to build my own house in the style I choose, I will do without additional connections to mains water, electricity, sewerage or road systems'.

Planning authorities would be given the power to designate any area PC Land, whether it was previously industrial, agricultural, military or even residential land. Conditions would be put on the number of dwellings per acre, roads and vehicles, and a height limit of structures appropriate to the site.[3]

Wrench supposes that in Year One of the scheme a number of trial areas would be designated and farmers would apply 'in their hundreds' for designation. He predicts that with this initial restricted supply, PC land would sell at about £10,000 per acre. However by Year Five, with PC land more readily available, prices would fall to around £4,000 per acre, about double that of good agricultural land. Clearly, if virtually all land (including urban land but barring National Parks and other ecologically sensitive sites) were declared potential PC land, then the price would stabilize at the actual use value of the land — above present agricultural values because there would be the opportunity of building upon it, but in rural areas not much above, because PC building land would no longer be scarce. The incentive to speculate would be almost non-existent.

Wrench goes on to predict a number of far reaching consequences of such a scheme. Environmental quality would improve drastically through an increase in tree planting, organic agriculture and the use of renewable energy; but at the same time, easy and affordable access to land would trigger a boom in low impact building which would reduce homeless figures, revive local economies, and solve many of the problems associated with smallholders, travellers and the homeless. Rural domiciles would become accessible, not only to rich urban commuters and retired people, but also to poorer people seeking to establish a livelihood. Fragmentation of farmland would accelerate, but instead of a moonscape of caravans, horseboxes and bunga-lows, a more wooded landscape would emerge providing the matrix for intensively farmed holdings practising more self-sufficient and sustainable forms of husbandry. As the land based rural population increased, so would local infrastructure, in the form of marketing co-operatives, community services, workshop facilities, local schools and public transport. In cities where degraded areas were declared PC zones, a new kind of urban environment would emerge — greener, traffic free, more creative, more human scale.

A contract of the kind described by Wrench represents a bargain struck between the citizen and the state. 'In return for the freedom to build my own house ...' the citizen agrees to abide by certain environmental constraints. Throughout British history, restrictions upon access to land have been at the root of many social problems, and currently these restrictions are imposed, ostensibly, for environmental reasons. Giving people access to land in return for a commitment to protect and enhance the environment is the key to the resolution of these problems.

Essentially this bargain is a form of what planners call 'planning gain'. The benefits derived by developers from the increase in the value of the land when it is accorded planning permission can, in part at least, be channelled back to the community by imposing certain obligations upon the developer. The archetypal situation is one in which the developer of a supermarket, in return for receiving planning permission, is obliged to construct or contribute towards the cost of a new road. The same mechanism operates with low impact development, except that the person receiving planning permission is obliged, not to provide expensive high impact infrastructure such as a new road, but to provide environmental protection, maintenance or improvements. The individual thus profits from an affordable place to live or work; the environment benefits from regulated low impact land use; and society benefits from the creation, at no public expense, of a new dwelling and/or livelihood.

This is not to suggest that all land should immediately become open to low impact development, but simply to point out what would happen if it were. Tony Wrench's vision of a new land use class is a proposal which no Government could introduce overnight because of the shock effect it would have on land prices. There are a number of reasons why low impact development needs to be introduced with great care; and there are other less radical means by which local authorities can release land for low impact development, using mechanisms which already exist within the current planning structure. It is through a measured use of these mechanisms that planners will be able to forge a sustainable rural environment that is open to rich and poor. However before we look at these, it is necessary to define the criteria by which the environmental impact of developments can be assessed.

Chapter 5

Nine Criteria for Low Impact

'Painful experience of past mistakes has made development a pejorative word
for many people in the countryside. This makes it all the more important to assess
the impacts of development upon the environment'.
White Paper, *Rural England.*

W HAT MAKES a building low impact? Is this a question that can be easily
answered? Or are we entering into treacherous subjective territory, much as
if we asked, 'What makes a building beautiful'?

Fortunately, we are not. Many matters pertaining to a building's impact are a
question of degree. How high is it? How much fossil fuel will it consume? There is,
admittedly, an element of qualitative judgment involved insofar as these factors
relate to an agreed standard of environmental quality. But since basic agreement
upon this standard has been reached by most of the world's governments at the Rio
Earth Summit, any disagreement is likely to revolve around interpretation of
Agenda 21, rather than its basic objectives.

Planners already possess one tool for environmental assessment: the requirement,
under EU law, that planning applications for certain developments should provide
an 'environmental statement ... for the purpose of assessing the likely impact upon
the environment of the development proposed to be carried out'.1 An environmental
statement can be required by the Secretary of State for a wide variety of developments ranging from breweries and poultry farms to roads and radioactive waste
dumps, but dwellings and residential estates are not on the list. Whether they should
be or not is of no great concern here since, by its nature, any planning application
for a low impact building will be an environmental statement in itself. What should
be noted are the broad terms of reference which apply. According to the Assessment
of Environmental Effects Regulations 1988 an environmental statement must
consider the likely 'direct and indirect effects' of the development upon 'human
beings, flora, fauna, soil, water, air, climate, the landscape, the interaction of any of
the foregoing, material assets and the cultural heritage'; and may include, by way
of amplification, 'secondary, cumulative, short, medium and long term, permanent,
temporary, positive and negative effects'.2

This is a fairly exhaustive list of all the effects that need to be considered in an environmental impact analysis of a hopefully low impact building. But it is not particularly helpful in telling us what a low impact rural building might look like, what it is likely to be made of, how it might operate and who might live in it. A considerable amount of work has been performed on these questions by a wide range of organizations, and it is possible to isolate nine features that are likely to characterize a low impact development. These are that the development:

- is temporary;
- is small-scale;
- is unobtrusive;
- is made from predominately local materials;
- protects wildlife and enhances biodiversity;
- consumes a low level of non-renewable resources;
- generates little traffic;
- is used for a low impact or sustainable purpose;
- is linked to a recognized positive environmental benefit.

Few buildings are likely to conform to all these categories. But a significantly low impact building is likely to conform to many of them, and they provide a useful check list against which planners and the public can assess the impact of any proposal.

Temporary

This category is in a class apart, since temporariness is only beneficial in certain cases. There is clearly no advantage in a project that is designed to have a positive environmental effect being short term.

Temporary accommodation is already firmly entrenched in the planning lexicon. After the war, many of the homeless were housed in temporary dwellings such as prefabs; similar constructions are now, typically, used to accommodate school classes by a cash-strapped education system. Temporary structures such as marquees or caravans are a permitted form of development for up to 28 days in the year.[3] In rural areas, temporary dwellings are authorized 'where there is evidence supporting an application for an agricultural or forestry dwelling but it is inconclusive'[4] and have become the rule rather than the exception when planning permission is granted for smallholders. Government policy states: 'A second temporary permission should not normally be granted. A trial period should be set that is sufficiently long for it to be clear by the end of the first permission whether permanent permission or a refusal is the right answer'.[5] In practice, planning authorities or appeals Inspectors frequently do renew temporary planning permission[6] and there are cases of small-holders who have lived for ten years or more in a mobile home.

Aside from the 28 day rule, the planning system therefore tends to sanction temporary development less for its low impact than as a stop gap or trial measure. There is one exception, although this has not yet been ratified: the South Somerset draft local plan acknowledges that 'some travelling people and others who wish to live an environmentally low impact life style live in 'benders', which are temporary

Hal Wynne-Jones' complex of adjoining yurts being erected at a festival in London, 1994.
The structure is made from coppiced, steam-bent willow and covered with canvas.
Photo: Nick Cobbing.

structures for which no conventional foundations are required. On removal of these structures, regeneration of the site to its former condition occurs in three to six months. Where temporary low impact dwellings cause no harm visually, environmentally or to the amenity of occupiers of adjacent properties, and where the site can be restored to its former condition, there would be no objection in principle'.[7]

The South Somerset draft policy (which may be withdrawn from the plan under pressure from the DoE) is a recognition of a view that has been put forward for some time now by many who live a nomadic or cyclical existence: that moving one's dwelling from time to time means 'living lightly on the land' — not least because a movable dwelling needs to be fairly light. Thus the inhabitants of Tipi Valley in Wales move their tents, not simply to dodge planning regulations, but to allow the spot upon which they have been dwelling to recuperate. Such a life style is particularly suitable for forest and coppice workers — indeed this was the traditional pattern of life for charcoal burners and the like in the not-so-distant past — and for nomads who may be following a cycle of work, involving activities such as fruit picking or providing services at summer fairs. However, as Helen Baczkowska, a professional conservation officer with experience of benders, warns, this lifestyle 'is only feasible in a large area and if the habitat is suitable'. She has observed that on the site of the original road protest camp on Twyford Down —which survived the ravages of the DoT's bulldozers — the outlines of the tents are still visible after four years and there is a significant change in the chalk grassland flora.[8]

A distinction needs to be made between sedentary people such as smallholders who are living in 'temporary' dwellings because they are stuck in a planning limbo, and those who actively seek a mobile way of life. The former tend to live, reluctantly, in 'mobile homes' which never move, which can hardly be said to be an asset to the landscape or blend into the vernacular, and which are often poorly constructed, subject to condensation problems and in many respects inferior to the permanent house that the incumbent would like to build. The latter, when they are not living in motor- or horse-drawn caravans, tend to inhabit tented structures — benders, yurts or tipis — which over the last two decades have become increasingly well designed, and which, because they are transported in 'kit form', can be discreetly sited. Forcing people to live in temporary accommodation is not necessarily a low impact strategy, whilst allowing them to do so often can be.

Small scale

It is self-evident that a small building will have less of an impact than a larger building of the same kind, and this is recognized by the planning system in the form of restrictions upon the height of buildings in certain areas, limits to the size of agricultural buildings that can be erected without planning permission and so on. The grandiose may have had its place in past eras, and may still have a place in the public domain, but in an overcrowded world, modesty is one of the hallmarks of an environmentally acceptable domicile. The humble dwelling that evoked pity in early centuries now demands respect. One development control officer recently described, with undisguised admiration, a rural shed inhabited by an ex-soldier as 'no bigger than this tiny office, but superbly organized'. Unfortunately the officer is carrying out an enforcement policy which views the matter differently. If the ex-soldier is evicted, he will probably move into a dwelling of much greater environmental impact.

The question of scale has recently arisen in one other related area, that of rural industry. The Rural White Paper has raised the possibility of 'a new Rural Business Use Class which would encourage local authorities to allow enterprise to diversify by reducing the risk of uncontrolled expansion'.[9] In other words non-agricultural businesses in the countryside may be acceptable as long as they do not get too big and generate too much traffic. This not very tacit admission that 'small is beautiful' is somewhat surprising coming from a Government that is committed to the expansion of industry and discourages small farms. It recalls a classic case of Planning in Wonderland when a farrier was refused permission to re-open an old smithy in a Wiltshire village 'in case he became too successful and wanted to expand'.[10] Quite how the Government intends to resolve this dilemma remains to be seen, but it is a sign that it is beginning to understand that where there are healthy local economies, enterprises can thrive at a local scale. Dare one hope that it may lead to a more enlightened approach towards small scale farming?

Unobtrusive

Unobtrusiveness — low visual impact upon the landscape — was, until recently, the aspect of environmental impact which most concerned planners. Other impacts, such as resource depletion, tend to lie out of sight and hence out of mind. To an extent, concern about obtrusiveness and the consequent tendency to screen any development that is likely to be obtrusive with a belt of trees, is a manifestation of landscape guilt.

Nonetheless, visual obtrusiveness is a real concern to anyone who has to look at a particular development, and even a small temporary structure such as a tent can be an unwelcome blot — or at least a spot — on the landscape. There has been a tendency from some architects and designers specializing in renewable energy (though by no means all) to dismiss the importance of the visual impact of their otherwise admirable experiments. There are many people in this country who would not welcome a proliferation of solar panels, and who would accept the prospect of climate change if that was the only way they could preserve a familiar townscape of tiled roofs or the atmosphere of their thatched village.

A planner entrusted with assessing the impact of a development may therefore have to balance the advantages of a low energy impact from, say, the use of wind generators or solar panels, against their visual impact. In such a case, the only resorts will be good design, clever siting and screening with hedges and trees (though even this is tricky with wind installations). The fact that screening is a dishonest form of architecture should not weigh too heavily in this assessment if what is being screened is a sustainable development rather than a polluting road or factory. Trees are an asset in their own right: they provide shelter from the elements, positive benefits to the environment, and contribute towards the Government's aim of achieving 'a doubling of the amount of woodland in England over the next half century'. Similarly underground or earth-sheltered architecture is not just a way of making a building invisible; it also economises on land and provides one of the most effective ways of conserving heat and energy.

Local materials

There are three main reasons why the use of local materials figures highly in any assessment of environmental impact — they are easily accessible, easily accountable and easily assimilable.

Firstly, local materials do not involve inordinate transport. Usually the most local material is earth dug out in the process of digging foundations and which can provide valuable building material with high insulatory properties. In many areas, until recently earth, either as cob (rammed earth) or as daub, was a primary building material and any endeavour to revive its use, through either traditional or more modern techniques, should be encouraged. Local timber, stone or thatch are also often available on site or close at hand.

Secondly, local materials are accountable. If a local quarry is becoming rapidly exhausted or supplies of local timber are becoming scarce, this can be easily observed and it will be within a local planning authority's powers to do something about it. On the other hand, if timber is being imported from Brazil or Canada, aggregate from Scandinavia, aluminium from South America and oil-based products from Nigeria or the Middle East, the planning authority can have no way of knowing whether these products are sustainably produced. 'We are keen to see local quarries in use', says Sue Clifford of Common Ground, 'because we believe it is important that people experience/appreciate the impact of their own expansions. It is more likely then that things are kept in proportion, that materials are regarded as precious, and appropriate use is made of them, rather than, for example, the grinding down of good building freestone for road ballast'.[13]

Finally, local materials are easily assimilable, both into the local landscape and into the vernacular architecture. A house built predominantly of stone, timber, thatch, soil or clay from the locality is, literally, part of the surroundings — and because almost everything built before about 1850 would have been constructed from the same local materials, such a house will fit naturally into the local vernacular.

For over 20 years, the planning profession, through Design Guides and guidelines in local plans, has tried to recreate artificially, usually with ghastly results, the architectural integrity that was natural in pre-industrial buildings. Nowadays even supermarkets try to don the vernacular, for example the discount shopping centre just off the M40 marketed as 'a development which would blend with and enhance the local environment ... The distinctive personality of the scheme is that of an English village street with its mixture of cottage style shops and premises modelled on traditional rural industries, such as the traditional blacksmith's shop'.

Such nonsense [writes Gillian Darley for Common Ground] re-iterated dozens of times weekly in planning applications clogging up the local authority planning office in-tray is smiled upon in the planning committee ... The functional nature of materials and techniques — tile hanging to protect rough and ready brickwork, soft plaster to weatherproof wandering mud-made walls, slates set to bounce the rainwater off a chimney or elsewhere, feet-thick rubble walls to minimize the

Use of local materials promotes local craftsmanship. Sophisticated shingle work on modern wood-frame dwellings in the USA. Photo: Art Boericke, from *Hand-Made Houses: A Guide to the Woodbutcher's Art*, Idea Books International, London 1975.

extremes of temperature — is long forgotten ... Superficial neo-traditionalism has gone a long way towards destroying and devaluing precisely the traditional qualities that professionals and the lay public alike believe that they are safeguarding.[14]

This failure arises because planners and designers have turned the question on its head. Traditional building styles developed by finding inspired solutions to problems that arose through access to only a limited range of materials. Modern architects, with literally thousands of building materials and products at their fingertips, instead paste skeuomorphic[15] detail over a non-existent problem. If we are to rediscover an architecture that is dynamic yet remains authentically traditional, then we can only do so by giving builders free rein to solve functional problems with a similarly

Residential development is not incompatible with wildlife protection. This self-built house is at the Holtsfield site near Swansea, which is on the edge of a nature reserve and has been declared a Conservation Area. Its occupants are presently facing eviction.
Photo: Nick Cobbing.

limited, but updated, range of basic local materials. And if such an architecture is to flourish, the obvious arena is that of low impact development.

Wildlife and biodiversity

When human beings move onto an uninhabited site, they increase its biodiversity by one species. But from then on they may have a highly beneficial or a highly detrimental effect upon the variety, the abundance and the stability of the wildlife populations that already abide there. If the human incomers plant gardens with a wide variety of plants attracting both pests and their predators, or if, in a heavily wooded situation, they thin out a few trees to increase the area of forest edge, then they may well be helping to increase the biodiversity of the site. On the other hand, if they plant large areas of monoculture, embark on major drainage projects, lay significant quantities of concrete across animal habitat, or suppress any vegetative growth that serves as cover, then they are likely to have an adverse impact upon flora and fauna.

Planners should be aware that while untrammelled industrial or suburban development is likely to destroy natural habitats very quickly, more modest forms of development may benefit valued wildlife. Barn owls, as their name implies, have benefited over the centuries from barns stocked with feed that attract the mice that they eat — this is one of the reasons why CPRE and other wildlife organizations object to the conversion of old isolated barns to dwellings.11 In certain cases, an alternative solution might be to grant planning permission for a low impact agricultural dwelling tied to the barn, on the condition that the barn continued to serve the purpose for which it was constructed.

However the impact of humans upon animal and plant populations is too complex and site specific to be subject to generalized rules. In some cases it will be clear that a development has a high and destructive impact upon a population, particularly in an SSSI harbouring a protected species. But where an intentionally low impact development occurs on a moderately sensitive site, it may be very difficult for planners to assess the long term impact upon flora and fauna. In such cases there is no reason why the planning department should not ask the applicants to draw up a management plan to be vetted by ecologists working for the district council. Such a management plan may then, if necessary, become subject to a Section 106 planning agreement.[12]

Resource consumption

According to the Town and Country Planning Association, 'if the energy used to make building materials and the energy used for travelling home to employment and shopping are added into the equation, the design and planning of the built environment probably account for more than three-quarters of fossil fuel use'.[16] Leaving aside the question of transport for the moment, there are two principal ways in which a building consumes resources: in its construction materials, and through its services.

Local building materials are preferable both because transport costs are lower and because of the easy accountability (see above). Hand wrought and less processed materials will also be preferable because of the energy savings. Sawn timber has been calculated to have an embodied energy value of 580 kilowatts per tonne; by comparison the energy value of bricks is four times as high, cement five times, plastic six times, glass 14 times, steel 24 times and aluminium 126 times. Hand-dug earth, by contrast, will have an energy value of next to nothing.[17]

Conventional buildings use an inordinate quantity of high embodied energy material. The architect Tony Thomson has calculated that a typical two storey dwelling house, with its road space and drains, uses 80 tons of aggregate (including 12 cubic metres of concrete), 10 cubic metres of fired clay, 9 cubic metres of kiln dried wood,12 square metres of glass, and significant quantities of more energy intensive materials. At the other extreme, a typical bender, designed to last ten years, uses little more than 75 square metres of hemp tarpaulin, up to 100 hazel rods and one or two recycled windows.[18] A permanent, wooden, cob or wattle and daub cottage with a thatched, tiled or turf roof will lie somewhere between the two.

The question of building services — the provision of power, heat and light, of water, and of sewage disposal services — is of greater significance. Domestic consumption of energy has risen since the early 1980s by some 20 per cent and is now greater than industrial consumption, which has fallen over the same period.[19] Fossil fuel is highly polluting, it contributes to global warming and its provision involves either an expensive and often unsightly infrastructure (electric pylons, gas pipelines) or else long range delivery by road, rail and sea (oil, coal). A low level of fossil fuel consumption — either through the use of renewable energies (wood, wind, solar, water) or through high levels of insulation — must therefore be a high priority for any low impact development.

The provision of water is also an important concern. In the UK about 80 tonnes of water per year (the equivalent of 50 gallons per day) fall on the roof of a house of 100 square metres; yet, in a feat of quite incomprehensible incompetence, the water authorities have managed to contrive a shortage from the hundreds of billions of tonnes that fall all over Britain. This disappearing act is partly achieved by channelling and pumping water from one place to another, a pointless exercise given that 'rain falls on rich and poor alike'. Even what is delivered is so polluted as to be undrinkable without the addition of chemicals. One answer to this problem is to supply at least a proportion of a household's water from the roof, a standard procedure in rural areas in some countries. The self-provision of water from a roof, a well or a spring is therefore a factor in assessing impact.

Conventional sewage disposal involves pumping the same liquid, now contaminated with organic wastes, back in the opposite direction, often to a situation where it will cause a pollution problem. The process is expensive and, in rural areas at least, quite unnecessary, since two alternative (and cheaper) on-site systems, reed beds and dry composting, regularly meet the standards of the environmental health authorities without any problem.[20] Of the two systems, reed beds can cope with larger amounts of liquid waste, while dry composting may be more suitable for those who wish to recycle the nutrients for agriculture.

One salient factor distinguishes all these low impact solutions to environmental problems associated with building services — they can be carried out on site. These 'autonomous technologies', as they are called, are potentially highly attractive to planners because they obviate the need for expensive and unsightly infrastructure for new settlements, yet so far they have generated little interest. Even renewable energies, which in 1993 received the Government's backing in Planning Policy Guidance 22, have been ignored in development plans. According to planning consultant Paul White: 'This lack of detailed policy advice on renewable energy developments is surprising, compared with the attention given to sustainability and land use planning elsewhere in development plans. Planning Policy Guidance 22 is almost three years old, and yet much of its advice remains largely ignored'.[21] Part of the problem is that PPG 22 ignores autonomous low impact solutions and concentrates on large scale projects. It contains 11 pages on wind farms and large scale wind generators linked to the national grid, and just two disparaging paragraphs on photovoltaic solar collectors (lamenting that they cannot be economically connected to the grid).[22] Local planning authorities, however, are likely to feel much more comfortable about solar panels of two or three square metres, which can deliver sufficient energy to light and power a low energy home, than about installing 30 metre high wind generators in a prominent rural location.

The planning system thus often proves a major obstacle for architects and designers working on autonomous technologies and energy efficient houses. David Olivier, of Energy Advisory Associates, pioneering an 'energy-efficient, ecologically-sound house' writes: 'Yes, planners are a problem (*the* problem). Had it been proposed in Ireland, France or Sweden, among other places, the project would have been designed in 1989-90 and built in 1991. It still hasn't started on site though we hope to start this autumn [1995]'.[23]

There are however exceptions. Newark and Sherwood District Council gave permission for an autonomous house of entirely traditional design to be built in a designated conservation area in Southwell, only 100 metres from the famous Norman minster. This house, designed by architects Robert and Brenda Vale, uses no fossil fuel energy, makes electricity from solar panels, collects rainwater from the roof and turns its sewage into garden compost. The Council was so impressed that it announced that it wanted to see a hundred such houses built by the year 2000.[24]

Hopefully the foresight of Newark and Sherwood DC will spread to other councils. The Building Services Research and Information Association is presently engaged in a comprehensive study entitled *Autonomous Technologies: Reducing Inefficiency by Design*. Its overall objective is to 'reduce the inefficiency and high waste production of the built environment, through the use of technologies and techniques which allow much closer control of the provision of resources. In practice we expect this to mean an organic 'low tec, high spec' approach'.[25] The report, to be published in 1997, will contain a review of existing technologies, feasibility studies, and a chapter on planning. Hopefully, by then, the Government will be working on a more robust version of PPG 22 that will give due credit to autonomous systems.

Meanwhile, planners should note that encouraging autonomous technologies on low impact sites is a relatively simple affair. A condition disallowing the supply of mains electricity, water and sewage services more or less obliges the occupants to investigate autonomous and renewable technologies, except insofar as they are willing to truck in oil, gas, coal or water. Such conditions are a useful way of stimulating demand for renewable energy and other sustainable technologies.

Transport

'Low residential densities are associated both with increased travel and the proportion of that travel undertaken by the car'. This statement is taken from a section entitled 'Residential Density' in the DoE's 1993 draft revision of PPG 13 on transport.[26] It reflects an opinion which has increasingly become an item of faith within the planning profession over the last decade. For many planners the quest for sustainability has become almost synonymous with reducing the demand for motor transport. Development in the countryside, where people tend to live at some distance from each other, is viewed as being intrinsically dependent upon the motor car, and hence unsustainable.

In a further section of the 1993 draft, entitled 'Settlement Size', the DoE continued this line of argument, asserting that 'small settlements tend to be less efficient in terms of transport because they are less self-contained. The draft proposed a package of policies designed to restrict dispersed development, which counselled planners to maintain or increase densities in urban and suburban areas; to 'constrain the incremental expansion of small settlements, especially those likely to accommodate relatively long-distance commuters'; to 'avoid the development of small new settlements which are not likely to be well served by public transport or which will not be likely to be largely self-contained'; and to encourage the 'juxtaposition of employment and residential uses' so as to 'make it easier for people to live near their work'.[27]

However, the final version of PPG 13 which appeared in 1994 was not a product of the DoE alone. It was a joint publication from the DoE and the DoT and in some ways it was a considerably changed document. The DoT did not disagree with the specific policy recommendations about urban densities, small settlements, and juxtaposing residences and workplaces, which are repeated with broadly similar wording — indeed a further recommendation was added: 'avoid sporadic housing development in the open countryside'.[28] But the heading 'Residential Density' was pulled out, and the generalizations concerning residential density and settlement size were dropped. Nowhere in the final version of PPG 13 is it suggested that a low residential density is associated with increased car use, or that small settlements are necessarily less self-contained. Instead, the final version states: 'If land use policies permit continued dispersal of development *and* a high reliance on the car, other policies to reduce the environmental impact of transport may be less effective or come at a higher price' [author's italics].[29] This wording suggests that low residential density may occur without high reliance upon the car and that this may be acceptable.

This important adjustment has not been absorbed by many in the planning profession. Faced with the complex question of traffic generation, too many planners are content with the simplistic answer — 'density equals traffic reduction' — and are therefore inclined to give an automatic thumbs down for any dispersed development in the countryside.

The notion that country life is necessarily dependent upon the motor car has long been an urban (or rather a counter-urban) myth, and if PPG 13 is misinterpreted then this myth is likely to become conventional wisdom. Certainly, it is true that more rural households have access to a car than do urban households, and that a higher proportion of journeys made in the country are made by car than in the town. But the fact remains that significant numbers of people (including the author) do live successfully in the countryside without regular access to a private car.[30] Access to supermarkets, hospitals and restaurants might be poor, but access to what the countryside has to offer is good. Country dwellers accused of car dependency could point an accusing finger at the streams of motorists fleeing London in their droves every weekend, or the daily passage of suburban dog owners driving their pet out to a place where it can freely defecate — and claim that the pot is calling the kettle black.

Moreover, DoT statistics show that people working in urban areas outside London are marginally *more* likely to drive to their work than people working in rural areas (69 per cent in urban areas, 68 per cent in rural areas). Twenty-two per cent of rural workers walk or cycle to their job, compared to seventeen per cent of urban workers, while urban commuters are more likely to take a bus or train. The average distance travelled is the same in both urban and rural areas, eight miles.[31] These statistics suggest that density does not necessarily promote an environment where the facilities people use are near at hand, while a dispersed community may still be a close one.

Given the complex and conflicting evidence on the subject, it would be wise to heed the reminder from the Royal Commission on Environmental Pollution that 'some evidence suggests that income and car ownership are more important determinants of travel demand than population density, and the extent to which population density acts as an independent variable is disputed'.[32] In a rural context, where low income people reliant upon public transport have been eased out of the countryside by an invasion of rich motorized incomers, to the detriment of the public transport infrastructure, this would seem to be the more accurate interpretation.

The final version of PPG 13 glosses over one other important aspect of the traffic generation debate. It advises against the development of small new settlements of less than 10,000 dwellings 'where they are not designed to be capable of being self-contained'.[33] However it neglects to point out that the prospects of a rural community being 'largely self-contained' are considerably higher than those of a large urban community. Virtually every material resource consumed by urban dwellers is at its origin either extracted from the ocean or grown or mined in the countryside; everything — from the cornflakes to the computer — has at some point been trucked in from ghost acres somewhere in the world. Small rural settlements on the other hand can aspire to being 'largely self-contained': they have the potential to supply for themselves the bulk of their food, their energy, their water and their furniture, whilst providing a surplus of raw materials to help sustain the millions of consumers in the cities. In this respect rural settlements are potentially less transport dependent than urban settlements; not, as PPG 13 implies, more so. PPG 13 paints a distorted picture of a universal service economy where everybody has to live close to everybody else, so that they can all earn their living from doing each other's laundry.

These important background issues need to be borne in mind when assessing the transport impact of a particular development. It is simply not sufficient to conclude that because a development is in the countryside it will generate traffic. A large number of different factors will dictate how much transport a particular low impact development is likely to generate.

There are three main ways in which a development can generate traffic: through its consumption (importing goods, access to services and leisure journeys), through exporting its production, and through commuting, travelling back and forth to work.

As regards consumption, in general the more 'self-contained' a settlement is, the less transport it will involve. If a community provides most of its fuel, food, water, entertainment etc. on site or close by, then it will not need to travel much to obtain sustenance, and what it is consuming will not have travelled far. Subsistence production is the epitome of the juxtaposition of residence, workplace and 'shopping' in one small area.

The issue of how much produce such a settlement exports is less relevant to planners, because the amount a commodity travels is primarily contingent on the distance between the source of a product and its market — and this is more a question of where the consumer lives than of where along the line the producer lives. Obviously the sale of goods locally is likely to generate less traffic than selling them all over the country. But, short of sending everyone in cities 'back to the land,' there is no way that the urban population can be provided with necessities without some measure of long distance transport. That is not to say that there are not some ways of distributing produce which are more transport intensive than others. For example a farm shop, where consumers are encouraged to drive out to buy a few items for their personal consumption, clearly generates more traffic than the producer taking all his or her produce to market in one weekly journey (and buying necessary consumer items there); or a 'box' delivery system whereby produce is delivered on a weekly basis to a number of subscribers, rather like a milk round.

As for the question of commuting, it is evident that the closer anyone lives to their workplace, the less they will need to travel. The case of the farmer cited in Chapter 3 who travelled 7 miles every day at 4 a.m. to milk his cows and did not return home to his family until 6 p.m. is clearly a travesty of planning justice. The difficulty for planners is how to assess the transport needs of someone who works part-time on the land and part-time elsewhere. Will driving out from a town or village house to attend to animals generate less or more traffic than living on the land and driving to the town to work? Such cases can only be assessed on an individual basis; but it should be borne in mind that it is in the interests of the applicant to reduce transport costs, and that this may be a strong motive in wanting to live on the land.

Aside from the amount of traffic generated by a proposal, the other factor to take into account is the mode of transport available. In general planners have been predisposed against proposals in the country which are not within walking or bicycling distance of services such as shops, schools and surgeries, and which are not served by adequate public transport. For instance South Somerset's draft policies for travellers' camps and low impact developments states that they should be 'reasonably related to schools and other community facilities'.[34] PPG 13 advocates planning policies which avoid the development of small new settlements 'especially where they are unlikely to be well served by public transport'.[35]

The wording in PPG 13 is interesting because it does not refer to the actual existence of public transport, but to the likelihood of it existing, suggesting that planners should be looking ahead to the not-too-distant future, when motoring costs will be considerably higher than they are today. If more non-car owners are allowed to live in the country, then there will be a greater demand for public transport.

To people applying for planning permission, particularly to those who do not own a car, or do not want to, the demand that they should site themselves close to a more or less non-existent transport system seems grossly unfair. It is not their fault that services such as schools have become more centralized, nor that in Herefordshire, for example, there are now only four railway stations, whereas in the 1940s there were 49.[36] Perhaps it is not the planners' fault either, although, in the case of railways, the planning system is indeed to blame for the greater crime of building on discontinued lines, and thereby scotching the likelihood of them ever being revived. Reluctant car owners are the victims of what Ivan Illich terms a 'radical monopoly ... when one industrial process exercises an exclusive control over the satisfaction of a pressing need, and excludes non-industrial activities from competition'.[37] To refuse people the right to live somewhere, on the grounds that a satisfactory transport infrastructure has been dismantled and replaced by an unsustainable one, is absurd and will do nothing to enhance the rural economy.

What is clearly needed is a 'post-industrial' rural transport infrastructure that is sustainable and supplies people's needs. One way to create it is perhaps to let people build it for themselves. Planners can best assist this process by letting people live and work in the country but applying stringent conditions upon the use of private cars, something that is well within their powers (see Chapter 8).

Sustainable use

Clearly, what a building is used for is an important factor in assessing its impact. From an environmental point of view, there is little to be gained from granting permission for an impeccably designed, energy efficient, low impact structure if it is going to be used to accommodate people or materials involved in activities that are ecologically destructive. At present, the use to which a building is put — agricultural, residential, industrial, recreational, etc. — is the main way that the planning system distinguishes between buildings. There is, as yet, little attempt to make a distinction between *sustainable* use and *unsustainable* use. As far as the planning system is concerned a barn is a barn, whether it is used to store hay or pesticides.

Some distinctions are made, however. In the case of applications for a workshop (and those classes of agricultural building requiring planning permission) planners can directly control the environmental impact of the use. For example a hen house, a farriery, or a small on-site sawmill, might be regarded by a planning authority as appropriate and environmentally low impact enterprises, whereas a broiler chicken factory, a car spraying workshop or a large saw mill dealing with imported timber might not. Many of these potentially high impact uses are listed in Schedule 2 of the Assessment of Environmental Effects Regulations, 1988.

In the case of residential dwellings, the question of sustainable livelihood is more tricky. When a residence is tied or in some other way associated with a particular enterprise or kind of operation — then the sustainability of that enterprise will clearly be relevant to the environmental impact of the building. For example, an organically run agricultural holding, involving a low level of external inputs and machinery, is likely to be of lower environmental impact and more sustainable than a highly industrialized operation, and more likely to provide the diverse and intimate kind of countryside that most people prefer.[38] Similarly, sympathetic or sustainable commercial management of an area of woodland, a lake or a quarry will be relevant to the assessment of the impact of any residence associated with it.

However, when it comes to applications for low impact residences from people who obtain a proportion of their income from working for enterprises unconnected with these residences, then the impact of these activities cannot be viewed as material to an assessment of the impact of the dwelling. Who can judge how sustainable or unsustainable these occupations may be, or will remain? Ideally their sustainability will be regulated by planning decisions concerning the sites at which these activities take place. Clearly someone working for nearby farms, forestry enterprises, quarries etc. is to be regarded as more eligible than someone commuting into town; but this is a question of transport issues and of enhancement of the rural economy.

Likewise, the reliance of the applicant on income support is not a planning consideration. However the Government and planners should look sympathetically upon those who are dependent upon income support while they build up the basis of a rural livelihood; and any endeavour to replace income support by subsistence production should be actively encouraged.

In summary, the use to which a building is put is an important factor in assessing its environmental impact — but this use is only accountable when it is tied in some degree to the building. In this respect, the Government's proposal for a new Rural Business Use Class[39] could be extremely helpful if it were drafted as a Sustainable Rural Businesses Use Class. There is scope here for drawing up a list of low impact uses, qualified by their scale, their transport intensity and their use of local resources and renewable energy, to which rural workshops and residences could be tied.

Positive environmental impact

Last, but not least, a development may be viewed as having a positive effect upon the environment. The other categories listed above refer to the low negative impact that a building may have on the landscape or the environment — its unobtrusiveness or its relatively low use of resources. But a development may also be judged to enhance the environment, or else to be linked with a project which enhances the environment.

The cases where a building itself is universally agreed to be an improvement to the rural environment are rare. There is no consensus, nowadays, as to what constitutes architectural quality or good design, and almost any new building is likely to generate some controversy. Against a rural background, the highest public accolade that any new building is likely to obtain is that it blends in well with its surroundings. The main exceptions are conversions of buildings that are generally regarded as a scar on the landscape. Much could be done, for example, to improve some of the dire concrete buildings on abandoned war-time airfields.

On the other hand, a rural building may well be associated with a project that is generally viewed as environmentally beneficial. In areas where there is an oppressive monoculture — notably in the extensive belts of conifer plantation and overgrazed pasture land in Scotland — the introduction of a human settlement may, in itself, act as a spur to biological diversity. Elsewhere, a rural building may be necessary to accommodate people carrying out some form of environmental improvement — for example establishing organic or permacultural agriculture in a degraded natural environment, or managing neglected woodland. There may be advantages to be derived from park rangers and conservationists living in low impact residences in the area they are managing (just as gamekeeper's cottages were often sited in woodland). And in still other cases, it may be the development itself which raises sufficient funds to pay for environmental improvement —this is the dynamic behind the Lowland Crofting experiments discussed in the following chapter.

Ultimately, this is the criterion that overrides all the rest. The previous eight categories are all concerned with low negative impact — with limiting the scale, the obtrusiveness or the resource use of rural developments that in other respects may be desirable. They are, in part, designed to accommodate our landscape guilt, our feeling that the countryside has been so under attack from human pressure that development should only be allowed under exceptional circumstances, and with exceptional safeguards. The fear is real — very real — and that is why so much space has been devoted to defining these circumstances and these safeguards.

Guilt is not a promising basis for action; low impact is a restraint, not an ideal. The object should not be to squeeze as many people as possible into the countryside without ruining it — that is what the present policy of building around towns and villages aims to do — but to reintroduce people to the countryside in a way that will help it to flourish, that will create new livelihoods by increasing the diversity and abundance of nature. Most of the proposals and visions that we shall examine in the following chapters should be viewed in this light: not simply as low impact exceptions, but as ways of re-invigorating the rural landscape.

Chapter 6

Four Examples of Low Impact Development

'We are also determined that imaginative schemes for isolated dwellings should not always be dismissed. There must be scope for the truly original and high quality building that enhances the environment'.

White Paper, *Rural England*, p.69.

THE PRESSURE FOR low impact development, or for something similar, has come from a range of interests and actors, some of whom might be viewed as strange bedfellows. This chapter examines four prominent experiments already under way in Britain. Each example is prefaced by more general discussion of its context and of the approach adopted by planning authorities towards such developments.

The examples have been rated for their impact in respect of eight of the criteria outlined in the previous chapter, according to a points system, ranging from 0 to 4. Zero points means minimum negative environmental impact, 4 points means maximum negative environmental impact. The ideal development will score zero, and the worst imaginable 32. Because there is no advantage in a development being short term if it has a positive environmental impact, the criterion of temporariness

	West Harwood	Hockerton	Tir Penrhos Isaf	Kings Hill	Conventional House
Small Scale	3	2	1	1	3
Unobtrusive	0	0	1	1	3
Local Materials	3	2	1	2	3
Wildlife	1	2	1	2	4
Low Resource Use	3	0	1	1	4
Transport	3	2	1	2	3
Sustainable Livelihood	3	1	0	1	3
Positive Impact	0	2	0	3	4
Total	16	11	6	13	27

has not been included: if it were, temporary developments (such as Kings Hill) would score better. The collected ratings are printed below, together with a rating for a standard village-perimeter detached house.

On no account should this low impact indicator be seen as anything other than an informal exercise. It gives no reliable indication of the relative worthiness of different schemes, which occur in varying circumstances and may have other objectives aside from low impact, for example affordability. Nor is it suggested that planning authorities should adopt a points system. The planning system is refreshingly free of the obsession with statistics and cost-benefit analysis that has plagued transport policy, and it should stay that way. These indicators are useful simply as a check list to ensure that all facts are being considered.

Lowland Crofting: West Harwood

Probably the most significant local authority led project for a low impact residential development is the Lowland Crofting scheme devised by West Lothian District Council, near Edinburgh, under the guidance of David Jarman. The project is not styled 'low impact' — from a visual point of view it has a high impact upon the treeless, overgrazed surroundings — but it comes clearly within the definition of low impact because its objective is to use the judicious allocation of residential planning permission outside the development zone to achieve environmental and landscape improvements.

The correct title for Lowland Crofting is 'Very Low Density Housing and Woodland Development'. West Lothian planning department observes: 'The term "Lowland Crofting" has caused some confusion. The title was coined by Dr. Jim Hunter, then chairman of the Scottish Crofters' Union, to describe how rural Scotland might be revived by increasing the population density to the levels found in crofting areas such as North Lewis. But Lowland Crofting will be very different from the Highland version'.[1]

There will be more to say about Highland crofting later on. The lowland version is designed to improve a somewhat dreary, deforested and depopulated landscape consisting of small to medium sized farms and nothing much else — although West Lothian Planning's claim that 'much of it is a "green desert" with every inch grazed by livestock' is a little exaggerated. Since many of the farms are economically marginal, few can spare any land for tree planting, and so the Council concluded that the only way to promote tree planting was to deal with whole farms.

The way that it has done so is quite visionary. The farms are divided up into three main categories of land. A minimum of 30 per cent is planted with trees; from 20 to 50 per cent remains as agricultural land; and the remainder is sold off as 'crofts' — smallholdings of from two to ten acres with planning permission for a house and outbuildings in which to operate a small business. The plots are sold at market price for development land (about £40,000 to £50,000) and the profit from the betterment pays for the design and implementation of the scheme and the planting of the trees. The ecological management of the land is secured by a planning agreement under

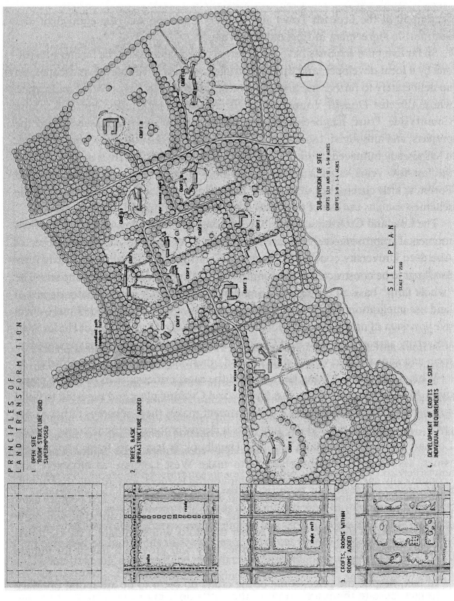

A schematic representation and site plan depicting the conversion of bare farmland into a wooded crofting site. If schemes such as these became widespread they would contribute significantly to the Government's target of doubling the area of woodland, at little expense to the taxpayer. The design, by architects Anthony Wylson and Munro Waterson of London, was entered in a competition for designs for Lowland Crofting sites, held in 1992. Many of the entries are published in *Fields of Vision: New Ideas in Rural Housing*, Royal Incorporation of Architects in Scotland, Edinburgh, 1993. Photo: courtesy RIAS.

Section 50 of the Scottish Town and Country Planning Act (the equivalent of a Section 106 Agreement in England and Wales).

So far five pilot schemes have been started, one managed by the farmer himself, one by a local developer, and three by an agency, New Lives New Landscapes, set up deliberately to further the lowland crofting vision. New Lives New Landscapes, whose director Donald Young was previously secretary of the Central Scotland Countryside Trust, has been the most dedicated and dynamic force behind the projects, and although it took on its three projects after the other two were initiated, it has already outpaced them. The agency has planted 240,000 trees in the region in the last two years, a substantial contribution to the projected Central Scotland Forest, at little cost to the public purse. It has also introduced other benefits into the schemes, such as the use of reed beds for water waste disposal.

The Lowland Crofting schemes have received considerable acclaim for the environmental improvements they have introduced. A study by Anthony Cooper of Aberdeen University concluded: 'Lowland Crofting will have allowed nearly forty dwellings to be constructed in the countryside, with positive landscape impacts. The "whole farm" basis of the restructuring has also allowed a much greater degree of land use integration than might be expected. This in turn has provided more effective provision of nature conservation'.[2] In another study, Martin Watt of Heriot Watt University agreed that 'Lowland Crofting is creating a scale of landscape improvement and nature conservation which would otherwise have been very unlikely'.[3]

Where Lowland Crofting has attracted the most criticism is in its social objectives. As Watt observes: 'The cost of Lowland Crofting plots and the need to build a rather large house to create a safe investment makes these schemes rather exclusive ... The cost of Lowland Crofting plots is clearly prohibitive to the young'.[4] West Lothian Planning's Lowland Crofting Handbook is less than frank about these issues, saying only that the object is to make West Lothian 'as attractive and economically successful as rural Perthshire or the borders' and adding that 'it will be nearer the cities and motorways — and well planned to meet 21st century aspirations'.[5] The aim appears to be to create an attractive landscape that will draw wealthy investors into the area. Whether the crofts will stimulate a trickle down effect into the local economy, or whether they will provide a haven for yuppie commuters, remains to be seen.

In fact, despite the price, some of the crofts do seem to be attracting ordinary people of moderate means who wish to set up up small rural businesses. On the West Harwood scheme, operated by New Lives New Landscapes, nearly half the buyers want to set up an enterprise on site, carrying out businesses such as livery, manufacture of horse blankets, a cattery, a joinery business and the rearing of game birds. Under construction, the West Harwood site does not at all resemble a standard edge-of-town private housing estate. The self-build element gives it a pioneering feel, not dissimilar to housing plot-land that can be seen on the edge of some small towns in Alaska. All the houses are different and invite the observer to guess as to their occupants. On one plot there is still only a caravan surrounded by chickens.

One of many designs proposed for Lowland Crofting sites.
Illustration: *New Lives New Landscapes*.

Donald Young has confessed that he is disappointed with the architectural standards of many of the houses built, and in future projects would prefer to specify architectural guidelines — a 'house style'. It is true that most of the houses are 'kit houses' of little intrinsic architectural merit. If they were all of identical design and the same level of architectural mediocrity then the result would be dire. But they are saved by the fact that they are all individual expressions of somebody's dream. West Lothian Planning also has opinions on this subject:

> If the croft house or the entrance or some other aspect is going to be visible and non-traditional, then it should be carefully designed and well thought out. What people see — in the countryside just as in an art gallery — is the complete picture. A successful crofting scheme will be judged as a picture: it must all hang together. There will be highlights in view, but it must not be too busy or crowded. The background all has to be filled in with care. Discordant touches are to be avoided (once built, they cannot easily be painted over).[6]

Not everyone will agree. The countryside is not an art gallery, and a living community is not a painting by numbers to be peered at by passing motorists. The West Harwood scheme will hang together as it develops patina and as the trees that are planted around the houses grow to maturity. What gives the community its life is the sense that at least some of the settlers may have found a measure of freedom in which to stake out a new life for themselves in a new landscape.

The Lowland Crofting scheme has been studied, not because it is the epitome of a successful low impact development — in some respects it isn't, and wasn't intended to be — but because it is a brave and imaginative development from a local planning authority; and because it breaks new ground in securing environmental benefits by allowing people to live in the countryside, particularly through its use of Section 50 Agreements. Any local planning authority in England looking to achieve similar benefits (for example with redundant county smallholdings) can learn a great deal from West Lothian's experience.

Rating: 16

Earth shelter: Hockerton

Earth-sheltered buildings, that is to say buildings that are completely underground, or whose roof and usually some walls are protected by a layer of earth, have a remarkable record in obtaining planning permission. By summer 1995, out of 75 applications for earth-sheltered buildings, 48 were successful either at committee level or at appeal.[7]

This is a good record in itself: but it is particularly interesting because 38 of these successful applications were recommended for refusal by the planning authority and 15 were contrary to the development plan. Moreover there are at least 17 recorded cases of permission for earth-sheltering on sites with a previous history of refusal, suggesting that earth-sheltered buildings are regarded as more acceptable than conventional ones.

The reasons for this are not difficult to discern. Earth-sheltered dwellings are easy to hide. Indeed, where it is thought necessary, they can be made completely invisible. At an appeal for an underground lecture theatre near Dove Cottage — William Wordsworth's home in the Lake District — the Inspector concluded that 'the character and the appearance of the conservation area would be preserved. Having said that, my conclusion would be based on the assumption that the lecture theatre would be completely buried'.[8] In some cases the invisibility of an earth-sheltered building has been used to avoid the planners altogether. One agricultural worker lived in his underground dwelling in Wiltshire for eight years until he was finally rumbled by the planners.

The value of earth-sheltered constructions as a convenient way of hiding industrial development was studied in a 1982 DoE report. One review of the report commented: '"Out of sight out of mind" is a facile expression but it is nevertheless accurate. Development can take place beneath areas with a sensitive or important surface environment, such as landscape amenity areas where it would be otherwise opposed'.[9] The ability of earth-sheltered buildings to assuage feelings of landscape guilt is unmatched. In the case of residences this may be regarded as benign; in the case of industrial processes which may be environmentally damaging in other respects than landscape impact, placing them underground should be regarded with suspicion.

Nevertheless, the architectural qualities of earth-sheltered buildings sometimes receive acclaim. A conversion of an old water reservoir in green belt land near Bradford on Avon was passed by the Secretary of State for the Environment partly because 'the design has been commended by the Arts Council and by the Royal Fine Arts Commission' and for 'enhancing its immediate surroundings'.[10]

The Caer Llan Berm house in South Wales, under construction. The mullion-windowed stone facade is in keeping with the main house from which the photo is taken. The roof of the terrace was covered with four feet of earth, sown with grass. The indoor temperature of the Berm House remains around 20° Celsius all year, without any subsidiary heating.
Photo: Peter Carpenter.

But probably the most important advantage of earth buildings is not their minimal visual impact but their minimal use of resources. They economize on land space (because the roof is usable land, an important consideration in urban situations); their often considerable construction costs are compensated for by longevity and low maintenance; and most of all, the extremely high level of insulation results in formidable heat savings. A well designed earth sheltered house with passive solar heating — in other words, south facing windows — needs no other form of heating to maintain a constant comfortable temperature. Peter Carpenter's Caer Llan Berm House in South Wales, a handsome stone faced terrace with well proportioned mullion windows, maintains a constant temperature of about 20 degrees centigrade without any subsidiary heating whatsoever. It once hit 24 degrees in a hot spell in June 1991, and dropped to 16 and a half degrees in a two week period of freezing fog in 1992.[11]

Recognition of the enormous energy savings that earth-sheltered buildings can achieve has recently become a significant factor in successful planning applications. The Bradford on Avon scheme was commended by the Secretary of State for its 'many energy efficient features which accord with the principles of sustainable development'.[12] And in the case of a complex of five earth-sheltered dwellings outside the development zone at Hockerton in Nottinghamshire, the planning authorities' recommendations for approval were largely based upon the scheme's energy efficiency, stating that 'in this *exceptional* case there is a justification ... because the applicants have outlined in some detail how the development would ... go some way towards creating a sustainable development'.[13]

The Hockerton scheme is particularly interesting, because it combines the advantages of earth shelter with other autonomous services including a reed bed sewage system and wind generated electricity, and it seeks to establish a sustainable lifestyle for its occupants. The project, consisting of five underground dwellings, designed by Robert and Brenda Vale, is sited on the edge of Hockerton village, by a busy road, but outside the village envelope. It was originally designed as a scheme that would provide a modicum of self-sufficiency for a group of relatively low income families, who would benefit not only from considerable energy savings but from small scale food production and a fish farm. 'The families involved will combine wildlife conservation, wood coppicing, organic food production for local householders, shops and restaurants, and animal husbandry — goats, chickens, geese and pigs'.[14] The project was greeted enthusiastically by Newark and Sherwood planning authority, and permission was granted at committee level.

The development is regulated by a complex Section 106 Agreement 'to ensure that the total project ... is maintained in the method in which it has been fully outlined'.[15] The agreement not only covers the environmental management of the land but also such matters as sharing of work amongst the different members of the community, restrictions upon fossil fuel powered vehicles on the land and the democratic decision making process.

It was hoped that the price of each unit would be in the region of about £50,000. However the costs of putting forward the planning application were hefty — according to the projects' builder, Nick Martin, over £18,000 — and other details, such as prolonged negotiation over the Section 106 Agreement and the siting of a wind powered generator, are threatening to more than double this expense. The saga of the relatively small 5 kilowatt wind generator has been particular trying for the developers, involving objections from Bernard Ingham of Countryside Guardians, a lobbying organization with connections to the nuclear lobby; the required translation of a report from Denmark on noise levels which subsequently proved to be unacceptable because the Danish method of measurement is different from the British; and the resiting of the generator to a position 150 metres, instead of 120 metres, away from a group of houses that lie within 20 metres of a trunk road carrying 6,000 vehicles per day.[16]

As the costs of the project have mounted, the developers have sought to amortise their expenditure by concentrating on long life and low maintenance and Martin acknowledges that the houses are not likely to be accessible to people in the lowest income brackets. While it is understandable that the local council should wish to obtain every possible guarantee that the project should meet and keep the environ-

Designs for the Hockerton Housing
Project, courtesy Hockerton
Housing Project.

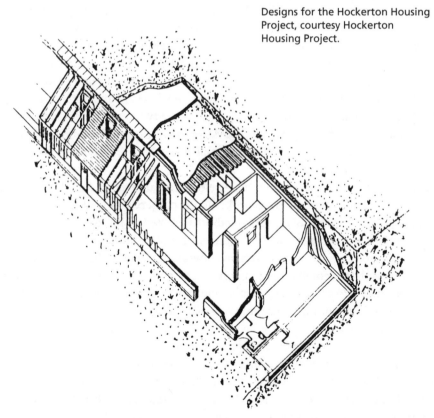

mental standards which gained it planning permission, it would be counter-productive if similar developments continue to be shackled by high bureaucratic costs. So
far, many earth-sheltered residences gaining planning permission have been expensive or even luxury residences (for example a house in Oxfordshire with an indoor
swimming pool on the market at £250,000). It is to be hoped that the experience
gained, both by the developers and the planning authority, from the Hockerton
project can be used in the future to speed through similar projects at a lower cost,
and achieve the Local Agenda 21 aim of 'tackling fuel poverty through improving
the energy efficiency of low income housing'.

   Rating: 11

Permaculture: Tir Penrhos Isaf

Permaculture is not just a system of agriculture: it is a form of land use. It is therefore
of particular concern to planners, and already permaculture as a land use system has
acquired something of a case history in planning appeals recently (see Appendix C).

   The term 'permaculture' was coined in the 1970s by the Australian, Bill
Mollison, to describe forms of land use which attempt to emulate nature.[17]
Natural ecosystems — a clearing in a wood, for instance, or a stretch of sea shore
— are resilient because they involve a high degree of interdependence between a
wide variety of different species. Monoculture does not exist in nature, nor does
waste, for whatever is waste to one species is food or habitat to another.
Permaculture casts human beings as part of such a system, rather than as external
managers; the object is not to produce a maximum yield of one or two species
useful to humans, but to increase the richness, the diversity and the interconnect-
edness of the entire system, with human activity, nourishment and waste
production as a contributory part. If the system thrives, so will the humans that live
in it. Therefore, 'there is no division in permaculture between farming and conservation. They are the same thing'.[18]

   Permaculture thus involves minimal use of external inputs, a high level of crop
and stock diversity, natural pest control, and the conservation and reuse on site of
resources such as water, solar energy and organic wastes. But this does not mean
that a permacultural system is self-contained. Like a natural system it flourishes
through a reciprocal interchange with neighbouring systems radiating outwards —
it is neither isolated, nor dependent upon a number of select long distance outside
inputs which tend to produce a corresponding surplus of waste. Neighbourhoods are
reciprocally self-supporting in the same way that species within each neighbourhood
are. Permaculture is a system of economics which emulates nature.[19]

   The permaculture movement has spread rapidly, not only to people in industrial
countries concerned about the overconsumption of unaccountable resources, but
also to people in southern countries, such as Nepal or Zimbabwe, with little access
to outside inputs, where enriching the local natural resource base often proves to be
the best strategy for survival. In Britain there are now over 60 local groups and over
50 farms and holdings operated on a permacultural basis.

One of these, Tir Penrhos Isaf in Gwynedd, Wales, concerns us particularly, not only because it is now fairly well established, but also because it has been so favourably received by local planners — even though it is sited in a National Park.

In 1986, Chris Dixon applied to live with his wife and son in a caravan on a seven acre site in a valley in Snowdonia National Park. The holding had been farmed in days gone by, but the original dwelling was owned by the Forestry Commission, who now lease it to the National Mountain Bothy Association. His application was turned down, and for the next four years the Dixons worked part-time converting the holding to a permaculture regime. In 1991, by which time their efforts were beginning to bear fruit, he applied again for permission, this time with a wealth of evidence explaining how they were building up a complex ecosystem, which took as its model a clearing of pasture and scrub within a diverse forest.

The submission outlined a programme for planting trees to protect the soil and provide fuel; described a project to capture surplus water running off the hills in 'swales' (low banks running along the contour) and divert it into aquacultural ponds; listed the indigenous and non-native fruiting plants, shrubs and trees that were being introduced to create an 'edible landscape'; and explained what livestock could be incorporated into this intensive natural system, including goats, cattle, pigs, ducks, fish and bees. Dixon argued that the multifarious activities involved in creating this ecosystem could only be sensibly carried out if the family lived on site. Among the many letters of support they received was one from their MP, Dafydd Ellis Thomas, stating that 'the park should promote these principles of balanced farming practices in Snowdonia which provide a variety of products and that it is in accordance with several fundamental objectives of the National Park'.[20]

The local authority officers were initially divided over the proposal, but in the end permission was granted for a temporary caravan, 'the project being viewed as a demonstration project, with the onus on the Dixons to 'sell' Permaculture to the council'.[21] Three years later, in 1994, the Dixons put in an application to renew permission for the caravan. The Park ecologist came to inspect the site and in Chris Dixon's words he was 'gobsmacked ... he told us that this was exactly the direction they were trying to encourage farmers throughout the Park to move in, with relatively little success'.[22] The Dixons obtained their renewal with almost no objection.

The Dixons are not self-sufficient, nor do they intend to be. They are dependent upon a certain amount of outside work to provide the capital investment for their holding — and they also earn money by conducting permaculture courses on the site. They run a car to connect them with the nearest community, four miles away, and to bring in materials; though after having survived two months when the car was broken down, Chris Dixon is confident that once the holding is fully established, it could operate successfully with horse, bicycle and the occasional hire of a van.

The Dixons eventually want to build a small house on their holding, 400 square feet in area, constructed from local stone, local timber and glass, with a turf roof. This may be a difficult pill for the planning committee to swallow. But the Government advises that 'it will normally be unsatisfactory to grant successive

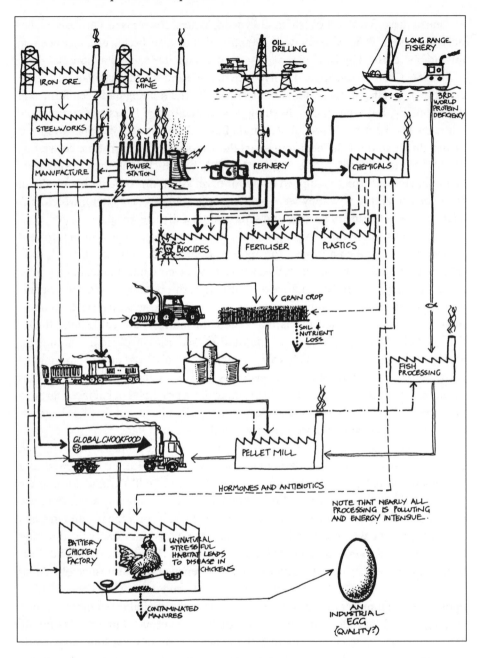

Industrial methods of producing an egg (this page); permaculture methods of producing an egg (facing page). From *Permaculture: A Designer's Manual*, Bill Mollison, Tagari Publications (Australia).

IRON ORE

COAL MINE

STEELWORKS

POWER

CHICKEN WIRE, DRUM, ROOFING GUTTERING.

SOURCE OF HARD SEEDS (PERENNIAL)

HIGH PROTEIN FRUITS (EG MULBERRY)

CLIMBING VINE WITH HARD SEEDED FRUIT.

FRUITING HEDGE SURROUNDING GRAIN PLOT

ANOTHER EGG

extensions to a temporary permission'.23 If the Dixons continue to provide a sustainable model for the enrichment of the Park's ecology, then it is likely that the Park's planners will eventually allow them to put forward a model for low impact Park architecture.

Rating: 6

Tent settlements: Kings Hill

Insofar as benders and other tents are acceptable to planning authorities, it is largely because of their temporary status. They are a low impact version of a caravan-style mobile home: less obtrusive, more mobile and not requiring hard standing. At least three planning appeals have confirmed that benders do not constitute 'operational development', in other words they do not class as a structure or building in the same way that a house does.[24]

This may in some cases make it easier to get planning permission for benders, and it exempts them from building regulations, but it also makes them legally less secure. Whereas councils cannot use the summary enforcement measure known as a 'stop notice' to prevent residents from living in a building or other structure, they can, through an amendment made in the Planning and Compensation Act 1991, use a stop notice to prohibit people from living in a caravan or anything else not classed as a building.[25] The logic of this amendment, which is clearly targeted against the travelling community,[26] is that if one's caravan or bender is subject to a stop notice, the best strategy may be to lay foundations and turn it as quickly as possible into a house.

Stop notices aside, benders and other tents offer a cheap and relatively acceptable form of temporary accommodation for those living on land without planning permission. It is therefore difficult to estimate what proportion of people living in tents do so out of choice, and what proportion do so because they have no other option. Probably the majority are happy living in a tent and, given the choice, a sizable minority would opt to continue living in one. Tent dwelling is by no means as uncomfortable as some might think, and it is healthy, a dry tent being in almost all circumstances preferable to a damp house. Because canvas breathes, there are no condensation problems, and provided fires are lit from time to time in winter, a sound canvas structure will not suffer from lingering damp. Rugs hung on the walls can provide a reasonable amount of heat insulation, and a small solar power unit can provide electric light at the flick of a switch. Over recent years some fairly sophisticated designs have appeared, based on the traditional English bender (a canvas draped over a cylindrical vault of hazel poles), on the cone shaped tipis of North America, or on yurts, round cake shaped structures from central Asia.

On the other hand, some people living in tents would rather build a house, but know that they have no chance of obtaining permanent planning permission in the foreseeable future. Usually the style of house envisaged is a small low impact shack, built out of wood, thatch, earth or other local and recycled materials, and with autonomous services — the sort of cabin for which there is at present no place whatsoever in the British planning system. For these people, a canvas roof over a light

One of the Kings Hill benders. It is in a prominent position, but trees have been planted round it. Photo: Ian Sumner.

wooden structure, perhaps embellished with windows, fitted cupboards and so on, is the nearest approximation.

There have been innumerable cases of people living in benders being forced by planners to leave land they owned or leased. Mostly these have been small individual or family settlements, whose inhabitants have not applied for planning permission either because they were too poor — a planning application costs about £160, about twice as much as a small bender — or else because they knew they had no chance of getting it. There appear to have been only two successful applications in recent years for planning permission for residential tents, both of them multiple applications, and both of them on land connected to a farmhouse. One was for an 'experimental low impact movable dwelling plot' at Higher Rockes Farmhouse, Butleigh, Somerset in 1992.[27] Permission was given on appeal for a year only. The site was privately owned by one individual and lay within the village, a situation that was felt to be unsatisfactory by the occupants, who did not apply for renewal. The other is a similar settlement at Yoke Farm in Herefordshire, where a farmer was given permission at committee level to rent out a field as a bender site, much as if it were a mobile home site. This settlement is still in existence.

By far the longest established tent site is the Tipi Village near Carmarthen in Wales, where since 1976 up to 100 tipi dwellers have been playing a cat-and-mouse game with local planners, moving their dwellings from one parcel of land to another to avoid enforcement. Despite the clear fact that the village is fulfilling a need, and the conclusion of an appeal Inspector in 1985 that the settlement was on balance beneficial to the environment, the Welsh Office called in the decision and refused it planning permission in 1987. At the end of 1995, the Tipi dwellers were still there awaiting the results of a decision, again called in by the Welsh Office, as to whether some of the plots of land now occupied for more than ten years should qualify for a certificate of lawful use as defined in the Planning and Compensation Act 1991.[28]

The Government has been persistent at calling in decisions on what Secretary of State for the Environment, John Gummer, styles 'hippy camps'.[29] In 1995, Gummer called in and dismissed the appeal for seven benders on an agricultural holding at Tinker's Bubble, Somerset, despite the Inspector's recommendation that planning permission should be granted. And the appeal by the Kings Hill collective for three years temporary permission for 20 benders upon a four acre site, also in Somerset, was also called in by the Secretary of State who, in March 1996, confirmed the Inspector's decision that the appeal should be dismissed.

The Kings Hill project is the clearest example of a residential bender site outside the development zone — in effect it is a self-built, low impact housing estate. About 16 benders, each about the size of a double garage, most of them with windows, are sited in a field, forming a circle around a central garden area. At one end of this open space there is a red telephone kiosk. The estate is hidden from the approach road, but can be viewed at a distance of a mile or more from the other side of the valley. The settlers have planted the site with trees, which in a few years time will screen it from this aspect.

One of the benders is a communal space where guests can sleep, the others are individual or family dwellings. The estate is run by a co-operative comprised of the owners of the bender plots who pay £600 for their share: private mortgage facilities at £5 per week for 120 weeks are available. Any share offered for resale must first be offered back to the collective to be repurchased by the remaining members, and new shareholders are only admitted by consensus agreement from all members.

Although there are a number of vegetable gardens dotted around, and the collective has plans for growing a greater amount of food on site, the project is not linked to any agricultural enterprise. Most of the inhabitants are ex-travellers seeking above all a safe place to live. The collective's appeal submission states that 'the choice of site was almost entirely determined by considerations of availability. It is very difficult to obtain sites for this type of project, and this difficulty is further compounded by the financial problems of a group of low income individuals without existing capital or mortgage eligibility'.[30]

The occupants also share a desire to 'progress towards a truly sustainable life style, minimizing resource consumption and maximizing recycling and food production',[31] and are frustrated by the difficulty of finding a suitable place to do this. 'It is crazy, there is no room for experimentation in this country', says one of the settlers, Brian Monger. 'We are trying to live as harmoniously with the envi-

Inside Brian Monger's bender at King's Hill. Photo: Ian Sumner.

ronment as is possible, but are not allowed to do so. I have repeatedly asked Mendip District Council where I can live like this, but they have never answered the question, so I have taken a shot in the dark'.[32]

Mendip Council have never answered this question because they view their task to be to tell people where it is unacceptable to live unsustainably, rather than advise people where they can live sustainably. 'The main role of the planning system', they state in their recommendation for refusal, 'in working towards sustainable development, is through demand management. This includes restricting development in the open countryside'.[33]

The collective's progress towards sustainability is realistic rather than ambitious and based on a low cost life style, rather than high capital investment in alternative solutions. The occupants are gradually acquiring renewable energy hardware, such as solar panels and a wind generator, piece by piece, whilst continuing to use paraffin for lighting and wood for heating. The site provides its own water and sewage services, in the form of composting earth closets, which are eventually back-filled and planted with a tree. The relatively low income needed to maintain this way of life is derived either from local casual or part-time labour, or from income support. Use of local facilities, trip sharing and cycling reduce the need for car travel; a survey carried out for the collective's appeal submission concluded that the 16 households generated vehicle movements equivalent to those normally generated by three or four average households.[34] Sensitive to the view that living in the open countryside generates traffic, the collective comments: 'We plan to reduce our vehicle use over the three year period: this project is part of a move away from vehicle based lifestyles. While we cannot achieve legitimate security of tenure on our own land, we must retain the ability to remove ourselves and our dwellings from it. Refusing applications from travelling people attempting to stop travelling surely cannot be justified by reference to a policy of "minimizing the need to travel"'.[35]

The Kings Hill bender site should be viewed partly as an answer to the problems of the travelling community, whose position is somewhat different from that of the majority of homeless people. The collective is following Government advice to buy land and apply for planning permission.[36] However the project should also be considered in the light of its environmental impact as a new settlement. It is true that its siting outside the development zone may result in a degree of visual impact and a certain amount of traffic generation that might not exist were the inhabitants to pursue a similar lifestyle on the periphery of a village — though this is open to debate. On the other hand, Kings Hill provides affordable accommodation for up to 20 households in lightweight structures on less than an acre. A standard development for 20 houses on the edge of a village would cover about double the area, would involve an extension of the peri-urban infrastructure in the form of access roads, electricity provision and drainage, would use thousands of tons of concrete and other building materials, and would probably generate a greater number of objections from the public than the handful of objections to the Kings Hill site.

The three previous examples in this chapter were all granted permission at committee stage; the Kings Hill bender site, on the other hand, was opposed at committee stage, went to appeal and lost. In his recommendation to dismiss the appeal, the Inspector agreed that 'a balance sheet of consumption and production would probably show that the site is contributing to a sustainable way of life'. However he did not feel that this outweighed the objections on transport and land-scape grounds: 'General movement to and from the site, the hubbub of children at play and adults doing daily chores, however attractive or picturesque, change the character and landscape quality of this former field'. Kings Hill was an interesting experiment, but in the Inspector's opinion one that 'could equally be undertaken in the grounds of a research institute or university, where results would be readily monitored'.[37]

Why the Kings Hill project should be felt to require academic monitoring, and why its 'hubbub' should be more problematic than that created by the occupants of West Harwood, Hockerton or Tir Penrhos Isaf, are not clear. All of these projects are taking place in former fields. Some people may suspect the appeal was dismissed because the residents of Kings Hill are travellers, acting on their own initiative. Whatever the reason, the Inspector's vision of a 'King's College bender site' is a bizarre response to Brian Monger's question, 'Where can I live like this?'

Rating: 13

Chapter 7

Five Visions of Low Impact

THE DIFFICULTIES EXPERIENCED by Gypsies and travellers seeking a place to settle in the countryside are in many ways similar to those met by other settlers. Nomadic people, however, face a particular set of problems. Over the past decades, almost all the customary stopping places for Gypsies have been shut off for one reason or another. According to the Friends Families and Travellers Support Group (FFT), 'between 60 and 90 per cent of traditional sites have been lost through encroachment, blockage and denial over the last ten years'.[1] Detailed studies of two areas in Somerset revealed that 92 per cent of traditional sites had been lost in the previous eight years in one case, and 72 per cent in the other.[2] Furthermore, many of the occupations traditionally pursued by Gypsies have declined over recent decades, in particular fruit picking and seasonal agricultural work which also provided secure temporary residence.

A future for nomads

The laws and planning policies governing traveller sites are not the same as those applying to other settlers. Since the 1960s a series of Acts and policy measures have made prescriptions which apply to 'Gypsies' or 'nomads', but not to other people. The difficulty, of course, has been to decide who is and who is not a Gypsy. In 1967, in a case called Wills v Cooper, Lord Parker came up with the memorable decision that 'a man might well not be a Gypsy on one date and yet be one on another', depending upon whether he was leading a 'nomadic life, with ... no fixed employment and no fixed abode'.[3] This definition was changed significantly in November 1993, when Mr. Justice Harrison ruled that a Gypsy was someone 'who moved from place to place with a purpose in mind as a necessary and characteristic part of their lives'. A commentary on this ruling in the *Solicitors Journal* suggested that the test was so defined as to exclude 'new age' travellers or indeed, in the words of another solicitor, anyone 'whose movements are dictated by evictions, rather than any economic or traditional 'purpose''.[4].

Failure to qualify as a Gypsy means ineligibility to benefit from the meagre concessions made to Gypsies in planning law. The Caravan Sites Act 1968 placed a duty on local authorities to provide adequate sites for Gypsies, and any authority which complied could apply for 'designated status' which would allow it to deal more effectively with illegal sites. However the relevant sections of this Act were repealed in the Criminal Justice and Public Order Act 1994, which at the same time makes camping on any unoccupied land or on the highway a potentially criminal offence.5 Instead, DoE Circular 1/94 encourages nomads to buy sites and apply for planning permission — in effect to stop travelling. As one travellers' organization points out, the 'nomadic requirement ... fogs the issue as the whole point of Private Sites is to allow Gypsy people to "settle"'.6

This is precisely what considerable numbers of those Gypsies who can afford to buy land have tried to do, though without much co-operation from the authorities. At the beginning of this decade, something like 90 per cent of applications by travellers for private sites were refused by local authorities.7 Today that figure may be even higher: a survey by FFT of 48 applications made between November 1994 and October 1995 revealed that only two were allowed by local authorities, lending weight to Lord Irvine of Lairg's contention that 'the Government's proposition that Gypsies should apply for planning permission for sites that they should buy is nothing other than a sick joke'.8

There is no space here to examine all the aspects of the Gypsy and traveller issue. Their demands vary considerably: some can afford to buy land, some cannot; some wish to settle, some to travel, and some want to travel part of the time. Some would accept living in a building, some are attached to living in caravans, and some wish to live in horse drawn accommodation. A large number of proposals which attempt to cater for all these separate requirements have emerged, particularly in response to the Government's 1992 consultation exercise on the reform of the 1968 Caravan Sites Act. The discussion here is limited to proposals for nomadic people which come under the heading of low impact. In describing them, there is no suggestion that these will meet all Gypsies' and travellers' needs.

The first of these proposals appeared in a document drawn up by a consortium of seven travellers' organizations in a document entitled *Alternative Proposals for the Constructive Reform of the 1968 Caravan Sites Act*.9 It contains a section headed 'New Forms of Site' which advocates, for rural areas:

• 'The expansion of Council Smallholding schemes, 'residential allotments' for small scale, single family agricultural developments.

• 'Self-help settlement schemes — basic amenity sites on unused land in public ownership, to be upgraded via standard housing improvement grants, providing own labour on a co-operative basis. Self-build projects for sites would be very attractive financially.

• 'Reforestation projects and other environmental improvement schemes of limited duration allowing workers and families to live on site ... productive and acceptable 'workfare schemes' for nomadic people'.

The authors conclude: 'the above all provide "a reason for being there", occupations, and a benefit to the whole community;' — they suggest ways of providing a livelihood as well as a place to live.

A woodland camp of Gypsy clothes peg makers in the early twentieth century. From *Romany Life*, Frank Cuttriss, Mills and Boon, 1915.

The first two of these suggestions, 'residential allotments' and self-build communities are solutions for travellers who wish to settle, and are examined elsewhere in this book. But the third proposal — residential environmental projects of limited duration — is aimed at those who wish to pursue a nomadic lifestyle. Environmental and conservation work is replacing agricultural work as the main form of manually skilled seasonal employment in the countryside; there are many environmental projects which badly need labour and there are travelling people who would be interested in performing this work in return for reasonable wages and a secure place to stay. Indeed there are travellers who already have such an arrangement with landowners on an informal basis. In response to a demand from travellers, FFT is in the process of setting up and securing funding for a woodland skills training programme for travellers.

However, as the authors of the report indicate by their use of the word 'acceptable', such 'workfare schemes' have to be undertaken with caution. They are vaguely reminiscent of the Training Centres instituted in the 1930s where unemployed people worked on 'forest clearing, road making, drainage, timbering, excavating, quarrying and levelling. Conditions were awful; beds were lousy, medicine and food inadequate, the men were accommodated in barracks and visits home or to local towns limited ... Many absconded; there were frequently demonstrations, strikes and walk outs'.[10] These work camps sprang out of a 1931 Royal Commission on Unemployment which noted that 'in Germany, some considerable success has been achieved in this respect and we believe that something of the sort is strongly desirable in this country' and which 'saw no objection in principle to the application of compulsion'.

It is therefore important that such schemes are initiated from the bottom up, rather than from the top down, otherwise they may begin to resemble labour camps. Perhaps the best way to catalyse such projects would be for a travellers' organization to approach environmental groups or organizations representing potentially interested land owners — the National Trust, Wildlife Trusts, the Small Woods Association, the Coppice Association, the Permaculture Association, Working Weekends on Organic Farms, for example — and explore the possibility of setting up an *ad hoc* agency which could put nomadic workers in touch with interested land managers. If in certain situations (namely those where residence was required for more than 28 days) it were felt necessary to lodge an application for temporary or seasonal planning permission, then the agency could assist with this task, and there should be very little reason for any local authority to refuse permission.

Such a project could mesh with another proposal put forward by FFT for temporary sites linked to Britain's neglected network of green lanes and droves which traditionally provided a cycle of stopping places for Gypsies.[11] FFT's draft document observes: 'It is within the context of a network of sites that traditional models of nomadic land use can be understood; they are used seasonally and in sequence, to eventually create a cycle. They are therefore temporary and permanent at the same time. Vacancy enables winter frosts to cleanse the soil and an undisturbed spring, summer and autumn promotes floral regeneration.' In recent years, as these traditional sites have been closed off, travellers have been forced to congregate in larger and more permanent concentrations, 'with all the environmental and social stresses which this creates'.

FFT therefore recommends that it should be permissible to put in a single planning application for seasonal use of a number of such sites: 'Section 24 of the Caravan Sites and Control of Development Act 1960 gives power to local authorities to buy or to compulsorily purchase land to provide sites. By acquiring sites which follow the traditional model outlined above, green lane and drove networks could be completed to enhance the amenity of all countryside users, and create habitat for a diversity of life... The larger the number of sites held in reserve, the greater the tolerance margin of the system and landscape concerned. Not only could sites be used in sequence, but also networks. This has potential benefits not only to the environment but also to the resident population who would be assured that site occupancy would be transitory only. Six sites in every 25 square miles of lowland rural landscape is a target figure attainable by most highway authorities."

This imaginative proposal bears some consideration, and invites some questions.

First, beyond providing much needed accommodation in a form which protects the environment and enhances public amenity, will these sites have what the Alternative Proposals document calls a 'reason for being there'? To what extent can they help to provide sustainable livelihoods for those wishing to pursue a rural nomadic life-style?

This matter is beyond the scope of the FFT draft proposal. But there seems to be

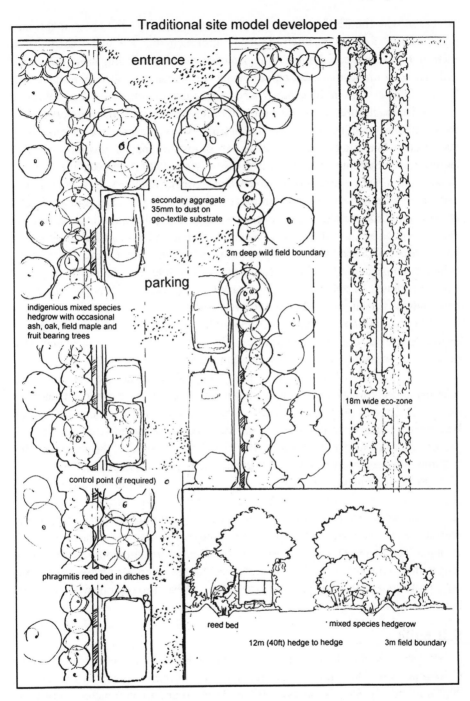

Traditional site model developed

entrance

secondary aggragate
35mm to dust on
geo-textile substrate

3m deep wild field boundary

parking

indigenious mixed species
hedgrow with occasional
ash, oak, field maple and
fruit bearing trees

18m wide eco-zone

control point (if required)

phragmitis reed bed in ditches

reed bed

mixed species hedgerow

12m (40ft) hedge to hedge

3m field boundary

A design for a low impact travellers site, surrounded by three metre deep hedgerows and
equipped with reed bed sanitation. The inset shows how the site might be incorporated into
an 18 metre wide eco-zone. Courtesy Friends and Families of Travellers.

no reason why the FFT's scheme should not be married to the above-mentioned proposal for sites where environmental improvements are to be carried out. Interested travellers could move through a cycle of seasonal occupations that might include, for example, tree planting, coppicing or snigging in the winter, fruit picking, fair and festival work in the summer, and apple picking, indigenous seed collecting and Christmas decorations in the autumn. In forestry in particular, possession of a working horse could be very useful. In such a network, a number of the temporary residential sites might be furnished by private or institutional landowners in need of labour, thus taking the onus off the highway authorities to provide all the sites.

Second, is such a network of green lanes conceivable? FFT estimate that a network of four or five green lanes around every market town in England would cost about £10 million. Much of the work involved in establishing and maintaining the network could be carried out by travellers. At the moment droves seem to be the only category of pre-industrial transport infrastructure that is not being rehabilitated. Britain's footpaths are being registered, repaired and maintained; the canal system, after being left for derelict, is being put back together again. Given that an entirely new 'post-industrial' network of paved cycle paths is being created with the help of the Millennium Fund, it should not be that difficult, at least in some areas, to revive an old network of droves and lanes. Can it be that these lanes have been neglected because they have become the favoured domain of social outcasts?

The feasibility of such a network serving a circuit of low impact sites certainly needs to be examined critically, particularly for winter months when ungravelled lanes can become boggy and grazing for horses is scarce. There is a danger that they might become race tracks for trials bike users and four-wheel-drive enthusiasts. Nonetheless, the attractions of such a project are undeniable. Large sections of the general public, including walkers, horse riders and mountain bikers would welcome it.

These two complementary visions, of an inventory of environmentally beneficial projects and a network of low impact sites, would undoubtedly require considerable review and experiment before they could be forged into any coherent policy. But they are visions of what might be achieved if the current attitude towards travellers changed. The obstacle is not simply timidity and lack of imagination within the planning system. At root it is a refusal to recognize that travellers are an asset to society, not a problem; and that the question to ask is not, 'What is to be done with nomads?' but, 'What can they do?'

Self-build

Between a third and a half of the world's population build their own homes. In Colombia over 500 self-help organizations are currently involved in building 90,000 homes. In Stockholm over 200 self-built homes are completed every year. Norwegian farmers customarily build their own homes. A recent report showed that self-help accounts for at least 40 per cent of the housing provision in Belgium, West Germany, Austria, Italy, France, Norway, Finland and Ireland. Only in the UK does it account for less than 10 per cent of completions.[12]

A Walter Segal design house, with a turf roof. Photo: The Walter Segal Trust.

There is no intrinsic connection between self-built and low impact housing, but nonetheless the two often go hand in hand. Most of the projects and proposals mentioned in this book are self-built. There are several reasons for this. Firstly, self-built houses save on labour costs and many seeking a low impact residence are on a low income. Secondly, a number of low impact proposals come from people who are not impressed by orthodox building methods and are actively interested in building their own experimental house. Thirdly, many self-built houses are timber framed, a method which often appeals to low impact builders. And fourthly, self-built housing, since it can be tailored to individual need and is not dependent upon economies of scale, can afford to experiment in environmentally sound design. The Diggers self-build scheme in Brighton achieved a National Home Energy Rating of 9.8 out of ten.[13] The Volume Self-Build Scheme achieves a similar NHER rating, with annual heating costs of only £30 per year, using passive solar gain, insulation made from recycled newspaper, and energy efficient boilers.[14] The Walter Segal Trust, a national charity which helps people to build their own homes has published a guide entitled *Out of the Woods: Ecological Designs for Timber Frame Housing*.[15]

Self-build is widely viewed as a solution to housing problems. It forms an important component of the Homeless Persons and Mutual Aid Bill which is being drafted by an alliance of environmental and social organizations. A number of councils have used self-build schemes to help alleviate a housing problem, most of them urban. Of nineteen housing schemes listed in the Walter Segal Trust's 1995 Developments List, only three were not in urban areas. The reasons for this are not entirely clear, since the need for affordable housing is just as great in the countryside as in the town, but it may be partly because rural councils do not feel that self-build schemes would fit in with vernacular village architecture. In at least two cases, smallholders have applied for permission to build their own energy efficient houses in the style pioneered by the Walter Segal Trust, and have been told by their local planning authority that only buildings using traditional materials and techniques would be acceptable.[16]

If this attitude is prevalent amongst councils, it is founded upon a somewhat selective definition of the word 'traditional'. While most buildings in villages are nowadays constructed in masonry, this has been a relatively recent development. Over 90 per cent of pre-Reformation buildings which survive today are timber frame constructions, broadly similar to those advocated by the Walter Segal Trust.17 Admittedly the Segal buildings are built with machine sawn timber, resulting in a geometrically regular construction that does not possess the attractive irrectitude of a medieval half timbered building. But then the same is true of modern masonry techniques. Where there is a distaste for timber framed buildings in villages, it seems to be based on an innate and misplaced conservatism (perhaps linked, in some cases, to the vested interests of the building industry).

Where the Walter Segal Trust has been successful, largely in towns, it may be partly because its function as a facilitating agency has helped make the development palatable to councils who might otherwise be afraid of what could emerge if individuals with a DIY bent were allowed to build for themselves. The self-build movement can claim another older pedigree, in a phenomenon which was anathema to planners because it was so unplanned, but whose virtues have long been advocated by one veteran commentator, Colin Ward:

> Nearly 20 years ago I urged that we should learn the positive lessons of the 'plot-lands' of South East England. The word is a useful bit of planners' jargon for those places where, during the agricultural depression from the turn of the century until 1939, speculators sold off plots in Essex, Kent, Sussex and the Thames valley to low-income Londoners to build their dream home, chicken farm, holiday shack or chalet. The existence of such places was one of the reasons for the rise of conservation bodies and comprehensive planning legislation.[18]

Colin Ward's enthusiasm for these individually designed and built homesteads (which were by no means special to South-East England) is shared by Sue Clifford of Common Ground:

In my 30 years as a planner, I have heard all of the arguments over 'squatted' developments from the Essex Plotlands to the East Lothian holiday camps and the beach huts of Portland. But early on I formed an opinion ... that the care and ingenuity which are hallmarks of these inventive shelters are far more important than the received aesthetic, usually driven by tidiness and fear of unfettered small scale decision making. The community commitment which they generate is envied. These are often rich vibrant places, fulfilling social as well as individual needs, they usually have a good impact on the ecology of the place, indeed they often support wild life displaced by farming practice and clinical development. Like allotments, they develop their own integrity and personality from hard work from within.[19]

The survival of the remaining plotlands became a national issue in 1995 when 27 chalets in Holtsfield on the Gower peninsula near Swansea were threatened with eviction by the owner of the land who wanted to build a housing estate. Some of the chalets 'were built in the 1920s and 1930s by people who hauled the timber, by bus, from Swansea and then walked two miles with it to the building site'.[20] Other chalets and extensions have been built using timber recycled from Swansea skips. In 1990 Swansea City Council declared the site a Conservation Area. The chalets are 'buried in lush and greenery ... on the edge of a nature reserve. It has owls, bats, cats, dogs and tame geese, all living in apparent harmony'.[21] What a contrast to the sea-front development, ten minutes walk away, described as a 'concrete and tarmac burger bar and ice cream paradise'.[22] The magazine *Perspectives on Architecture* praised the dwellings as 'the perfect example of community architecture in action' and 'a model for a more sensitive, socially responsible way of developing the countryside'[23] — a verdict that *The Independent* observed was 'an architectural accolade that comes a bit too late'.[24]

Unfortunately the DoE does not share the general enthusiasm for this kind of development. A health survey conducted in 1991 found all the chalets unfit for habitation, mainly on water and sewerage grounds, even though the inhabitants use compost toilets, a method that normally meets with no objection from health inspectors. Moreover, the residents, who own the chalets, but not the land, are not accorded full tenants' rights because their residences are not viewed as proper dwellings. The irrational nature of the prejudice against this kind of dwelling can be observed in a rather sinister recommendation in DoE Circulars 1/85 and 11/95 that it may be 'necessary to prevent the permanent residential use of holiday chalets which by the character of their construction or design are unsuitable for continuous occupation'. No explanation is given in the circulars as to why buildings that are deemed to be suitable for occupation some of the time are not suitable for occupation all of the time.[25]

Sadie Bowens, Holtsfield's oldest resident, interviewed by a reporter on the day of the first attempted evictions of the chalet community, October 1995. Photo: Nick Cobbing.

Late in 1995, some of the chalets were evicted, despite large scale public protests. The resistance was not as violent as that in the 1970s at a similar site at Boudigou near Perpignan in the south of France, when a number of bulldozers brought in to destroy timber and bamboo chalets were fire bombed overnight. Instead, in pure Ealing comedy style, the local vicar was reported to have chained himself to one of the chalets. In an Ealing comedy, the vicar and the Holtsfield community would have won. In Britain in 1996 they may yet lose. The Holtsfield episode shows the British planning system in its worst light, an accomplice in the destruction of widely admired low impact homes for the benefit of a developer profiting from the site's suitability for high impact development.

Colin Ward has championed the cause of the plotlands because he views them as a model for new forms of rural development. In 1975 he wrote:

> We are once again in a period with a huge range of ideas in the air, especially amongst the young. There is enormous interest among the young in what has become known as alternative technology ... There are large numbers of people interested in alternative ways of making a living: looking for labour intensive low-capital industries, because capital-intensive industries have failed to provide them with an income.[26]

Nineteen years later, writing in the magazine *Town and Country Planning*, Ward reflected:

> If I was optimistic in 1975 about the number of people disowned by the employ-ment system and the housing system who ... yearned for a chance to develop their own expectations in the margins of our big-spending wasteful society, I certainly do not exaggerate their numbers today... . What I urged was a 'do-it-yourself' new town: an area with waivers on the planning and building legislation, where it would be possible to operate some kind of 'usufruct' which would enable people to house themselves with a means of livelihood, while not draining immense sums from central or local government.[27]

Ward goes on to explain how the modern political situation has provided poten-tial sites for such a DIY new town:

> The happy end of the cold war, for example, has left a series of redundant military air bases, publicly owned and provided with roads and mains services. Here's a marvellous chance for a great public gesture to make NIMBY-free land available for groups of unemployed people to build their own dream houses, with work-shops and chicken runs, kitchen gardens and tree planting. In no time at all there would be food co-ops and community buses. Wind generators would spring up.

Among the unemployed who might fruitfully colonize one of these abandoned air fields are the considerable numbers of travellers who are roaming the country in buses and horse drawn wagons, and who, if they can afford it, are buying land upon which they hope to settle. Colin Ward is certainly not the only person to muse upon the suitability of derelict military property for low impact settlement: the very NIMBYs that he refers to are also keen on the idea. As one objecting neighbour to the Tinker's Bubble project wrote in his submission to the planning appeal: 'There must be many more suitable tracts of land available for such a development ... Abandoned farms or airfields immediately come to mind'.[28]

There is a danger that, with the best of intentions, scheduling an air base as a 'NIMBY-free' site for social misfits could have a ghetto effect which might even antagonize relations between NIMBYs and travellers, rather than healing them. The travellers' problem is caused by lack of access to land, and an 'out-of-sight, out-of-mind' solution is not necessarily the best way of integrating them into rural society or of taking advantage of what they have to offer.

Nonetheless, the use of such sites as self-build settlements certainly has great potential. With a certain amount of grant aid for tree planting on these often grim and wind-swept spaces, there are tremendous opportunities for environmental improvement and social experimentation. There is no doubt that, within 20 years, untrammelled human ingenuity could turn one of these dreary concrete and tarmac anachronisms into something as lush and as vibrant as Holtsfield.

Colin Ward ends his article with the comment: 'The planners' dilemma is that of how to accommodate these dreams of self-help and sustainability, while excluding those whose interest is in unsustainable profitability'. In fact this is not as great a dilemma for planners as one might think: as we shall see in the next chapter, an ideal mechanism for accommodating such dreams was drafted into the planning process in 1986 in the form of Simplified Planning Zones. Anybody can apply for one.

The Second Great Wood of Caledon ...

The Highland area of Scotland presents a rather different rural situation from the rest of Great Britain. The process of enclosure in northern Scotland in the nineteenth century, known as the Clearances, was of a different order from that in England, or perhaps anywhere in Europe — more on a par with the annihilation by British colonists of the aboriginal population in Tasmania, or Sadam Hussein's recent attempt to burn out the marsh dwellers in the south of Iraq. In order to provide pasture for sheep and hunting estates for the aristocracy, the inhabitants of the high-lands were literally shipped off to Canada or carted away to Glasgow, while their homes were burned or razed to the ground.[29] Today much of the Highland area is deserted, and owned by a handful of landlords — 4,000 people own 80 per cent of the whole of Scotland. The fate of the Highlands was described most poignantly by the Canadian novelist Hugh MacLennan, in an essay called 'Scotchman's Return':

> The Highland emptiness only a few hundred miles above the massed population of England is a far different thing from the emptiness of our North-West Territories. Above the 60th parallel in Canada, you feel that nobody but God had ever been there before you. But in a deserted Highland Glen, you feel that everyone who ever mattered is dead and gone.[30]

The disappearance of human settlements from the Highlands has not provided an opportunity for the resurgence of wilderness, or a niche for the wolf and bear that roamed the country in primeval times when it was covered with forest. On the contrary, severe grazing by sheep and by deer kept for hunting has resulted in large expanses of deforested and degraded pasture land that support a very limited range of species as well as very few humans. As Sir Frank Fraser Darling wrote in a survey published in 1955, 'the Highlands are a devastated countryside... and that is why there are now few people and why there is a constant economic problem'. What reforestation has occurred has been based upon the establishment of vast monocul-tures of conifers, usually Sitka Spruce, which further diminish the level of bio-diversity and provide little in the way of employment for local people.[31]

A vision, from the Highland Green Party, of how the Highland economy could be invigorated. Photo: Paul M. Thomas, Highland Green Party.

The initial response to the problem of desertification was the support given to crofts — small rented farms which provided a basic livelihood for the rump of the Highland population. The 1886 Crofters Act gave crofters heritable security of tenure with controllable rents throughout the seven northernmost counties of Scotland, and 90 years later, the Crofting Reform Act of 1976 gave them the right to buy their land at a price 15 times the controlled annual rent. Today there are some 17,000 crofts averaging from about three to seven acres in size, but these are concentrated mainly in and around the Western Isles of Scotland; the rest of the Highlands consists primarily of large hill farms and sporting estates.

The crofts have provided a basic livelihood for a population that otherwise might have completely disappeared. According to Martin Watt:

Crofting today, such as on the isle of Lewis, supports the most densely populated part of the British countryside, outside the semi-suburban South of England. If the agricultural and economic strategies which transformed most of our countryside had controlled Lewis, we would be seeing probably 30 large hill farms in operation there, instead of the several thousand smallholdings which we see today.[32]

Crofting is not a planning regime; it is a system of tenure. But nonetheless it has resulted in a more liberal approach towards planning than exists elsewhere in the UK (except perhaps in Northern Ireland). According to one study, crofters on average obtain only 10 percent of their income from the croft, and the rest is derived from other forms of part-time or even full-time work.[33] Yet despite this low income, a croft is regarded as 'viable' in terms of the rural economy, and crofters are therefore able to acquire planning permission for projects more easily than part-time farmers in other areas of Britain. Whether this lack of planning restraint has resulted in environmental benefits is open to question: the initiators of Lowland Crofting are anxious to dissociate their scheme from 'the worst visual aspects of Highland crofts — the abandoned vehicles, the rush-grown pastures, the obtrusive new bungalows'.[34]

A more searching criticism of both the environmental and economic aspects of present day crofting appeared in a 1989 Scottish Green Party publication, *A Rural Manifesto for the Scottish Highlands*, which observed:

Crofting as a type of mixed husbandry involving a high degree of self-reliance has, at least on the Highland mainland, become almost extinct in the last 50 years ... The typical croft today has an income derived from at least one job off the croft, and from the provision of tourist accommodation. Agricultural activity is mostly part-time ... and comprises the running of sheep alone. Even the provision of seasonal vegetables and fruit for the kitchen is now an uncommon part of the croft economy. The decline of crofting husbandry has gone hand in hand with the ... loss of contact with the productive capabilities of the land.

These observations form part of a growing consensus in Scotland that the revival of the rural economy requires not only changes in tenure rights and land reform, but also a reinvigoration of the region's ecology. The Green Party publication was subtitled 'Creating the Second Great Wood of Caledon' and it proposed the creation of a 'forest economy' in Scotland:

Where open moor and denuded peat can only support a few animals, a few plants and therefore little agriculture, population and employment, a forest can support an abundance of economic activity in proportion to the relative abundance of its biomass. The Second Great Wood of Caledon would comprise an enormous range of tree and shrub species, providing a correspondingly great range of food (animal and vegetable), fodder, fuel, timber, industrial, craft and even medicinal products.[35]

In 1991, the pressure group Reforesting Scotland was formed to bring the concept of a forest economy into the public arena. According to one of its founders, Alastair McIntosh, some of the impetus for the group came from British forestry development workers in the Third World who came back home and realized 'that the

A log home in Washington State, USA. It was built in the 1970s at a cost of $200. The materials to build such dwellings are now abundant throughout Scotland and in many parts of Wales and England.
Photos: Art Boericke and Barry Shapiro, *The Craftsman Builder*, Simon and Schuster 1979.

progress which has been made in some community forest projects in Nepal or Papua New Guinea, for example, is not only absent in Scotland, but positively ridiculed as having no relevance to areas such as the Highlands and Islands'.[36]

The barrier of ridicule was breached in 1993 when 31 representatives of Scottish organizations, including Scottish Natural Heritage, the Highland Regional Council and the Forestry Commission participated in a two week tour of Hordaland in Western Norway, an area geologically and climatically similar to the highlands of Scotland. The participants observed that the forest economy of Hordaland, based on farms with on average 10 hectares of farmland and 56 hectares of forest, supported over three times as many people per hectare as the Highland economy could support. The tour also noted that 'a high proportion of sawn timber is processed in local sawmills or on the farm. Unlike Scotland, the vast majority of Norwegian buildings are both timber framed and clad. Farmers frequently build their own houses and farm buildings from farm produced timber'.[37] This is a far cry from Scotland, where crofters can see 'huge barges of timber being hauled off the hillsides and towed to processing plants in the English Midlands'[38] while planners wince at the proliferation of 'obtrusive new bungalows' and 'kit houses' (the prototypes of which were imported from Norway).

Three years after the Norway tour, the project of community forestry in Scotland is no longer ridiculed as a Third World anachronism, but has become conventional wisdom, even within the Scottish Office. 'We've won,' wrote the editor of the magazine *Reforesting Scotland*. 'After just five years of promoting our once radical view of a reforested and repopulated land, the seminal Forests and People in Rural Scotland (FAPIRS) report, published recently by Rural Framework and endorsed by the Scottish Office, concurs with everything we've been saying about forestry and community'.[39] The author of the FAPIRS report, Robin Callander, had been a participant on the Norway tour. In December 1995, the Scottish Secretary, Michael Forsyth, agreed to allow the villagers of Laggan, in Inverness-shire, to buy 3,000 acres of forest from the Forestry Commission and manage it themselves. The Laggan Community Association (which had sent a local farmer, Graham Grant, on the Norway tour) persuaded the Scottish Office that the plantation could be 'exploited more imaginatively to provide work which will ultimately replace the bulk of the 36 forestry jobs lost since the 1970s'. Another villager, David Campbell, described the local forest as 'like a Glasgow tenement that is abandoned and empty while there's hundreds of homeless people all around ... It's been very frustrating to watch the forest lose value from under-management, while the local people, who could have done the work, were left unemployed'. The Scottish Secretary not only agreed to the demands of the community, but spoke of returning 'the land back to the people who can manage it best'.[40]

If, as seems both sensible and likely, the Highland region gradually moves towards a forest economy, more akin to that of Norway, then more people will need to be accommodated in the countryside. The main hurdle to be overcome is not planning policy — which, as regards development in the countryside, can afford to be relatively lax compared to the rest of Great Britain — but land ownership. At the moment most land in the Highlands is not owned by 'the people who can manage it best', but by absentee landlords and the Forestry Commission. Buying them out will take time.

Nonetheless, some Scottish planners are looking ahead at the ways in which future planning policy can positively influence the development of a richer Highland ecology and economy. Thoughtful people are looking at the sterile banks of Forestry Commission or private coniferous plantations draped over Scottish hillsides and musing that small sheltered clearings — 'rooms', in planning jargon — could be carved out of these monocultures where a pioneer forester/farmer could use the income from the maturing trees to create a more diverse and productive natural habitat. A group called Building in the Forest, formed to look at such possibilities, held its first field day in September 1995.

Similarly, sooner or later, one of the remote moorland estates will be bought up, not by another international investor, nor by a local village association, but by a dedicated body whose aim is to plant a variety of trees, enrich the local ecology and settle people upon the land. One group, Natural Resources Scotland Ltd, is already looking at an estate in Perthshire and seeking funds to develop just such a project. New Caledonia, as the scheme is called, will sub-divide the property into 50 acre holdings, restrict sheep use, plant community forests and explore the commercial potential of wildlife, such as elk.[41]

The Scottish planning system has an opportunity to elicit a considerable amount of environmental planning gain from such situations. Planners cannot buy the land back from those who presently own it; but, once it is bought, they can help ensure that settlers, in return for the opportunity to live on this land, enhance the diversity of the local ecology and in other respects maintain a beneficial impact upon the environment. Planning permission is valuable and it can be used to subsidise the labour necessary to diversify the forests and reinvigorate the degraded areas of the Highlands. By laying the groundwork for such a policy now, Scottish planners will help to open the doors for the land reform that is so urgently required.

... And reforesting Albion

In the rest of Britain, land reform is not such an urgent priority, nor is the countryside so barren. However tree cover is lower than in Scotland (or any other country in the EU, except Ireland), and forest regeneration has become a national policy. The Government has proposed a 'National Forest in the Midlands' and 'would like to see a doubling of woodland in England over the next half century' from about seven per cent of the total area to about 14 per cent.[42] A 'Second Great Wood of Albion' may not yet be on the political agenda, but it is not that far off. English land use planners will need to adapt, and they could learn much from the Scottish experience, just as the Scots have learnt from the Third World and from Norway.

So far the Government has been vague about who will plant this new forest, who will manage it, and what it is for. It talks blithely about 'an economic resource ...

One of the illustrations from Sir James Hall's little known treatise *On the Origin and Principles of Gothic Architecture.* Hall's theory that Gothic architecture is a skeuomorphic adaptation of ancient wattle and daub techniques (in the same way that classical Greek architecture mimicked earlier wooden structures), though conjectural, is nonetheless fascinating. Coppice wood construction is a 'soft-bodied' technique that leaves few archaeological traces, so its historical influence may be underestimated. From *Transactions of the Royal Society of Edinburgh*, Vol. IV, 1798.

new opportunities for recreation and leisure, for wildlife conservation and enhancing the landscape'[43] — but it has so far made little serious attempt to assess the profound affect upon the rural economy that a doubling of woodland area throughout the country will have. In particular, little attention has been devoted to working out how this 'economic resource' can be exploited economically.

At present the UK imports about 85 per cent of its timber requirements, and is therefore heavily reliant on ghost acres of sometimes virgin forest in other parts of the world. This is partly because Britain simply does not grow enough timber, and in this respect a doubling in the area of woodland is to be welcomed. An increase in recycling rates of paper and other pulp products would also do much to reduce the deficit. But if quantity is lacking, so is quality. Most of what is supplied domestically is at the lower end of the market: pulpwood, fencing, rough sawn timber (although the UK industry has been effective at turning low quality timber into panel boards). Almost every other product one can think of made of wood — matches, charcoal, plywood, toys, furniture, windows etc. — is likely to be made from foreign trees. Good quality sawmill grade timber accounts for about 40 per cent of the UK's timber trade deficit by volume and far more by value.[44] Much of the tree planting carried out in Britain since the Second World War, has been prompted by tax advantages, particularly to people in the higher income brackets; the result has been considerable areas of conifer plantation extensively managed for low grade timber or in some cases simply neglected.

With the rise of environmental concerns and the changing of agricultural priorities, the tax and grant advantage of planting woodland has now shifted from conifers to broadleaves. However there is no guarantee that this new generation of deciduous woodland is likely to be any better managed than the preceding coniferous one. According to Peter Wilson of the Timber Growers Association (who also went on the Reforesting Scotland tour of Norway): 'The strategic context is completely lacking. People are being given a dollop of money to plant politically correct woodland, but no money for ongoing management. With the final payback so far down the end of the road, the result will be that they will plant too wide, and will skimp on thinning and general management. Unless this changes, you are not going to get good timber'.[45]

The Timber Growers Association would like to see considerably more research into ways of 'pushing English timber up the value-added ladder'. Wilson considers that the production, for example, of veneer quality oak is perfectly possible in the

Building in the woods. The roof timbers are Douglas fir thinnings, too flimsy for sawmill purposes and of little market value; but the reciprocal cone-shaped structure braced by its battens will be strong enough to support a heavy layer of thatch.

UK, given the will. The Timber Growers Association is presently working on a report examining the economic feasibility of reviving coppice industries such as hazel hurdles and split chestnut paling; some of these traditional 'green wood' activities could play an important role in providing an ongoing income from the thinnings taken out of a wood as it grows to maturity. Wilson observes: 'There are high quality niche markets, but people need to have much more imagination. There will need to be new people coming in to take that forward'.

These concerns are not as far removed from the domain of the planner as might first appear. A doubling of the area of woodland raises significant questions about land use, both as regards the environment and the rural economy. As we have seen in the case of Lowland Crofting, the use of planning gain can stimulate the planting of significant amounts of woodland at little expense to the taxpayer (an idea that has been taken several steps forward by Julian Pitts' suggestion of planting community forests for their 'hope value' as potential sites for future sustainable development).46

The question of forest management and reforestation is also of importance within the context of the fragmentation of farmland. This is most likely to occur in marginal hill and dairy areas, especially to the west of the country, which also happen to be climatically propitious for timber production. Planting new woodland may well be a feasible option for redundant farmland; and existing (and frequently neglected) woodlands are sometimes sold separately from the holding to which they were attached at a fairly low price. In such areas intensive woodland management might prove to be a long term option that could enhance the local economy — something has to be done with the land — and also serve to mitigate the impact of the 'shackery' that has been identified as a by-product of fragmentation (see Chapter 3).

The research for this book suggests that there is an upsurge of highly environmentally aware people interested in obtaining a livelihood through the intensive management or planting of small woods. A number of organizations (Coppice Association, Association of Pole Lathe Turners, Marches Greenwood Network, etc.) with committed environmental aims have been formed to represent their interests. Martin Kibblewhite of the Marches Greenwood Network writes: 'Green woodwork suggests working with wood that is 'green' or unseasoned. It could also mean woodwork which is 'Green' in the social and environmental sense. Working with unseasoned wood requires no fossil fuels, since all its operations can be performed by muscle power. Transport is minimized as the work is done in or near the woods, and can employ people in the countryside close to their homes ... Overheads are low or non-existent while the premises are the woods themselves. So workplaces are cheap and job creation need not be costly'.47 Kibblewhite also points out that recent improvements in mobile sawmills mean that timber can be economically sawn and dried in the forest, eliminating the need for transport to a sawmill.

Unfortunately, while the workplace may be cheap, available dwelling space may not be. After agricultural smallholders, as a profession, it is coppice and other woodland workers who are experiencing the greatest difficulty with rural planning restrictions, particularly with regard to on-site dwellings. A small woodland

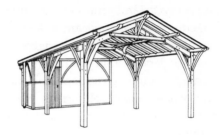

Two designs for traditional wooden buildings: *left* an English cruck frame structure being built in Leigh woods near Bristol (S. Daniels), and *right* a traditional French design which can be constructed from lighter coppice timber (P. Garland and P. Nichols).

enterprise, at least at its outset, may offer enough income to obtain a livelihood, but not sufficient to pay the costs of renting a property at some distance from the wood and commuting to and fro. 'We do need local accommodation while working in our wood', writes Hugh Ross, a coppice worker in the Midlands, living in a caravan; 'we are not generating enough money to rent or buy a house locally'.[48] Permission to live in a small working wood will help to make it pay, and as the saying goes, 'the wood that pays is the wood that stays'. Given that building materials are usually freely available on site, and that the landscape impact of building a cabin in the woods is virtually nil, the draconian restrictions upon forestry dwellings presently being advocated by the DoE's consultants (see Chapter 3) seem counter-productive.

A judicious relaxation of planning restrictions for low impact woodland buildings could also provide a fillip to the timber construction industry. The government acknowledges that 'building standards can affect the demand for timber' and that they may need to be reviewed.[49] The low impact dwellings that some small woodland operators are keen to build are mainly constructed from the materials at hand. They are likely to combine traditional techniques — log cabin (in conifer plantations), half timbering, weatherboarding, wattle and daub, shingle walls or roofs — with some modern techniques such as laminated wood, and levels of insulation and lighting that meet existing building standards. Given that there is a need to identify higher value uses for English timber (particularly coppice and thinnings), that a sustainable forestry policy requires the optimum use of indigenous supplies, and that half timbered cottages are in great demand in the housing market, there is an excellent opportunity here for developing Britain's forest resources. It would be a shame if this opportunity were denied by blind adherence to an outmoded planning orthodoxy.

In the near future, planners and other policy makers will need to recognize that a doubling of the area of woodland does not simply entail an improvement in amenity for day trippers, and a contribution to the nation's global warming account, but also presages a radical change to the rural economy and culture. More woodland in England means more woodland employment, more woodland production, more oak and ash and thorn in people's daily lives. Planners would do well to look to our neighbours in Scandinavia: to Finland, where a third of the population have access to family forests; or to Norway, where small farm-forestry holdings are supported much as crofts are in the Highlands. And they would do well to consult colleagues in Scotland, where it is becoming recognized that a community forest — a concept derived from sustainable development projects in the Third World — is a shared resource providing sustainable livelihoods for local people, not just a country park. South of Hadrian's Wall there is an urgent need for pressure groups entitled 'Reforesting England' and 'Reforesting Wales' to follow the trail blazed by Reforesting Scotland.

Sustainable settlements

The major objection to small scale low impact projects outside the development area, is that they lead to dispersal, and hence to an excessive use of transport. For this reason many advocates of sustainable land use nonetheless disapprove of low impact development in the open countryside and favour policies which make planning permission for farm dwellings even harder to obtain (though usually without having considered the social questions raised in this book). For example, the authoritative design guide *Sustainable Settlements* recommends that planners should 'refuse permission for farm based dwellings unless the case for round-the-clock presence is very clear and likely to be needed indefinitely. Rather encourage "farm villages"'.[50]

Unfortunately the authors do not elaborate on what they mean by farm villages; but it is not difficult to guess. If a number of sustainable low impact farm holdings are sited in a cluster, there are great benefits to be gained from co-operation. Personal transport can be pooled, and goods can be imported and exported from the village collectively through what are in effect embryonic public transport systems. Childcare can be shared, and in a larger village this service could develop into an infant or primary school. The larger the community, the greater its potential to satisfy its own needs for manufactured goods (e.g. cheese, bread), services (e.g. mechanics, computing) and entertainment. Such farm villages would not be very different in essence to the villages that existed in England before they were colonized by urban refugees.

This argument against dispersal is a strong one; the problem is that there is no end to it — or rather there is only one end to it, megalopolis. The transport benefits derived from social clustering can be used to justify communities of any size, in relation to a smaller one, until the logical process ends at the vision of a total compact city (which, paradoxically, imports virtually all of its produce from the countryside). Along this continuum lie a number of positions, all of which can be made to sound convincing.

One step up from 'farm villages' (and also 'eco-hamlets') is the 'sustainable village'. This concept was pioneered in Britain by the Stroud Sustainable Village Project, a group of individuals who in the 1980s decided to pool their resources in order to establish a new sustainable village for 150-200 households near Stroud in Gloucestershire. The project fell through — not least because of the 'inevitable obstacle of planning restrictions'[51] — but the group has continued as a lobby working

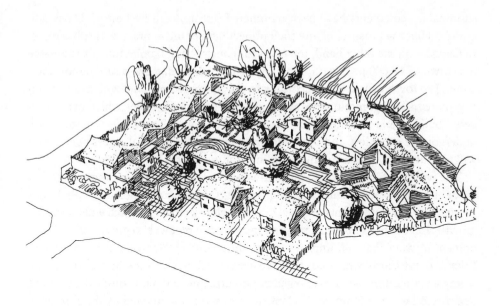

A number of small contemporary settlements with aspirations towards sustainability have emerged out of the self-build movement. MW2, at Maaspoort in the Netherlands (above) uses a Finnish system of lightweight log cabin style construction, with turf roofs. Fences are made from living willow woven into screens. There is an emphasis on eliminating health risks from radioactive, electromagnetic and chemical sources.

Lightmoor community, near Telford in Shropshire (left) is a self-build scheme supported by the TCPA, comprising mainly timber framed houses. The project benefits from special permission for mixed uses on the site through Section 7.1 of the New Towns Act 1981 and offers smallholding opportunities.
Drawings by Brian Richardson, from *The Self-Build Book*, Jon Broome and Brian Richardson, Green Books, 1991.

to influence the formation of structure and local plans. Its activities have since been reinforced by the formation of the Sustainable Villages Group and the Action for Sustainable Rural Communities network.

On a bigger scale still are 'sustainable settlements', complete new towns of 10,000 dwellings or more. These, their proponents argue, will be sufficiently large to be self-contained in terms of employment and facilities. The concept continues the tradition initiated by the Garden City movement of the early nineteenth Century, precariously maintained in the New Towns built after the Second World War and still put forward by the TCPA.[52] In the UK, criteria for designing and specifying sustainable settlements have been hammered out in detail by Barton, Davis and Guise,50 but the prospect of any such project happening in practice is still remote. In Canada, on the other hand, the plans for constructing Bamberton, a sustainable new town of 12,000 people on Vancouver Island, are being given serious consideration. The town will be built according to the 'Bamberton Code' which lays down five fundamental commitments and some 300 design principles which every resident, builder and architect will be invited to sign. 'The project is currently undergoing a very slow and thorough process of environmental assessment which will take until 1998, as a condition of final zoning approval'.[53]

The vision of new settlements, however, is opposed by another school of thought which views density as a prime environmental objective. CPRE has condemned new settlements of this size as a 'high risk strategy' which will fuel traffic growth, and counsels instead a programme of urban renewal 'to provide new development in ways that can improve the environment'.[54] This view is supported by Friends of the Earth, who argue that 'we need to debunk the rural image' and create 'compact cities' through 'urban regeneration utilizing and refurbishing derelict and underused land and building'.[55] Compact cities are championed by the European Union in their *Green Paper on the Urban Environment*.[56]

The argument between the decentralist advocates of sustainable settlements and the centralist advocates of sustainable density can be followed week by week in the pages of the planning press and is not a main concern of this book. The two positions are not mutually exclusive — it is perfectly possible to have denser greener cities *and* smaller sustainable communities co-existing. Valuable work is being carried out on either side to make both cities and smaller settlements more sustainable, and it is somewhat disconcerting that effort is sometimes spent decrying the objectives of the opposing camp.

This onrunning debate serves above all as a reminder of the extent to which planners assume they have the right to decide where people live. Common sense dictates that different sized communities will serve different people's needs; but a worrying proportion of planning strategists believe that it is their job to direct where and in what concentrations people should live — although this is perhaps more true of the compact city advocates who would 'debunk the rural image' and 'ensure that those returning to our higher density urban areas outweigh those leaving'.[57] This is nothing new: for the last 50 years the planning system has been labouring under the apprehension that successful communities can be imposed from above. History tells us differently: hamlets, villages, towns, cities have usually grown organically, according to people's needs. Romulus and Remus, one imagines, first installed themselves on the banks of the Tiber in something not unlike a bender. Essex Man can trace his origin back to the plotland shacks that provided the basis for Basildon.[58]

If we accept that people nowadays are expected to live where planners put them, CPRE are probably right to state that new settlements are a 'high risk strategy'. It is all very well for planners to design a community to be sustainable and self-contained, but as CPRE points out, this will mean little if the people who are moved in are not committed to that ideal, and take advantage of cheap travel costs to commute to other centres.[59] A sustainable settlement could quickly turn into a dormitory town. Similarly, the advantages of a compact city are less obvious if its inhabitants opt to drive out to the country every weekend.

The difficulties of imposing top-down sustainable settlement have been illustrated by the Ecolonia development of 101 'green' houses, within a larger settlement, at Alphen an den Rijn, between Rotterdam and Utrecht in Holland. Here, many of the new residents did not identify with the environmental measures imposed, and simply changed them. For example, 22 of the 101 fitted kitchens were replaced by owners within the first year; private fencing and security screens of tropical hardwoods were erected in open spaces; and the streets that were designed for walking and cycling have attracted quite high levels of car use that have posed a danger to children.[60]

Clearly, if settlements are to stay sustainable, it will help enormously if the people who move in are committed to sustainability. The Bamberton Code is one way of trying to achieve this; but in the UK at present, it is perhaps more likely to happen where the project originates from the bottom up, rather than being imposed upon a more or less random section of the population by well-meaning planners. Initially most of these dedicated grassroots proposals are bound to be fairly small — and there are obvious advantages in conducting any experiment on a small scale. Unfortunately it is precisely these small scale, idealistic projects that fall foul of the planners, because they are in the 'wrong place', because they do not fit in with preconceived notions of what scale or kind of settlement is likely to be sustainable, or because they do not have the contacts and the financial clout to force their application through the planning process.

In the absence of a British Bamberton, it is from small scale independent settlements of committed people that we are likely to learn much about sustainable lifestyles in the coming years, and such experiments should be given a great deal more encouragement by planners. This does not mean that they should be idealized. There are many ways in which such projects can founder, or simply slide back into conventional, unsustainable behaviour; and this is where planners can play a useful role. The purpose of the planning system should not be to discourage such experiments from taking place, but to provide guidelines and provisos that oblige such communities to live up to their commitments. The mechanisms for doing this — conditions, Section 106 Agreements, Simplified Planning Zones, and possibly a new land use class — are described in the following chapter.

Chapter 8

The Tools for the Job

However favourably planners may view a low impact project in the open countryside, however much they may accept that the project is a worthy one and a
warranted exception to the structure plan, they will still be inclined to refuse it. There
are two reasons for this, both of them fairly good.

Firstly, planners need to be reassured that a project that starts out low impact will
stay low impact. However well intentioned the original applicant may be, that
person may go bankrupt, die or simply decide to sell up to another proprietor who
is not so well intentioned. What starts as a fairly innocuous or sensitive development
linked to an organic smallholding may, they fear, metamorphose over time into
bijoux bungalows for commuters, or some highly unorthodox monstrosity.
Moreover, as one planner suggested, 'if permission were granted for an earth-sheltered structure on land which was not allocated for development and the building
was never built — that site would then carry a history of planning consent which
could be misused at a future appeal'.[1] Planners, who through bitter experience are
constantly on the alert for 'ruses and wheezes', are likely to view low impact projects
as a potential Trojan horse for further development.

The problem here for planners is that there are no weapons in the planning armoury
specifically designed to ensure that low impact buildings remain low impact. This is
because planning law does not make any statutory distinctions between different kinds
of building. Instead it differentiates between buildings according to their use — agricultural, retail, industrial etc. — as defined under the Town and Country Planning (Use
Classes) Order 1987. These distinctions can be quite precise: for instance a stall on a
smallholding selling home produced vegetables will change from agricultural to retail
use class if it starts to sell imported bananas.[2] But no such distinctions exist between
different kinds or scales of building. An underground house, a wooden shack, a
converted barn, a bungalow, a three storey house, a high rise block or a palace are all
lumped under the same heading: 'residential dwelling'. There is no Town and Country
Planning (Classes of Building) Order, and hence no robust distinction between them.
In other words, development in the countryside has in the main been restrained not by
regulating the quality and scale of the constructions, but by restricting certain uses to
certain areas. The concept of low impact development — limiting development
according to the impact it has on the environment — is not catered for by this structure.

This is not to say that local authorities cannot influence the size or the quality of buildings that are constructed in their area. They can and do, through stipulations made in local plans and through the application of conditions and planning obligations. But these do not have the force behind them that the Use Classes Order does. It is difficult to acquire planning permission for change of use from agricultural to residential. Once that permission has been won, it is a rather easier process, over time, to change the nature or size of the building by a series of minor applications for 'improvements', annexes, car ports and outbuildings, by overturning planning conditions, or by making additions that do not require planning permission.

A second problem that concerns planners is the question of precedent. Once one low impact dwelling has been built in the open countryside, will there not be a rash of further applications for others? The Secretary of State has argued in one case that 'the impact ... on the landscape or local highway conditions may not in itself be great ... Nonetheless, to grant permission would be likely to encourage similar applications for other rural sites in this locality which, if allowed, would have a serious cumulative impact upon this area of landscape value'.[3] Advocates of low impact might respond that 'a good precedent is a precedent worth setting'[4] and that the object should be to achieve a benign cumulative impact. Whether or not similar applications would in fact be forthcoming is a material consideration, whose significance is covered in some detail by the ruling in *Poundstretcher v. Liverpool City Council*.[5]

The question of precedent also masks delicate issues of social justice. As one development control officer put it: 'There is the problem of balancing equity of access to the countryside. For example, why should outsiders come in and start a low impact project while a local villager may not be able to erect a house for his son in the village he lives in?'[6]

The low impact dweller might retort by asking why wealthy outsiders should be allowed to come in and buy up houses in the village — is that equitable? The villager's son could of course apply for a low impact project on the same footing as outsiders, which would invoke questions of precedent and cumulative impact. On the other hand, the villager's son may not be at all interested in a low impact dwelling; he may well, however, have a greater need to live in the immediate vicinity than the low impact outsider. It is understandable that planners may wish to avoid making invidious decisions and opt for restrictions on all developments, on the grounds that 'everyone dances — or no one dances'.

For such reasons, planners are rightly wary about granting planning permission for agricultural and low impact dwellings. However, playing safe is not going to achieve the standards of sustainable and low impact construction that Agenda 21 demands: it merely stifles all forms of experimentation. The planning system may not be designed for low impact developments, but its great merit lies in the fact that it is flexible enough to absorb them. A number of tools that can be used to regulate low impact projects already exist within the planning system and these can be used as they stand with only very minor 'tweaking'. These tools are outlined in the rest of this chapter.

Temporary permission

Temporary permission is already widely used by local authorities to assess experimental and agriculturally linked proposals. Even when, on its own merits, a project may appear to planners to be sensible and sound, they will be most reluctant to give outright planning permission, and will usually only accord it temporary permission for a period of three or five years. Temporary permission can be tied to one occupier which effectively makes the development unsaleable.[7] There is nothing wrong with this; it is a sensible means of assessment and a deterrent to speculators.

However PPG7 states, in respect of agricultural dwellings: 'It will normally be unsatisfactory to grant successive extensions to a temporary planning permission. In considering applications for temporary accommodation, authorities should normally work on the basis that it will be translated into a permanent dwelling if the agricultural unit prove viable. Thus they should not normally grant temporary permissions in locations where they would not grant a permanent dwelling'.[8]

Despite these recommendations, planning authorities and appeals Inspectors very frequently extend planning permission for a second term, so frequently in fact that one wonders whether, in many cases, the authority originally had no intention whatsoever of permitting a permanent dwelling, and granted temporary permission the first time round in the hope that by the time three or five years had elapsed, the applicant would have given up and gone away. Indefinite renewal of temporary permission is not a satisfactory way of regulating schemes that depend upon a permanent structure to achieve their full potential.

Trusts, housing associations and co-operatives

The formation of a trust or some other body which will monitor and safeguard the low impact of a development is not something that can be imposed by planners. But the existence of such a body as a component of a planning application should help to reassure the local authority that the low impact of a development can be maintained, even when there is a change of occupant. Housing associations are already the standard means for ensuring that affordable housing stays affordable. Government policy states: 'Most commonly, the best way of ensuring that affordable housing will be enjoyed by successive as well as initial occupiers of property is by the involvement of a housing association or other social body (e.g. a trust) providing housing for rent or shared ownership; the body's continuing interest in the property will ensure control over subsequent changes of ownership and occupation'.[9] What is true for affordability can equally well be made to apply for low impact, or the linkage of a development to an agricultural project.

There are many forms that such a guardian body could take. To give one example, James Clarke of the consultancy group Ecoconsult has drawn up a draft outline for a housing co-operative where permanent low impact dwellings are saleable on the open market. 'This ensures accessibility and puts low impact dwellings firmly in the conventional spectrum', writes Clarke. 'The problem is then to maintain low impact with high impact residents/tenants'. Ecoconsult's solution is as follows:

> A housing group or co-op buys the land for a group of houses. Part of the land is divided into plots for housing, and the bulk transferred to a land co-operative or trust.
>
> The plots are transferred to builders, self builders or a Housing Association (for rented accommodation). Covenants are put on that transfer to assure low impact construction and use (covering materials, insulation, solar design, waste disposal, noise, further development, car use, use of co-operative land, etc.).
>
> The land co-operative runs the land along sustainable lines to protect wild spaces, produce sustainable food and fuel. Members of this co-operative would comprise those who contribute work to the land, whether or not they live in one of the houses. There is a strong incentive (cheap and wholesome food and fuel, and recreational space) for all householders to participate in the land co-operative, but they are not bound to do so. There are no strictures on house sales, apart from the covenants which remain in force to protect the common land and the other householders ...
>
> The land co-operative trust is set up in perpetuity, with bye-laws to encourage a mutually supportive community, with sustainability as its central aim.[10]

This proposal is only one of a number of variants that could be drawn up. In site-specific cases, the local authority could be involved in drafting the constitution of a suitable trust for the property. And the covenants held by the trust could be reinforced with planning conditions or (as indeed they are at Hockerton) a Section 106 planning agreement.

Planning conditions

Planning conditions are the standard mechanism by which planning authorities can control the appearance or impact of a building development. In a formula known by heart to planners: 'Conditions should only be imposed when they are (a) necessary, (b) relevant to planning, (c) relevant to the development to be permitted, (d) enforceable, (e) precise and (f) reasonable in all other respects'. These six criteria are explained in some detail in DoE Circular 11/95: The Use of Conditions in Planning Permissions.

Conditions are frequently imposed to control the use of a building in ways already discussed, for example by tying it to agricultural use, or to seasonal use, or by restricting the permission to a temporary period. But there are a large number of other ways in which planning authorities can use conditions to ensure that a development conforms with some of the criteria for low impact defined in Chapter 6.

Scale

In a situation where architectural plans are not submitted, conditions can be used to control the size or the extent of a development. For example, in a temporary tented or similar settlement, restrictions can be imposed upon the size of tents, their number, and the area in which they can be pitched. In the case of more substantial buildings, conditions can be imposed revoking normally permitted rights to add extensions or change the appearance of the building.[11]

Numbers of people

It is rather less clear whether conditions can be imposed upon the number of people who inhabit a development. Circular 11/95 states that a condition 'restricting the number of persons resident at any one time in a block of flats would be impracticable to monitor' and hence would not be acceptable.[12] However, in allowing the appeal for benders at Higher Rockes, the Inspector imposed a condition of no more than 16 residents, and in the Tinker's Bubble appeal, the Inspector recommended a condition of no more than 12 residents. The implication is that a low impact dwelling site is easier to monitor than a block of flats.

Landscaping

Provided that the work is directly related to the physical appearance of the building or the site, conditions can be used to force developers to plant trees, hedges or perform other landscaping measures. They can also stipulate when such planting should be carried out and what steps should be taken to replace planted trees that die or become diseased.[13] However, conditions cannot be used to secure the planting of trees as an environmental benefit in a situation where they are not directly related to the appearance or impact of the development.

Building methods and materials

Conditions may be used to control the materials or methods of construction used in a building in order to limit its impact or ensure that it conforms to a local architectural style. However, it would not normally be acceptable to impose such conditions, for example, on the grounds that use of local timber benefited the local economy.

Traffic generation

Conditions concerning traffic have normally been intended to ensure that access roads and parking spaces are adequate to accommodate the estimated traffic generated by the development. However conditions can be used to achieve the reverse — to limit the amount of traffic generated. In Edinburgh, a new housing estate is being constructed where tenants sign an agreement renouncing possession of a motor car; as a result Lothian council decided not to require the construction of a feeder road for the estate.[14] Such a tenancy agreement could be reinforced by a planning condition restricting car ownership. The inspector at the Tinker's Bubble Inquiry agreed to a condition limiting car ownership to three cars between up to 12 adults (the appellants at the time shared one van between seven adults). In the Avoncliff earth-sheltered housing appeal the Secretary of State rejected as 'unreasonable and unenforceable' a condition proposed by the local authority that no vehicles should be driven up to, or parked beside, the dwelling, except in cases of emergency. It is to be hoped that in future such conditions may be regarded as reasonable, and that it will be recognized that they can fairly easily be enforced by forbidding construction of a convenient everyday access.

Paraphernalia

Paraphernalia is a planning term which has never received statutory recognition, meaning all the accoutrements of a modern residence which may be visible to neighbours or passers-by. The classic example of paraphernalia, and one that causes a disproportionate amount of controversy, is the washing line, but the term also covers items such as motor vehicles, children's toys, garden equipment, business equipment, holiday caravans and what West Lothian Planning call 'salvaged materials of doubtful usefulness'.[15] The concerns about paraphernalia are particularly critical in connection with smaller dwellings such as benders and caravans, since by virtue of their smallness, a greater amount of this paraphernalia is likely to be left outside. Moreover a number of the inhabitants of such buildings may make a proportion of their living by salvaging 'materials of doubtful usefulness': the main objections to the visual aspects of Gypsy sites often do not relate to the caravans themselves, but to the recycling and other activities carried on around them.

The Government explicitly rules out conditions prescribing that the site should be kept tidy on the grounds that 'this is vague and likely to be incapable of enforcement'. It does however sanction conditions which limit the storage of materials, giving as an example: '[Scrap] material shall not be stacked or deposited to a height exceeding __ metres'.[16] Conditions can also be imposed which prescribe hedging or other forms of screening. One district councillor who objected to the Avoncliff scheme suggested that 'perhaps one of the conditions should be earth-sheltered garaging for cars?'[17] — but this idea was not taken up by the Secretary of State.

Similar problems arise in the sphere of agriculture. What researchers for the Department of the Environment have called 'shackery' — makeshift sheds, lorry containers, moribund tractors etc. — is basically agricultural paraphernalia. As noted in Chapter 3, the response of some councils has been to give planning consent for a dwelling with conditions attached limiting the amount of shackery.

Once again the issue of landscape guilt rears its head. The problem of modern paraphernalia is similar to the problem of modern architecture. People simply do not like it, particularly in a rural setting. Few people object to the paraphernalia of pre-industrial societies — to the sight of Bedouin rugs hung up in the desert breeze, or fish drying on racks at a summer congregation of Inuit. But for some unfortunate reason, the agglomeration of washing lines, pushchairs, plastic buckets, toy tractors, bin bags, barbecue stands, lawnmowers, caravans, ailing motor vehicles and what-have-you that are likely to be found in the back garden of an average modern residence (not to mention the heavy gauge junk that congregates on farms and in rural backyards) is regarded as obtrusive. The reason probably lies in our means of production, the phenomenal amount of stuff that is produced and bought, and the rate at which it becomes obsolete; but this is not a matter that planners can regulate. For the most part, all they can do is enforce ways of hiding it.

Planning agreements

Ostensibly, Section 106 planning agreements (also called planning obligations) are similar to conditions because the owner of the site receiving planning permission is required to abide by certain restrictions or perform certain tasks. Often they refer simply to the use to which a building is put and they are a common way of tying a building to an agricultural or other purpose.

But they differ in one respect from conditions. Planning agreements can be used to extract commitments from developers that do not relate directly to the development itself, but to the impact that that development may have upon the surrounding infrastructure and community or as the relevant Government circular rather clumsily expresses it, when 'what is required … is … community provision, the need for which arises from the development'.[18] For example — and this is the classic example repeated in towns around Britain — a supermarket development may increase the levels of traffic on surrounding roads and therefore the developer may be required to build a relief road or contribute a sum to the construction of such a road.

Planning agreements are thus a way for the community to extract planning gain from the development — a way of diverting some of the profit that the private developer derives from being given planning permission into another public development. The extent to which this actually happens and the extent to which it should or should not happen is the subject of a very extensive literature. On the one hand some commentators view planning agreements involving financial contributions or the provision of a road or other community infrastructure as 'the sale of planning permissions' or 'cheque book planning';[19] at the other extreme, a research report from the DoE concludes that 'there is almost no evidence that agreements are used to secure wider planning or non-planning objectives'.[20] Nonetheless, at the time of writing, the DoE is drafting a new version of Circular 16/91, designed to ensure that 'planning obligations should never be used as a means of securing for the local community a share in the profits of development'.[21]

From an environmental point of view, the endless and barely comprehensible quibbles about the legitimacy of planning gain are secondary. It really does not matter very much whether the infrastructure subsidized by Section 106 agreements is properly related to the development or whether it is a council scam. What does matter is whether it is sustainable or not.

Usually it is not. The DoE research report analyses all the Section 106 agreements made by a sample of 28 local authorities in England between 1987 and 1990. Out of a total of 852 agreements, 290 involved some kind of highways improvement (including 81 new roads) while only 18 involved traffic restraint, 12 involved an improvement for pedestrians, and none was specifically for the benefit of cyclists or public transport. There were 153 environmental measures, of which 103 were some kind of landscaping or 'clearance'. And there were 79 agreements for full or partial provision of community facilities, including 37 lighting, safety or security measures, 6 open spaces, 3 play spaces and no child care facilities.[22]

A low impact curiosity: a World War I prisoner of war logging camp at Rhos Dingle in Montgomeryshire, Wales. The single storey thatched huts were commissioned by the camp commandant, Major Hancock, who had served for many years in South Africa.
Photo: Ray George Collection.

The matter is as clear as daylight. As far as provision for the community is concerned, Section 106 agreements have been used primarily to accommodate an increase in road traffic; environmental measures come way behind, and provision of community facilities a poor third. Planning gain has been used to secure car-orientated, high impact community infrastructure to accommodate the pressure caused by high impact development. The revised draft of Circular 16/91 allows for contributions towards public transport facilities such as bus shelters and 'even additional bus or rail stations', but the most common examples it anticipates are 'new access roads, improved junction lay-outs and extra parking'.[23]

In an era when sustainable development is a priority, planning agreements and planning gain can instead be used to secure environmentally and socially beneficial community development. The DoE, in its test for the reasonableness of planning agreements, specifically 'welcomes the initiatives taken by some developers in creating nature reserves, planting trees, establishing wildlife ponds and providing other nature conservation benefits. This echoes the Government's view that local authorities and developers should work together in the interest of preserving the natural environment'.[24] This should not simply mean the provision of a token green feature to compensate for a high impact development. Section 106 agreements have been used to ensure that building projects remain low impact and provide genuine environmental and social improvements for the community.

Planning agreements have thus been at the core of several pioneering low impact developments. The Lowland Crofting experiment is founded on a comprehensive Section 50 agreement (Scottish Town and Country Planning Act) which ensures, among other things, that major landscape improvements will be carried out before the housing development is undertaken, that the woodland and other natural areas will be maintained and remain exempt from future development and that public access will be guaranteed. The developer's compliance is secured by a £30,000 bond.[25] A similar Section 106 agreement has been drawn up for the Hockerton earth-sheltered site 'with terms that ... ensure that the way in which the application has been presented is the way in which it is carried out and maintained in the future. Without this legal assurance there would be no way to prevent the house being sold for purely speculative purposes and the strive towards sustainability being forgotten'.[26] In the case of Tinker's Bubble, a Section 106 agreement, based on a Five Year Conservation Management Plan for the holding drawn up by the appellants and the local authority in concert, was agreed upon 'without prejudice' prior to the appeal for temporary planning permission, which was, however, dismissed by the Secretary of State.[27]

Both the Lowland Crofting and the Hockerton agreements will serve as valuable models for future low impact developments. They are designed to ensure that the development not only starts low impact but stays so, and any planning authority worried about the long term stability of a low impact proposal would do well to consider them. Similarly, applicants for low impact developments, if they are confronted with an obdurate local council, may wish to propose such an agreement 'unilaterally', though they should be warned that if it is accepted there may be some legal costs involved.

One other issue concerning planning agreements is relevant to the question of sustainability. Until recently there was no right of appeal against Section 106 agreements. But now, in England (though not in Scotland) under the Planning and Compensation Act 1991, 'anyone against whom a planning obligation is enforceable' can, after a period of five years, apply to the local planning authority to have the obligation discharged; and if the local authority does not consent, they can appeal to the Secretary of State. The present Secretary of State, John Gummer, has justified the five year period on these grounds:

> It would not be reasonable to allow an obligation to be reviewed very soon after it had been entered into. This would give no certainty to a local planning authority which had granted planning permission on the understanding that a developer would meet certain requirements ... On the other hand, where over a period of time the overall planning circumstances of an area have altered it may not be reasonable for a landowner to be bound by an obligation indefinitely. Allowing the five year period to stand appropriately reconciles these various considerations.[28]

This comment shows how far the Secretary of State for the Environment is from understanding the meaning of the word sustainability. The sort of economy where 'overall planning circumstances' are allowed to change within a period of five years is the antithesis of a sustainable one. Planners may very likely be less than certain about the usefulness of an agreement which safeguards woodland from development 'in perpetuity', but which may be revoked after five years.

There is some disagreement amongst planning experts as to whether, in practice, the robustness of planning agreements will be undermined by this new right of appeal. The answer seems to be to 'wait and see'. The problem is a difficult one; while there have been calls to abolish the right of appeal against planning agreements,[29] there are likely to be circumstances when a Section 106 agreement does need to be altered, as for example when a prescribed environmental measure is subsequently found to be counter-productive. It may make sense to rely solely on agreements being renegotiated between the owner and the planning authority, rather than entrusting the decision to a Secretary of State whose vision of sustainability may extend no further than the next general election. On the other hand, if a planning agreement is renegotiated bilaterally to the disadvantage of the local community (for example if it is decided that woodland originally safeguarded in perpetuity can after all be built upon), should not representatives of the public also have a right of appeal? There may be a case for making certain kinds of agreements subject to appeal, and others not. The entire question should be reviewed in the light of the need to guarantee sustainability.

Simplified Planning Zones — a planning serendipity

The above mechanisms — temporary permission, land management trusts, planning conditions and planning agreements — can all be used to ensure that a low impact development stays low impact. However there remains the other concern of planners: how to prevent a low impact development creating a precedent which might stimulate a rash of applications that, if accepted, could have 'a cumulative effect upon the landscape'? There is one planning mechanism which, by accident rather than by design, is tailored for this job — Simplified Planning Zones (SPZs).

SPZs were introduced by the Housing and Planning Act 1986. They are a relation of Enterprise Zones and are designed to stimulate private sector development by designating an area where, over a period limited to ten years, 'developers can know with certainty the precise type of development that can be carried out within the zone without having to make (and pay for) a planning application'.[30] They have been assiduously promoted by the DoE — unlike planning agreements and other 'weapons in the armoury' they have a Planning Policy Guidance all to themselves (PPG 5) — but they have been just as assiduously ignored by most planning authorities. By 1992 only six schemes had been adopted and another ten were in preparation, mostly on old industrial sites which needed regenerating.

In part, planners are suspicious of SPZs because they view them as an unnecessarily heavy weapon to deal with a comparatively minor problem — 'using a sledgehammer to crack a nut' as a representative of one planning authority put it. He and a colleague objected that SPZs occupy 'great swathes of countryside' and that they are not accountable to parish councils and similar bodies. SPZs are viewed as a rather high impact form of development, unsuitable for a rural area.

These comments reveal the extent to which SPZs have been associated in planners' minds with Thatcherite schemes to pump-prime economically depressed areas. Yet there is nothing in the legislation that says that SPZs necessarily involve high impact industrial activity. On the contrary, PPG 5 is at pains to explain that their 'versatility' means that 'both the size and the character of SPZ schemes can be varied to suit different objectives and prevailing local circumstances'. They can be used for many purposes, including new residential areas and large single ownership sites. They do not necessarily involve 'great swathes of countryside', as 'there are no restrictions on the size of SPZs'.[31] To date the biggest (in Corby) is 178 hectares and the smallest (in Dingwall, Scotland) is 4.75 hectares.[32] They can be set up anywhere except National Parks, SSSIs and other statutorily designated areas. And they can be applied for by 'anyone', including, one assumes, a parish council.

There is no good reason why SPZs should not be used to control sites allocated for low impact development, either residential or mixed use. There are two main advantages. Firstly, the occupants of the SPZ are free to build anything, anywhere, within the constraints laid down by the scheme, thereby combining maximum scope for ingenuity with minimal interference and paperwork. And secondly, the development is a 'one-off', a clear exception to the planning regime in the rest of the district, and therefore cannot be used as a precedent.

There are two forms of SPZ, the 'specific scheme' which 'specifically itemizes the types of development permitted and the limit imposed'; and the 'general scheme' which 'gives a general or wide permission covering almost all types of development, but listing the exceptions'. It is the first kind that will normally be suitable for low impact developments.

PPG 5 gives two model examples of SPZ agreements for specific schemes, one for a mixed use development and one for a residential development. On the opposite page we have taken the first of these and amended it so as to be suitable for a self-build project of the kind envisaged by Colin Ward in Chapter 7. The site of this imagined low impact development does actually exist; it is a small abandoned aerodrome in a flat, windswept, marshy area two miles from any village. An area adjacent to the aerodrome has already been turned into a singularly unpleasant warehouse estate, whose buildings, because of the security risks imposed by the remote location, are surrounded by 10 foot high fences and floodlit at night. The low impact SPZ covers a section of the aerodrome, about 12 acres in size, which has never been redeveloped and is scattered with derelict buildings.

This example does not deviate greatly from the model given in PPG 5, except that fewer uses are permitted, a number of conditions have been added while others have been adjusted, and the landscape zoning is more robust and more oriented towards protection of wildlife. It is clear that by adjusting these elements, the SPZ agreement can be made to cover other kinds of multiple development. There is no reason, for example, why an SPZ should not be used to regulate a 'lowland crofting' site, a

EXAMPLE A*

Boundary of the SPZ scheme

The area of land to which this SPZ scheme relates is delineated on the map attached.

Planning permission

Planning permission is granted by this SPZ scheme for development for the purposes of the retail sale of goods, the sale of food and drink, general industry, storage, dwelling houses *except*

(a) development which falls within any of the descriptions included in Schedule 1 to the Town and Country Planning (Assessment of Environmental Effects) Regulations 1988 (SI No 1199);

(b) development for any purpose mentioned in Schedule 2 to the 1988 regulations unless, in the case of any particular development not otherwise excluded from this permission, the authority notify the developer in writing that it would not be likely to have significant effects on the environment;

subject to the following conditions:

(i) no activity shall take place which may give rise to the presence of a controlled hazardous substance (as specified in the Planning (Hazardous Substances) Regulations 1992, nor land used for the laying or construction of a notifiable pipeline;

(ii) no single new building, retail unit, or residence shall exceed 'x' square metres in floor space.

(iii) the buildings and structures shall not be more than 'x' metres in height ; outside storage shall be restricted to no more than 'y' metres in height;

(iv) motor vehicle use shall be limited to no more than 'x' vehicles kept permanently on site and limited to the specified area, as described in Appendix W attached to this scheme;

(v) noise levels shall not exceed those as set out in Appendix X attached to this scheme;

(vi) no building materials shall be used for the outside fabric of the buildings other than recycled materials from on site, recycled materials from the district and building materials produced in the district as set out in Appendix Y;

(vii) water and sewage provision shall be autonomous to the site, and conform to Health Authority standards;

(viii) all electric power used on the site shall be produced autonomously from renewable sources.

Landscaping and Wildlife Sub-Zones

This SPZ scheme contains landscape and wildlife sub-zones connected by wildlife corridors, comprising in total 60 percent of the site, where no development shall take place. No development shall take place on the remainder of the site until a scheme for tree planting, landscaping and wildlife protection in these sub-zones has been submitted to and approved by the local planning authority. Annex Z sets out, for illustrative purposes, the type, details and time scale of landscaping which the authority consider to be appropriate to these sub-zones.

Normal planning procedures

Full planning applications are required for development proposals which fall outside the terms of the general planning permission granted by this SPZ.

Other permissions and licences

This SPZ only grants planning permission. All other consents (e.g. listed buildings) and compliance with Building Regulations should be sought in the normal way. In particular, the following building is listed:

The hangar marked on the map attached.

---

* A model agreement for a hypothetical Simplified Planning Zone on an abandoned rural aerodrome. This is an adapted 'low impact' version of the model agreement 'Example A' provided by the Department of the Environment in PPG 5: 'Simplified Planning Zones'.

bender site, or a residential estate consisting entirely of earth-sheltered buildings. There also may be grounds for extending low impact SPZs over wider areas of rural land comprising a number of marginal farms and other plots of neglected land (where such a scheme might incorporate a commitment to conversion of the land to organic production in accordance with the standards laid down by the Soil Association). The object of such an SPZ would be to stimulate the regeneration of land-based rural businesses whilst ensuring that any development remained low impact and within the appropriate vernacular framework, and that the zone did not become a magnet for commuters. Not, perhaps, such an easy task. On the other hand it is not at all difficult to imagine how a low impact SPZ could be used to reinvigorate a run-down urban area with self-built dwellings and workshops, permaculture garden schemes, solar power, compost organic waste disposal, car free zones, tree planting and so on.[33]

So far, it seems, only one local authority has indicated any interest in low impact SPZs. The report Developing Sustainable Communities, published jointly by Devon County Council, the Community Council of Devon and Designed Visions, proposes 'that the County Council actively seek to simplify access to planning permissions by creating, with District Councils, a series of Simplified Planning Zones designed to encourage sustainable development'.[34]

The report also observes that 'the act of working on the specification for these SPZs will provide a wonderful opportunity for planning professionals to become conversant with sustainability'. It would also provide a good opportunity for environmentally concerned people to become conversant with the problems that face planners. Readers are invited to take the model agreement and imagine how they would adjust it to regulate a specific low impact project on a specific site that they know.

A new land use class?

The advantage of SPZs at the outset is that they constitute an exception to the planning regime and hence are less likely to be viewed as a precedent for untrammelled development in the countryside.

But if a number of low impact SPZs (perhaps they might be called 'low impact planning zones' or LIPZs) were established, proved to be a success, and were followed by others, what would emerge would be something close to a new tier of planning permission, separate from conventional permission. It could, in fact, be a new category of sustainable land use similar to Tony Wrench's concept of 'Permaculture Land' discussed in Chapter 4.

Wrench's suggestion is now being examined by other people. Robert Hopkins of the University of the West of England has outlined how the General Permitted Development Order and PPG 7 could be amended 'so as to introduce the possibility for Local and District Authorities to both permit and encourage sustainable rural projects'.[35] He has also drafted a model set of criteria 'showing how Permaculture could be included in local plans as a use class of its own'. These criteria are reproduced in Appendix D.

The potentialities of such a new category, as Wrench and Hopkins point out, are far reaching: a greener and more forested landscape, a sustainable and more locally based agriculture, a more vigorous local economy, improved access to land, a decline in the number of homeless and a decline in the number of unemployed. However, whereas Tony Wrench pictured a hypothetical situation where Permaculture Land was suddenly introduced by a visionary government, it is more realistic to foresee permaculture land, or any similar category of land use, gradually growing out of the existing system. The legislation is already in place to experiment in the form of SPZs and planning agreements. All that is needed is the vision and the will from local authorities — and a Secretary of State prepared to countenance local initiatives.

Looking ahead

At the moment we are still at the experimental stage. It may be felt by some who read this book, that low impact development only addresses the demands of a pioneering minorities — greens, permaculturists, smallholders, travellers and the like. In one sense this is true, and if this is regrettable, it is also fortunate. The fact that demand for low impact dwellings is at present relatively small means that experiments can be undertaken without any threat to the *status quo*. Changes tend to begin at the margins of society: the organic farmers who thirty years ago were regarded as cranks are now given grants by MAFF; the 'alternative technology' pursued by hippies in the early seventies has now become 'renewable energy', the subject of a Planning Policy Guidance. The advocates of low impact land use may be few at the moment, but they should be listened to.

For in another sense low impact development addresses the demands of a great many people. As planning officers so often remark to low impact settlers: 'If we let you live here, then everyone will want to live here'. Millions of people — be they agricultural contractors, hoteliers, landscape painters, computer operators, single parents, retired people, even planners — seek an affordable home in a green and healthy environment. The pressure on the countryside is immense and comes from all sides. That is precisely the problem that the rural planning system was set up to solve. If it is to be solved, then a way will have to be found of accommodating people in the open countryside and on the edge of villages and small towns, that is sustainable and low impact — otherwise the countryside will be eaten away piecemeal while strategists indulge in fruitless debates about whether future high impact development should take place in new small settlements, on the edge of larger settlements, or through urban infill.

Sooner or later all development will have to be sustainable. That is the objective of Agenda 21 and there really is no other choice. A separate tier of sustainable or low impact planning permission would not be an end in itself but would provide an intermediary step between the present and a point in the future when unsustainable development is phased out completely. At the moment we are nowhere near that stage; we are still at the point where experiments in low impact development are

strangled at birth by planning measures which are designed to prevent the proliferation of high impact development — yet which are manifestly failing to prevent this
proliferation.

There is a danger that planners will duck their responsibility to encourage such
experiments and instead seek shelter beneath the facile equation that population
density equals sustainability. Richard Tiffin, a Hertfordshire town planner, is simply
being more frank than his colleagues when he advises them : 'Forget sustainability
as a practical concept, it is far beyond us. As planners, the best we can do is to try
and secure an improvement in future environments by looking for reductions in
consumption through movement. We may flatter ourselves that this amounts to a
sustainable approach, but this is plainly not the case; we are simply buying time'.[36]

Tiffin may be honest, but he is incorrect. Planners can do a lot better than this,
not by adopting a *dirigiste* approach to where people should live, but by encouraging,
regulating and monitoring whatever experiments in sustainable living may come
their way. Sustainable development 'as a practical concept' may well be beyond the
scope of the average planner at present, or indeed the average person; but that is no
reason for quashing the efforts of the growing numbers of people who are trying to
develop it in practice, now, because they don't believe in 'buying time'.

If more support is not given to experiments in sustainable living, and if more
attention is not paid to these concerns, the planning profession may find itself in
trouble. Until now, environmental protest has been directed at other sectors of the
social economy: in the past five years, it has been the Department of Transport's
absurd attempt to double the amount of road traffic that has taken a drubbing. But
the DoT's roads programme is now being lowered into its grave (partly thanks to the
planners). The growing numbers who believe that implementation of Agenda 21
demands direct and immediate action will be focusing their attention upon other
targets; and near the top of the list may well be the DoE's 'self-fulfilling' projections
for yet more unsustainable housing, stretching the tentacles of the octopus deeper
into the countryside. It would not be surprising if the environmental direct action
movement, in the next few years, were to shift its focus to the greenfield land already
bought up by housing developers for the construction of more houses, more service
roads, more unsustainable suburbia. If this is where the radical environmental movement concentrates its attack, then it will gather considerable support from the
NIMBY element, those who over the years have consistently, but unsuccessfully,
objected to such developments taking place on their patch. The wise planner will be
looking ahead.

The object of this book has not been to bury the present planning system, but to
praise it. It has attempted to show that the system introduced in 1947 is flexible
enough to accommodate the radical new forms of development that the quest for
sustainability demands; and to outline some of the ways in which local authorities
can foster experiments in low impact rural development — some of them carried out
at the margins of society, others designed to cater for more conventional people.

These experiments — the failures and the successes — will be necessary to provide the groundwork which will enable the planners, environmentalists and country dwellers of the next millennium to co-operate in the creation of a genuinely sustainable rural economy and environment.

Chapter 9

The Legacy of a Makeshift Landscape

Drawn from the book Arcadia for All: The Legacy of a Makeshift Landscape *by Dennis Hardy and Colin Ward. This material ought to have been presented in Chapter 1.*

Arcadia for All — the cover.

Few places have had as much invective heaped upon them as Peacehaven. A 'two-mile strip of bungaloid horror,' Geoffrey Moorhouse called it, 'perched on a cliff top between the Channel and the Sussex Downs. It should have been a home for heroes and it became a monument to rapacity.' Three writers in the 1930s labelled it respectively 'a dreadful blot', 'a disgusting blot on the landscape' and 'a monstrous blot on the national conscience' and Nairn and Pevsner were later to call it 'a rash on the countryside — there is none worse in England.' 'The poison begins at Peacehaven,' was the verdict of another.[1]

It was, as a less choleric author observed, 'the place most people love to hate.' Peacehaven was a caricature of itself, and of a hundred other settlements like it, and like all caricatures it exaggerated what many people didn't want to see. It was a mirror that reflected back in horrible detail the contradictions and conflicts that underlay the development process in an Old World aspiring to democracy.

'A Garden City by the Sea'

In 1915, a speculator called Charles Neville bought 415 acres of land on the top of chalk cliffs between Brighton and Newhaven. He subdivided this land into plots of 25 foot by 100 foot, laid out on an American style grid basis. Through a bogus 'competition', advertised in the press, he awarded the plots to 12,500 'winners' whose conveyancing charge for this 'free' land yielded Neville a decent profit. Neville was sued by 114 plotholders championed by the *Daily Express* and his plans were shelved.

But after the war Neville's scheme began to flourish. The national call for 'Homes for Heroes' was not met by an effective Government response, and the plots Neville offered at the 'Garden City by the Sea', which he christened Peacehaven, appealed to many who had returned from the war with small gratuities — particularly to those who sought a healthy environment or respite from experiences they had undergone.

Within a few years Peacehaven had become a frontier township offering prospects, independence and a simple life to people who otherwise would never have been able to afford them. One long term resident, Mrs Sayers, whose husband had been injured in the war and advised to seek a more bracing climate outside London, moved to Peacehaven in 1921 after failing to find anywhere affordable in Surrey. The couple built a house on the plot in 1922 and opened a

Cartoon in the *Peacehaven Post.*

post-office and grocery in 1923. Interviewed in 1980, she commented 'it seemed as though we had emigrated.'

Development proceeded at a brisk pace. A brickworks, a concrete block factory, a sawmill and joinery were all built on the site. The Peacehaven Water Company was formed in 1921, and the Peacehaven Electric Light and Power Company followed. A hotel was opened in 1922 and a theatre in the following year. Shops were sited along the main road. There was a private police force and a fire service operated by the residents. The township's own newspaper, the *Peacehaven Post,* published its first issue in 1921.

Despite this dynamic start, there were shambolic sides to the project. Many of the plots were not taken up, giving the gridiron layout a gap-toothed appearance, while overprovision of shops led to many closures. There were more than 20 miles of unmade roads for 650 houses spread over 650 acres, leading the district authority to complain that six postmen were needed to service a population which could have been served by one, were it more densely packed.

Much the same could be said for other municipal services including waste disposal and drainage, and this led to a mounting dispute with the local authorities who were unwilling to take on the costs of such provision, yet anxious to gain some hold over the development to stop it spreading. This, combined with the outcry from rural preservationists and aesthetes, led to increasing calls for the settlement to be brought under the control of an effective planning process. Peacehaven became the *bête noire* around which the forces campaigning for a national planning system rallied.

During the 1930s, the authorities prevaricated over a number of alternatives for taming the settlement, but nothing was decided before the outbreak of the Second World War. After the war, the 1947 Town and Country Planning Act provided all the legislation that was needed for the authorities to bring Peacehaven under their wing. Roads were paved, drainage laid on, vacant plots filled, apparently without any great objection from the residents whose pioneering spirit had perhaps been jaded by time. By the 1960s, Peacehaven had begun to resemble any other seaside retirement settlement except that it was still perched obtrusively on a cliff top and its inhabitants had acquired an inordinate predilection for garden gnomes.

Arcadia or abomination?

Peacehaven became 'the byword for everything that is objectionable' because Neville flaunted it, both through exaggerated exposure in the national press and by plonking it on one of Britain's best loved cliff tops.

East Londoner Fred Nichols bought a plot of land in Bowers Gifford, Essex for £10 in 1934, pitched a tent on it and brought timber and tools bit by bit from London strapped to a bicycle. The house is called 'Perserverance' (sic).

But Peacehaven was only one of hundreds of similar but less conspicuous plotland developments that were spreading around the country. *Arcadia for All* focuses on the South Eastern plotlands, but there were similar settlements to be found all over Britain, for example in Devon, along the Severn and the Wye, at the Gower peninsula near Swansea, in Cheshire, Northumberland, Yorkshire and within range of Glasgow. Even today, once one recognizes the telltale signs — a string of small dispersed bunga-

lows, some still wooden, with names like 'Homestead' or 'The Haven', sporting advertisements for dog kennels, horse manure, free range eggs or azaleas — one starts to spot little pockets of former plotland style development all over the place.

Some of these settlements (for example those at Jaywick, Canvey Island and Laindon/ Pitsea) were as large as Peacehaven and pioneered by populist developers in the Neville mould, though none matched his cheek and flair. Others began with a few beach huts on a pebble spit or rural shacks on squatted or redundant land, and gradually grew into communities. Most began as temporary holiday retreats (at least ostensibly, because these were more likely to be tolerated by the authorities) but many graduated into permanent settlements providing poor people with a retirement home or a dwelling close to work opportunities on the coast, or a smallholding or other small-scale enterprise in the countryside.

They spread with rapidity because an abundant supply of cheap land made available by the agricultural depression coincided with a rising demand for access to rural pleasures and 'a simple life' both on a part-time and a full-time basis. This demand spread across all social classes, but while wealthier members of society could buy up existing houses in the countryside, or avail themselves of the hospitality of country house owners, artisans and thrifty members of the working class could only afford a small plot, upon which they would deposit a railway carriage or construct a shack from timber and glass, sometimes carried miles on their back or ferried down from the city at weekends by bicycle.

Inevitably, these lower class 'greenfield' developments attracted the criticism of rural preservationists. Not only did they spread over substantial tracts of the countryside without any apparent order or plan, but also they exhibited a lack of taste and an architectural anarchy that offended those who believed that the mantle of rural preservation lay upon their shoulders.

Critics highlighted 'the straggly patches of bungalows, villas and shacks', the 'hideous shacks thrown haphazard like splodges of mud against a hillside once covered with trees', the 'artistically deplorable ... wooden shanties' and the 'congeries of discordant huts and caravan [whose] cumulative effect is to produce a shoddy, unplanned and unsightly blight... The worst places are those where the huts and caravans are used for permanent or semipermanent occupation.'[2]

This chorus of voices culminated in a wartime Ministry of Planning and Works survey of coastal development, by the Cambridge geographer J A Steers, which devoted an entire chapter to 'Shacks, Huts and Camps' and referred frequently to such structures throughout the rest of the text.[3] Steers had little regard for the vocabulary of objectivity and restraint one expects in Government reports: 'Certain fields are set aside for the reception of caravans, huts, old buses and shacks of every description. A horrible and unsightly mess of heterogeneous structures. There is no plan, no order and usually no adequate sanitation.' More formal townships such as Jaywick, Canvey Island and Peacehaven were characterized as 'aesthetically and in other ways ... abominable'.

However accurate all these criticisms may have been, they are somewhat undermined by the fact that many of the preservationists who made them were as attracted by the 'simple life' and the holiday weekend as were their social inferiors whose vulgar tastes they decried. The Bray estates at Shere, near Guildford, provided weekend cottages for many of the great and the good, including the majority of the members of the first Labour cabinet. Among the weekend residents there were several crusaders for the protection of the countryside, including Clough Williams Ellis, editor of *Britain and the Beast* (1938), from which a number of the expressions of outrage quoted above are taken.

Another weekend incumbent was social historian G. M. Trevelyan who lamented that 'the State is socialist enough to destroy by taxation the classes that used to preserve rural amenity, but is still too conservative to interfere in the purposes to which land is put by speculators to whom the land is sold.'

Hardy and Ward comment: 'Many other part-time champions of rural England deplored the desecration of the countryside, and at the same time had their own second home, correctly built to blend with its surroundings; but there is something unattractive about the way they took for granted that they were entitled to have a country retreat while wanting to deny, on aesthetic grounds, the same opportunity for people down the hierarchy of income and opportunity.'

The preservationists had a strong ally in the municipal authorities who had to deal with the arrival of these makeshift communities. Although local authorities could also be scathing about the aesthetics of the plotlands, their main concern was fiscal. The plotlands, in their eyes, constituted a public health threat; sooner or later they would have to pick up the tab for provision of sewage, drainage, roads, refuse disposal and other services, including (in the case of Canvey Island and Jaywick) sea defences. Sooner, rather than later, was what they preferred, because the longer such developments were left uncontrolled, the larger they grew and the greater liability they became.

Unfortunately for the authorities the Planning Acts which existed prior to World War II did not give them very great powers for enforcing control; and they were understandably unwilling to provide services without receiving a measure of control in return.

The situation was further complicated by an ambivalent response on the part of the plotlanders. Most of them were keen to have roads that did not become quag-mires in winter and relief from the chore of emptying Elsans. But there were many who cherished 'the simple life' and who considered that such inconveniences were a small price to pay for independence from the bylaws, building regulations and bureaucracy — not to mention the increased rates — that would inevitably accom-pany their provision.

Part of the problem for the plotlanders was that there was no officially recognized middle way. Either the plotlands stayed outside the system and provided their own sometimes inadequate services; or they submitted to the bylaws and standards of the local authority, which in effect meant development into a normal suburb. As late as 1957 Essex County Council was assessing the cost of providing 54 miles of proper roads in an area where, it was claimed 'the lack of a decent carriageway means that most of the dwellers in these areas are without the normal services taken for granted by other people.' But, as one of these deprived residents commented:

'If they were worried about our roads and the fact that we couldn't afford road charges, it wouldn't make much of a dent in the council budget, just to put down a concrete strip, and there wouldn't be any reason why it should be built to the usual council standard.'

But this solution was not what the council wanted, for the annexation of the plot-lands offered them a much more important prize. The dispersed development of the plotlands had opened up new tracts of development land, or in modem parlance, had converted greenfield sites into brownfield sites. Allocation of land for residen-tial development in South East Essex had been delayed until the County Council completed their survey of the plotlands. The belt of 'hideous shacks' was in fact a vast landbank waiting to be developed. The plotlanders had conveniently taken the flak for despoiling virgin countryside; the councils and developers now stood to win

Old Tom's bus which served plotlanders in the Pitsea Laindon area. Photo courtesy of G. Ward.

plaudits and profits for bringing this despoliation into line.

The taming of the plotlands

These conflicts between plotlanders and councils were the subject of much negoti-ation throughout the 1930s, almost all of it inconclusive. It was in the New Britain that emerged out of the upheaval of the Second World War that the fate of the plot-lands was settled. The chief mechanism for taming the plotlands was the 1947 Town and Country Planning Act.

Much of the impetus for the new Act had come from the rural preservation move-ment, which for the previous two decades had waged an articulate and well-financed campaign, not just against the plotlands, but against ribbon-development, jerry-building and all other incursions into the countryside that threatened their sense of beauty and order. The Act gave extensive and universal powers of development control to local authorities and instituted a system of development plans designed to provide long-term strategies for rural development.

The strategy most frequently adopted for the plotlands was absorption into main-stream suburban development, though this took a number of guises. In some cases there were strong pressures for the plotland dwellings to be compulsorily purchased and replaced, but the expense involved and the prospect of fierce resistance from the plotlanders usually deterred authorities from pursuing this option. Only two major plotland sites in the South East were systematically cleared in this manner: the shacks around South Woodham Ferrers in Essex for an upmarket new town; and those in Havering, on the fringe of London, for a country park.

A number of beach settlements, including those at Camber and Shoreham were destroyed, not by planners and developers, but by the army for beach defences during the war. In Shoreham, many of the plotholders whose huts had been destroyed by the army returned after the war in the full expectation of rebuilding their properties. To their alarm, they found that West Sussex County Council was proposing a parliamentary Private Bill to compulsorily purchase their land and construct a more upmarket residential estate.

The plotholders managed to stave off this bid, but their victory was shortlived, for in the following year the new Planning Act gave local authorities the power to compulsorily purchase through normal development plan procedures, and this is precisely what happened. In order to hurry along the procedure the County Council drew up a 'Part Development Plan' for the area before the Act had even reached the statute book. Hardy and Ward comment: 'It is surely no coincidence that the eventual plan for Shoreham Beach proved to be the first to be approved anywhere under the new system.'

Two other large scale plotlands, were profoundly changed, not by war but by natural disaster. In 1953, 307 people on the East Coast died in floods resulting from heavy storms. The two worst affected spots were the plotlands at Canvey Island, where 58 people died, and Jaywick, where the toll was 35 — ''an illustration of the contention that 'natural' disasters affect people with few choices of where to live.'

The subsequent rebuilding of the two settlements and reinforcement of the seawalls gave added force to the councils' project to restructure the communities. Roads were improved, rates raised and pressure put on plotholders to improve their properties or sell up. By the early 1980s, both communities had become ordinary suburban housing estates, except for a few pockets of resistance, such as an area in Canvey Island known as Sixty Acres. In 1980 a reader wrote to the local paper:

'If one wants to get a glimpse of what Canvey Island looked like, say 50 years

Two structures at Canvey Island in the inter-war period. Photo courtesy of F. McCave.

'The First Step Towards Peace, a Home and Happiness' — a cartoon in the *Peacehaven Post..*
Compare this to the 'Dig In for Victory' illustration by Tristan Mitchell of King's Hill, c.1995.

ago, the place is Sixty Acres. I wonder how long it will be before that too is turned into a concrete jungle.'

But the most systematic approach taken towards the absorption of the plotlands was in the inland Essex area around Pitsea and Laindon where the estimated population of 27,000 consisted largely of plotholding refugees from East London. Both Essex County Council and Billericay District Council petitioned the Minister of Town and Country Planning that the area should be included in the first wave of New Towns (the only other local authority in the UK that actually requested a New Town was Easington in Co Durham).

'Basildon was built on heartbreak' was a saying amongst old inhabitants of the area in the 1980s and people spoke bitterly of the lingering death of Laindon as the shops in the High Street closed down one by one. The first general Manager of Basildon Development Corporation, had stated in 1953 that:

'Any solution which includes the wholesale demolition of substandard dwellings cannot be contemplated. However inadequate, every shack is someone's home... and as often as not the curtilage is sufficient to provide... garden produce and to house poultry, rabbits and even pigs.'

But some level of compulsory purchase was inevitable and the terms were largely non-negotiable. Some former home owners were left with an implacable sense of grievance — particularly, one imagines those who had consciously sought out an

DUNTON
PLOTLAND
TRAIL

BASILDON DEVELOPMENT CORPORATION

Remaining plotlands are now often conservation areas. The Dunton Plotland Trail is in Basildon.

independent life, But for others, particularly older people who had spent years struggling to improve their lot, it was marvellous to suddenly find oneself in a new flat with easy access to the shops.

Precious remains

In Wales, the North of England and Scotland, there are still plotland areas that remain much the same as they were 50 years ago. They tend to be on land that is rented, rather than owned, by the occupants, who therefore call themselves 'hutters'. In the South East pressure for development has been so great that very few of the plotlands have been allowed to survive intact.

Where some vestiges remain they are now treasured for their environmental benefits, The settlement at Petts Level on the south coast which J A Steers in his wartime survey called a 'painful eyesore' was described by Rother District Council in 1977 as:

'an area where nature predominates and man-made structures are very individualistic Only a small proportion of the ground surface is 'man-made' — even the narrow tracks are rough. Large areas of plots are in informal garden use. The area is something of a mini-wildlife sanctuary.'

The Canvey Island that Steers characterized as 'an abomination... a town of shacks and rubbish' was thirty years later prized by residents for its few remaining 'old, bungalows with their beautiful gardens which are a joy to behold' in contrast to the 'concrete jungle' which had replaced most of them.

The plotland development at Cranmore which Steers pronounced a 'dreadful mistake' was viewed by the Isle of Wight County Council in 1973 as having:

'a particular character which is largely the result of the low housing density, fairly extensive tree cover and the informality and narrowness of the unmade roads. It is considered to be important to retain as much of this character as practicable.'

To an extent, this 180 degree shift in viewpoint can be attributed to nostalgia and to the grace bestowed upon buildings by patina and the passage of time. Nonetheless the aesthetic prejudices of the preservationist middle class, which so profoundly influenced the formulation of our present planning system, now appear to have been at best short-sighted, and at worst hypocritical. Most people (and apparently most planners) now agree that what replaced the plotlands has, from an aesthetic and an environmental point of view, often been a good deal worse.

As for the plotlanders themselves, they were by no means without their own sense of aesthetics, as can be seen in some of the photographs in *Arcadia for All*. But this was not their main concern. The plotland movement was united (and occasionally, in its dealings with the authorities, divided) by a dual motivation. One was to improve one's standard of living by making use of the limited means available. The other was to seek out a simple and independent life away from the oppression and grime of the city, In a sense, there were two sorts of plotlanders: those who came by choice and those who came because they had no choice. At first their interests coincided. But when society moved in to improve and upgrade, the upwardly mobile were rewarded, while the Arcadians were dispossessed.

Even in 1938, East Sussex County Council could recognize that Peacehaven 'appealed to persons wishing to live the Simple Life untrammelled by restrictions as to the type of house; the making up of roads arid the disposal of sewage,' As Hardy and Ward comment: 'The question remains — where do they find the 'Simple Life' now?'

All the facts, quotations and photographs in this chapter are taken from *Arcadia for All: The Legacy of a Makeshift Landscape*, by Dennis Hardy and Colin Ward, first published in 1984 by Mansell and now republished by Five Leaves Publications, PO Box 81, Nottingham, NG5 4ER, www.fiveleaves.co.uk. Full references are provided in the original book. The interpretation of these facts follows the line taken by Hardy and Ward, but I have taken the liberty of extending some of their arguments. Many thanks to both authors.

Chapter 10

Low Impact Development in the UK, 1996-2008

A LOT HAS HAPPENED but not much has advanced. When I was preparing the first edition of this book I was hard pressed to find photos of examples in the UK, and had to raid sources from other countries, in particular the seminal collections of photos taken in the USA by Art Boericke and Barry Shapiro.[1] Twelve years later there is no difficulty whatsoever finding images of low impact buildings in the UK. There are hundreds of them of all different kinds: yurts and super-yurts, benders and super-benders, timber-framed barns, straw bale cottages, cob buildings, thatched roundhouses, reciprocal roofed structures, turf-roofed buildings, timber-framed mobile homes, reconstructed shacks and many more. Some are houses, others are barns or workshops, and a few are showpiece homes that are not supposed to be lived in. Some were given permission before they were built, some gained permission retrospectively, and some have no permission at all.[2]

Collectively they are starting to form what historians one day will recognize as the 'low impact' architectural style. Its binding feature is the post-industrial use of renewable, mostly local or recycled materials. The resulting forms tend to be organic and shun straight lines. As is often the case with architectural movements, the more obvious features have been adopted as affectations on mainstream developments — grass roofs on factories, wooden siding on blocks of flats, wattle hurdles for street furniture.

Low impact building is, to borrow Bernard Rudofsky's phrase, an architecture without architects.[3] There are some biggish names

Ben Law's house, built almost entirely out of chestnut from his forestry holding in West Sussex.

involved, such as Ben Law, whose chestnut timber-framed house was featured on the television programme Grand Designs; Tony Wrench, whose widely copied turf-roofed roundhouse in Pembrokeshire has only just received planning permission after a ten year battle; and the strikingly named Amazon Nails and Chug Tugby, two of the pioneers of straw bale building. But these are all builders, rather than architects, and many of them began as self-builders.

The suitability of low impact structures for self-builders is a large part of their attraction to the public. Their organic forms are more responsive to a diversity of individual tastes and tolerate a level of precision lower than that demanded from a professional brickie or chippie. Courses in straw bale building, timber-framing or cob construction are mushrooming around the country at establishments that also provide tuition in permaculture, self-sufficiency, renewable energy, rural crafts and other aspects of a low impact lifestyle.

Demand for LID

Over the last 12 years I have been in a good position to observe this increase in demand. The publication of Low Impact Development prompted myself and a few like -minded people to set up the Rural Planning Group of The Land Is Ours, which in 1999 changed its name to Chapter 7. Our mission was to promote 'access to land for all households… through environmentally sound planning', a quote drawn from Chapter 7C of Agenda 21, entitled 'Human Habitation Settlement'.

Chapter 7 has two main roles. One is to provide free planning advice to low impact developers, self-builders, smallholders, downsizers, permaculture communities, caravan dwellers, hermits and other low-income rural misfits — a job which no other organization has yet shown willing to undertake. The other is to campaign for planning policies that will provide for the modest needs of these people. Our progress in both of these fields is monitored in our magazine *Chapter 7 News*, which after 16 issues was absorbed into *The Land*, where it still occupies the rear 20 pages.

While LID represents a new architectural movement it is a mistake to view it as a new social movement A sizable proportion of the people who contact Chapter 7 are what might be called 'old school' — they usually have a regional accent, keep livestock and are still living in the area where they were brought up, sometimes on the very same plot of land. Some have been fighting a low intensity war with the planning department from their shack or caravan for 20 years or more, while others have only recently fallen into the planners' net, as a result of an overzealous enforcement officer, complaints from an incoming neighbour, or a change in their circumstances. Low impact living is neither a new phenomenon, nor restricted to any social class — it is the way that most people have lived throughout human history — though the old timers and working class are under threat and their number is diminishing.

Of the spectrum of people who contact Chapter 7 asking for free planning advice, roughly a third are involved in a reasonably serious attempt at making a living from their land. It may not always be full-time (only a minority of farmers are nowadays) but working the land productively is what drives them. I like helping these people

Earth-sheltered affordable housing at Honingham, Norfolk, designed by Jeremy Harrall. Photo: CPRE Norfolk.

not only because I applaud their aims, but also because they are the easiest to help. Planning policy is often on their side, and frequently it is perverse opposition from planning officers, rather than government guidance or development plan policy, which is causing the problem. Normally, they get the permission they seek in the end, but after a prolonged and wearing struggle.

Another 25 per cent or so are people who have no overriding aspiration to work the land but are in need of modest accommodation that they could build or provide for themselves, if the local authority would only allow them somewhere to do it. Usually they are living harmlessly in a caravan, a yurt, a shack or a converted agricultural shed, and have been discovered by the planners. Others are lodged in insecure or unsatisfactory rented accommodation and would like to buy a plot of land and build their own sustainable house — but find that the few building plots which aren't already owned by the large house-building companies sell for five or ten times as much as it would cost them to build a dwelling.

It is these groups — diehard rustics, smallholders, and low income caravan and shackdwellers — who are most in need of Chapter 7's services. It is a national disgrace that there is no organization more competent than Chapter 7 devoted to assisting these people, even when the roof above their head is at stake. The Citizens Advice Bureau is completely at sea on this issue, the National Farmers' Union is unwilling to help, and Planning Aid, the Royal Town Planning Institute's free planning advice service, is mostly staffed by off-duty and former planning officers, who are neither keen nor competent to support applications which they have been trained to turn down.

The assistance currently available to low impact dwellers facing enforcement compares starkly with that available to the other major social group in a similar position, gypsies and travellers. As a senior senior planning officer once complained to me, 'the travellers always get the best lawyers.' Gypsy and traveller law has become a specialism in its own right with its own academics, conferences and books. The Community Law Project in Birmingham fields a team of dedicated and brilliant lawyers, secures legal aid for its clients and operates a travellers' helpline funded by Community Legal Aid. No parallel service exists for low impact dwellers and smallholders. Just Chapter 7, which is not much more than a bloke with no funding and no legal or planning qualifications on the end of a telephone.

Low impact dwellers seeking planning assistance beyond what Chapter 7 can offer must either fend for themselves, or cast around for a planning consultant in the private sector, if they can afford one. There are some good consultants who have a grasp of the special issues relating to smallholdings, caravans and self-built shacks, but there are a good many more bumblers who are more familiar with infill bungalows and granny annexes, and an alarming number of shysters who make a living from fleecing the gullible. Once a case advances to appeal or to the courts it is possible to get legal aid. But the number of firms willing to secure legal aid for planning appeals of this nature is tiny, and demand is such that they frequently turn people away.

As a result a significant number of people find themselves fighting a legal battle to stay in their home without any representation whatsoever. Some people rise to the occasion and become adept at planning law; some people have the ability to show a duck's back to whatever shite their planning authority may rain down upon them. But for many others the whole business is deeply stressful, and there are casualties. In the past few years Chapter 7 has encountered one suicide directly attributable to enforcement proceedings, several cases where a fatal illness was attributed to the planning stress, and a number of cases where interminable planning uncertainty was held responsible for a couple or family splitting up.

The good news is that there is an increasing number of 'bush planners' — people who, like myself, have learned how the system works by fighting their own planning battle, and who are willing to help out others in a similar position. This is what I have been trying to encourage because, fascinating though the planning process may be, I have no intention of ending my days as a planning consultant, and am only too happy to devolve this work to others. To this end, Chapter 7 publishes a 100 page *DIY Planning Handbook*, as a guide for those dealing with their own low impact planning problems or helping others.

Three acres and a car

The other 40 per cent or so of people seeking advice are mostly drawn from a range of middle-class, counter-urban downsizers, and they are on the increase. They want to lower their ecological footprint by building their ecohome on a few acres of land in countryside, complete with solar energy and compost loo. They have probably seen programmes like the 'Grand Designs' feature on Ben Law's house, or 'It Isn't Easy Being Green'. They may even have read *Low Impact Development*, though nowadays they are more likely to have found Nick Rosen's book *Off Grid*.[4] They often want to be 'self-sufficient', though that may not involve much more than growing vegetables and keeping chickens and a goat or a pig. And many of them, when they phone up for advice, are not on their land facing an enforcement notice, but thinking about it from the safety of an existing dwelling.

Although they are well-meaning, and I have considerable sympathy with their aims, these are the people I have most difficulty with. A number of them have not thought through the implications of their lifestyle change very thoroughly. When I ask those who aspire to 'self-sufficiency' where their Wellington boots are going to come from, not to mention their wheat and their computer, it often emerges that they have a sizable alternative source of income. There is nothing wrong with this, but it hardly justifies buying and living on a spread of land in the middle of the open countryside, especially if they need to commute to work. 'My car runs on veg oil', is a justification sometimes given by those who intend to commute, but the oil is more likely to be coming from clearings in the Amazon or Indonesian rainforest, than from home-grown rape. A worrying number of people have bought quite sizable tracts of farmland without having any more than the haziest idea how to farm it.

The three-acres-and-a-car lifestyle to which many of this group aspire does not set a sustainable pattern of land use. There is one acre of land for every person in the UK, from which, in an equitable world, we ought to be producing our fair share of food, fibre and fuel. The US-scale rural suburbia that would result from a proliferation of this kind of development — for which there is potentially enormous demand — might well benefit wildlife, improve biodiversity and create a magnificent architectural tradition of zero-carbon, straw-baled dwellings and oak-framed garages, but it wouldn't pay our ecological bills. Part of our work at Chapter 7 is explaining to people, as plainly and politely as possible, that in this respect, the planning system has a point, and perhaps they should think a bit more deeply.

Nowadays Chapter 7 advises such people to group together to buy a plot of land on the edge of a village with good facilities and transport connections; to site houses fairly densely with gardens about the size that rural council houses used to have; to hold an area of agricultural land in common to meet the subsistence and agricultural needs of residents as and when required; and to provide a collective renewable energy installation and a mandatory car share scheme. In short a development similar to Hockerton Housing Project, described on pages 76-80.

The trouble is that since 1994, when Hockerton was given planning consent, thanks to a sympathetic Chief Architect on the district council, no similar project has been allowed. This is not for lack of trying. Over the intervening years I have encountered at least a dozen similar projects, some of which are still progressing. But the combined problems of finding the right people, coming to an agreement about

For three years, Future Roots Co-operative, a group of would-be self-builders in South Somerset, struggled to get permission for a site for their own wood-framed mobile homes. They had land lined up on the edge of the town of Langport, they had the people, they had the design, they had money. But the project has been shelved because of (a) land costs, (b) the successive obstacles to planning permission posed by the local planning authority, and (c) the rising costs of having to provide infrastructure that the co-operative didn't want — for example, tarmacked road access to every unit. Photo © Future Roots.

the project, finding somebody with the time and energy to push the project through, amassing the finance, locating and securing the land and getting planning permission tend to drag on for year after year. Eventually committed people, who can't wait for ever, find some other opportunity, or lose enthusiasm and drift away in despair. Corporate developers can afford to wait the average of five years that it takes to get a housing development off the ground: if their architect or senior planner decides to emigrate to New Zealand they simply hire another. People in need of housing or seeking a change of lifestyle cannot afford to wait that long.

It is partly sheer bureaucracy that kills these projects, but partly also the lack of provision for them in planning policy and local plans. The people responsible for drafting national planning strategy have refused to recognize the growing demand for rural downsizing, failed to acknowledge that it represents a rational response to problems of urbanization and overconsumption, and neglected to investigate ways of providing for the needs of these people without inflicting damage upon the countryside. Hundreds of thousands of people would like to live in low impact, relatively self-reliant rural settlements, and the government hasn't even begun to think of how this should be done, let alone come up with any policies.

That is why, aside from Hockerton, the only low impact housing developments to gain permission so far have been tented or caravan communities who have moved onto the land first, and applied later, 'retrospectively'. They usually succeed in getting planning permission, and they are more common because there is little risk involved in moving a tent or caravan onto land without planning permission, compared with constructing a permanent structure.

National policy

The royal road to introducing changes to the planning system is to campaign for changes in national policy statements which will then cascade down through the hierarchy of national policy, regional strategy, and local development plans (or frameworks as they are now called). This ought to be the quickest route since it is a lot easier for an interest group to lobby one national policy guidance than a dozen regional ones, or 500 local authority planning departments.

However, in England, this road does not appear to be open to the advocates of LID. For the last 12 years Chapter 7 and other voices have been doggedly submitting evidence to a succession of government consultations — on planning policy guidance, on affordable housing, on new planning bills, on the Barker review of housing,, on the environmental impact of the planning system etc — and in every case the government has paid not a blind bit of attention. In no English national planning document anywhere is there any recognition that LID exists, or could exist, or that people would like it to exist. The only time I recall the government employing the term 'low impact development' was in regard to the Business Planning Zones it proposed in the 2001 Planning Green Paper, which are about as high impact as you can get.[5] (These proposals were eventually folded into new legislation on Simplified Planning Zones in Section 45 of the *Planning and Compulsory Purchase Act 2004*. This section withdraws the right for an individual to apply to the Secretary of State for an SPZ, as described on pages 123 to 126 of this book.)

The main opportunity for changing policy in recent years was in the revision of Planning Policy Guidance 7 (PPS7) on the countryside, in 2004. The year before, Chapter 7 convened a group of 16 people which drew up a 52 page document called *Sustainable Homes and Livelihoods in the Countryside*.[6] The report included 80 short case histories of people who had suffered planning difficulties, and made 21 proposals for policy changes. It was endorsed by 23 organizations including Friends of The Earth, the Town and Country Planning Association, DEMOS and the Centre for Alternative Technology.

When the new PPS7 came out there was still no reference to low impact development or the special problems of smallholders. Only one of our recommendations was accepted, that subsistence agriculture should be regarded as being potentially viable — and that was because this view had already been imposed upon the planning system through case law.[7] Our other success was to persuade the ministry to revise the statement in Annex I of PPG7 that 'normally it will be as convenient for farm or forestry workers to live in nearby towns as it will be for them to live where they work'. In every one of the cases we documented living away from the holding

A harmless but unlawful mobile home on a permaculture holding in Dorset, now removed. Photo © Aranya.

was extremely inconvenient. When the new version of PPS7 came back, hallelujah! 'Normally' had been changed to 'often'.

Chapter 7 is not alone in being brushed off by those responsible for drafting national policy. Other groups such as canal boat dwellers, and squatters also pass 'under the radar'. Most scandalous of all is the persistent refusal to acknowledge the self-build sector. I challenge anyone to find a single mention of self-build housing in any one of the hundreds of national planning policy documents, even though it constitutes over eight per cent of all owner occupied housing in the UK, and over 40 per cent in most countries in Western Europe.[8] The civil servants who draw up national planning policy have in mind a world driven by developers, architects, housing managers, and consultants, and populated by consumers. Anyone who prefers to create their own living-space without the help of overpaid social engineers is a non-person in their eyes.

Once again, the one marginal group that has successfully managed to penetrate this curtain of denial is the gypsy and traveller community which has been the subject of much government pontification, culminating in the changes introduced by Circular 1/2006. Virtually every local plan now has policies for travellers, whereas hardly any have policies for low impact lifestyles. The travellers have been successful largely because they have not been afraid to take direct action in large numbers, or to become a visible public nuisance. Smallholders, low-income self-builders and so on have remained too dispersed and discreet to cause an outcry.

Circular 1/2006 reversed the appalling legislation against travellers introduced by the Conservative party in the *Criminal Justice Act 1995*. Local authorities are now obliged to make provision for gypsy and traveller sites, and if they don't (and so far few have) then they are encouraged to give planning permission to travellers on private sites, provided certain criteria are met. This is to be welcomed, but shamefully, no such indulgence is granted to low impact applicants who do not have gypsy or traveller status. We now have a kind of reverse discrimination, where one section of the population wishing to live in caravans or other temporary structures benefits from exception policies, while another section of the population also wishing to live in caravans or similar structures doesn't have access to such policies.

Sustainable development

The biggest change in the last 12 years has been the increased emphasis on 'sustainability' — a term favoured by the two most influential secretaries of state for the environment over the last 15 years, John Prescott and John Gummer. By 1997, PPG7 stated that sustainable development was 'the cornerstone of both the Government's rural policies and its planning policies'; though this cornerstone was still so ill-defined that it was difficult to build anything upon it that would stand up.

In 2001, Prescott was replaced by Stephen Byers, with a brief to make the planning system more amenable to business. His Planning Green Paper, designed to streamline the system in the interests of 'competitiveness', only mentioned sustainability in passing and made no attempt to define the term. Fortunately, Byers was dismissed for burying bad news in the wake of 9/11, and Prescott was reinstated, to the relief of more green-minded civil servants in the ministry. Prescott got rid of Byers' proposal to take large infrastructure projects out of the public inquiry system (later reintroduced by Blair after Prescott had been duly disgraced and sacked) but blundered on with the rest of his predecessor's half-baked schemes to overhaul the planning system, most of which eventually became enshrined in the 2004 Planning and Compulsory Purchase Act. Prescott did, however, introduce Section 39 into the Act which states that everybody involved in regional or local planning should 'exercise their function with the objective of contributing to the achievement of sustainable development.' Sustainability became a statutory objective of the planning system.

Since nobody in regional or local planning had any clear idea what sustainable development was, the government had to come up with a definition. The new *Planning Policy Statement 1*, revised to reflect the 2004 Act, explained that the four aims of sustainable development were:

'- social progress which recognises the needs of everyone;
- effective protection of the environment;
- the prudent use of natural resources; and,
- the maintenance of high and stable levels of economic growth and employment.'

This definition helped to confirm 'sustainable development" as the world's most contentious oxymoron, it being clear to most people (except economists) that in a finite world, the pursuit of economic growth and the prudent use of resources are inimical, if not totally incompatible. It neatly reflects the New Labour strategy of being all things to all people and thus is of service to everyone from builders of airports to off-grid hermits in their respective quests for planning permission. The same schizoid approach is now emerging in regional spatial strategies, and will no doubt be reflected in local development frameworks. It has not so far resulted in any policies supporting low impact development, or providing for the needs of the people who come under that heading. But it does make it easier for low impact projects when they apply for permission or face enforcement proceedings.

In December 2007, the ministry introduced a Climate Change PPS which supports the sort of small-scale renewable energy that is an integral part of low impact development. The disdain for micro-generation that we noted in the 1990s (see page 63) is a thing of the past, and permitted development rights are being altered to make it easier for householders to erect small wind turbines or for solar panels.

The government also wants to make 'all new homes zero carbon from 2016 with a progressive tightening of the energy efficiency building regulations — by 25 per cent in 2010 and by 44 per cent in 2013 — up to the zero carbon target in 2016.' This proposal to make one of the criteria for LID compulsory for all new homes should be applauded — but what does the government mean by 'zero carbon'? The energy embodied in the building materials of a house is currently equal to about 20 years of its use of energy for heating etc. So far the government has shown little inclination to rid the building industry of the concrete and brieze blocks that make up a large part of its carbon emissions.

Local policies

New policies do not necessarily have to filter down from central government. For example, much of the impetus for the change of attitude towards microgeneration originated in local authority development plans, notably 'the Merton rule', first formulated in a Merton Borough Council policy obliging developers to source at least 10 per cent of their energy from renewable sources. The policy was so widely copied and amplified by other councils, that the government eventually felt obliged to endorse it, despite a campaign by the House Builders Federation to get it axed from the Climate Change PPS.

Occasionally local authorities have tried to introduce low impact policies into their local plans. These innovations have not met with great success. An early attempt by Gloucester County Council was scrapped by the regional government office of the South West (GOSW), and two other low impact policies, in South Somerset and Milton Keynes were emasculated by their respective regional governments. In the case of South Somerset, GOSW rendered a useful policy for low impact houses wholly irrelevant to anything actually happening in the district, by making it only applicable to tents. A potentially useful policy in the Oxford City plan has gone unused because nobody interested in low impact development could ever afford to buy land there, and this factor probably also limited the appeal of the Milton Keynes policy.[9]

A more recent and little known policy in Babergh District Council's local plan has fared better with at least one application given consent. Pembrokeshire's Policy 52,

The roundhouse at Tinker's Bubble, South Somerset. This is the building pictured under construction in the photo on page 107. South Somerset's development plan has a low impact policy, but Tinker's Bubble does not comply with it, because the Regional Government Office for the South West insisted that the policy should only apply to tents. Nevertheless Tinker's Bubble was given renewed temporary permission for ten years in 2005.

has attracted a great deal of attention, and four applications have so far been lodged, of which one has been allowed. But this policy was forged in the very different policy climate currently evolving in Wales, and I will deal with it later.

The performance of these local plan policies is, so far, disappointing. Their failure is due mostly to the fact that they are being drafted by maverick local authority planners in a policy vacuum where the ramifications of a low impact policy remain unexplored, and misunderstood.

Development control

Despite this policy vacuum, most low impact developments which go ahead without planning consent do manage to get retrospective permissions. A minority of these applications are allowed by the local authority, but this is nearly always thanks to the elected committee voting against a recommendation for refusal by the planning officers.[10]

More frequently the committee will agree with the officers' recommendation to refuse an application and it will go to appeal. Whereas the average success rate for all appeals is around 40 per cent, the success rate for low impact appeals is probably more like 66 per cent. Competent smallholdings which have been refused by their local authority regularly get permission at appeal. Virtually all of the large-scale low impact communities that have applied for permission in England — Kings Hill,

The timber-framed and thatched barn at Fivepenny Farm, an organic smallholding in West Dorset, shortly before completion. Fivepenny Farm won permission at appeal after refusal by the local authority.

Tinkers Bubble, Brickhurst, Steward Wood and Land Matters — were refused at committee and subsequently allowed by an appeal inspector. Since these five communities, and many other low impact projects, are blatantly in conflict with development plan policies, this is an impressive record.

Why do planning officers so often refuse low impact applications which are likely to get permission further down the line? This is not how they behave in regard to larger developments. When a supermarket puts in an application for a contentious retail development in a market town, planning officers will often let it sail through on the grounds that: 'Frankly, we don't like this development, but if we are taken to appeal we will lose'. But more than once I have heard planning officers dealing with a low impact application confide: 'We are turning you down, but between you and me you will get it at appeal.' Some local authorities seem to enjoy taking a pasting and come back for more. West Dorset District Council, having lost the Fivepenny Farm appeal after their agricultural consultant, in the middle of cross-examination, reversed his views about the need of the appellants to live on their land, two years later sent a similar application from smallholders Dan and Natalie Newbury to appeal, employing the very same agricultural consultant... and lost again.

There are many possible reasons for this behaviour, and a full understanding of the psychology of development control officers can perhaps only be achieved by posing as a planner and getting a job in a local authority. But anybody rash enough to pursue this line of research needs to be careful not to get drawn into the culture. The *DIY Planning Handbook* states:

> 'Development control planners are a very odd bunch. Within a year or two of graduating from college they get sucked into an institutional value system that is arcanely masonic in the hold it has upon them. They are bound at every step by government guidance and development plan policies, their every action is liable to be vetted by their superiors and they are subject to pressures from all sorts of vested interests. Being human, they have their likes and dislikes, but these sympathies can only be expressed through circuitous advice and perverse signals. Like a crab constricted by its carapace, they find it easier to walk sideways.'[11]

Some applicants would judge that the writer here was being a bit too kind. As part of her PhD thesis, Lucy Nichol recorded the views of farmers and forestry workers. About half expressed dissatisfaction with their planning authority, often vehemently. Here are comments from ten different respondents:.

'Blinkered, petty minded, inflexible.'

'Not happy (understatement).'

'Totally unjust and bent'.

'Clumsy, slow, bureaucratic, unhelpful, illogical, lacking in continuity and objectivity, costly.'

'It stinks.'

'Totally arbitrary.'

'Oppressive! Intrusive! Fascist!'

'Stinks.'

'I feel totally demoralized by it.'

'In one word, sick.'[12]

Naturally, one has to view these responses with caution. Nobody likes being held back by rules designed to protect the public good, any more than they like paying taxes. But I know from ten years experience of planning officers that a great many of them go well beyond the call of duty in their dealings with smallholders and low impact applicants. For example, the instances of officers demanding a full planning application, when all that is required legally is notification for permitted development, occur far too frequently to be mere mistakes. A culture of contempt for individuals who deviate from suburban norms often seems to prevail: one former planning officer told me that in his department planners who betrayed sympathies for awkward rural customers were judged to have 'gone native'.

The Planning Inspectorate

The longer I have been involved with planning, the more I have come to see the Planning Inspectorate as a rock of sanity in a system which otherwise is a sea of muddled ideas, conflicting advice, competing interests, and impenetrable jargon. The appeal process stands out as efficient, exhaustive and impartial, all of which local authority planning departments manifestly are not.[13] It is because of the consistency with which these virtues are upheld that appeal inspectors have looked more favourably upon low impact development than any other part of the planning system.

The appeals system is impartial — as much as anyone can reasonably expect — because it takes a planning application out of its local context, away from the vested interests, professional allegiances and class prejudices of local politics. Planning inspectors in the course of their duty encounter as many incompetent or mean-spirited planning officers as they do unscrupulous or devious appellants and are usually equally inured to the importunities and blandishments of either side. There is nothing to suggest that inspectors have any inbred tendency to side with local authorities, or with developers of any hue.

There is, it is true, a policy bias towards economically grandiose schemes offering 'employment', which most planning inspectors defer to, and which means, for example, that an organization like Centre Parcs will find it easier to win an appeal for 100 holiday cabins in a wood, than a family providing woodland retreats for a handful of people will for one cabin. But appeal inspectors do sometimes grant permission for one-cabin families if they think the project is promising, and they do so more frequently than local authorities.

As well as a reasonably fair hearing, the low impact applicant who goes to appeal can expect a full one: the generous amount of time freely allowed to appellants to unfold their case at a public inquiry is probably unmatched anywhere else in the field of bureaucratic decision-making. At local authority level most applications are delegated to the officers, in which case there is no public airing at all; but even when an application does get heard by the elected planning committee, the applicant has

Tree house for educational purposes in Devon, built by Stuart Barnes Watson, and refused permission on transport grounds, even though permission is regularly given to companies like Centre Parcs for developments involving scores of holiday cabins. Photo © Barnes Watson.

just three minutes to make a case and to respond to whatever misconceptions the planning officer may have been spreading about their proposal.

At appeal hearings or public inquiries on the other hand, appellants can introduce as many witness as they like, who may give evidence for as long as they like, provided there is no repetition or deviation. If an inquiry is scheduled for two days, but runs into three or four days, then so be it, an extension is allowed. Appellants have the opportunity to unfold the complexities of their proposals, explain misunderstandings, and challenge false allegations, whereas at committee meetings mostly all you can do is bite your tongue.

Most surprising of all, considering it is a government bureaucracy, is the standard of efficiency and decent public service. If you phone up the Inspectorate you will be greeted, after minimal voice-mail, by a receptionist who has a full understanding of the workings of the organization, and who can either answer your question immediately, or else knows who to put you through to. This is a far cry from most government agencies and a very far cry from many local authorities whose receptionists often have never been taught the difference between the Planning Policy department and Development Control, and who sometimes are briefed to ensure that you are not put through to the very department you know you want to get to. Unlike local planning authorities, the Inspectorate runs to a strict timetable. Deadlines are scrupulously observed when they are necessary to the efficient running of the system; but they are informally extended when there is no prejudice to either party. Public inquiries are modelled on adversarial court cases, but dispense with intimidating formalities and legalese. I never cease to be impressed at the competence and pleasantness with which Inspectors can run two or three day inquiries, often with an audience split between two rival camps, single-handed and without any help from clerks and ushers. Order is maintained, not by the presence of police officers ready to march away aggrieved individuals who get rowdy and charge them with contempt of court, but because inspectors are trained to run hearings where all parties come away feeling they have had a full opportunity to say what they want, and that it has been taken seriously.

The inspectors themselves are even more inscrutable than development control officers, largely because during the course of an appeal they are not allowed to talk to anyone from either side except for administrative purposes. If everyone involved is lunching in the same pub, then the inspector has to sit in a corner on their own. My hunch is that a lot of inspectors are people who are used to exerting a decison-making role, but who become disillusioned by the political compromises and vested interests that bear down upon anyone in a position of responsibility in the real world. Certainly, for anyone sensitive to such pressure, the option of becoming an appeal inspector, and writing decision letters in the seclusion of one's own home is an attractive one.

A few years ago I was invited, along with James Shorten of Land Use Consultants, to give a talk at the Inspectorate's annual beano, at Warwick University. When I arrived in the evening, I was greeted with the sight of 150 planning inspectors swarming around the bar. I felt like David Attenborough might, peering through the jungle foliage at a previously unwitnessed congregation of rare and reclusive primates. Once they've had a few jars, of course, they become less shy, and I learnt a good deal more about these curious creatures than I had known before.

James and I were invited to the Inspectorate's gathering to give a talk on low impact development, one of a number of presentations from people outside the Inspectorate. The Inspectorate's administrators had presumably observed an increasing number of appeals for LID, and decided that inspectors needed to learn more about it. This is in sharp contrast to the Secretary of State's policymakers, who have never once elicited any views on low impact development from myself, or, as far as I know, anybody else. However it should be borne in mind that the Inspectors are representatives of the Secretary of State, so it may be a case of the ministry testing out in the field what it is wary of laying down in policy.

Whatever the case, it is thanks to the Inspectorates' openness to ideas and its institutional impartiality that a high proportion of the LID appeals have been allowed. In a number of instances, inspectors have reasoned that although a development does not sit easily with development plan policies, it reflects the aspirations for sustainability which are increasingly dominant in national planning policy. The Petter and Harris decision, which, in regard to a subsistence smallholding, advises that Inspectors should look to the 'underlying purpose of planning policy' rather than just applying policy specifications to the letter, has been influential upon some of these decisions.[14] Of course, not all LID appeals are allowed, by any means; but the reasons given for refusal have usually been understandable, and it is hard to find more than a handful of outrageously bad refusals in England. The harshest judgments have often been where the land is owned by someone other than the appellant, or when a consultant has poorly represented a client.

Wales and Pembrokeshire Policy 52

Strangely, LID in Wales has taken almost exactly the opposite course from that taken in England. Appeal decisions, on the whole have not been helpful. Chris and Lyn Dixon, of Tir Penrhos Isaf (see page 80) lost a 2004 enforcement appeal for a wooden cabin, in what was a travesty of an appeal decision, though they did eventually get permission through the local authority. The long running saga of Brithdir Mawr, the Pembrokeshire farm in Wales where Tony Wrench and others have erected low impact turf-roofed roundhouses, was strung along for twelve years by a series of refused appeals.

Instead, and in sharp contrast to England, there has been some progress, partly promoted by the Welsh Assembly, towards getting a low impact policy in national planning policy guidance. This initiative was prompted by the Brithdir Mawr episode, and other refusals for low impact development in Pembrokeshire Coast National Park, which contrasted shockingly with the Park's keenness to allow the construction of 350 wooden holiday homes at the Bluestone theme park. The National Park, together with the Countryside Council for Wales and the National

Assembly commissioned a report on LID in Wales from the University of the West of England, and Land Use Consultants.[15] The report concluded that

'In terms of overall sustainability, the environmental performance of LID is undoubtedly strongest. Its social contribution is clearly positive, and its economic contribution, whilst undeniably small, is also positive. Considering the sustainability of LID as a whole, it is important to note that LID does not undermine any aspects of sustainability... Development which performs environmentally, socially and economically is unusual. Development with economic or social benefits often carries environmental harm.'[16]

In the light of this positive verdict, the National Park Authority (while its development control team were carrying out enforcement proceedings against Brithdir Mawr) commissioned another report, this time from Baker Associates of Bristol, investigating how LID policies could be drafted.[17] Out of this work emerged Pembrokeshire Coast's Low Impact Development Policy 52.

The good things about this policy are: (a) that it lays down, in detail, criteria that in a sustainable society ought to be observed by any rural land-based development; and (b) that its supplementary planning guidance explains very clearly what information the applicant is expected to provide in order to satisfy the planning officers.

The bad thing is that those who drafted it have been so cautious (though possibly caution has been imposed from above) that the policy is little more than the standard agricultural workers' dwelling policy, with a raft of extra environmental restraints imposed on top. The functional test in respect of whether or not there is a need to live on the land, is more flexible in the LID policy than in the agricultural dwelling policy. But as regards the financial test, it is a matter of debate whether the requirement in Policy 52 to meet 75 per cent of basic needs from the land, is more or less demanding than the standard agricultural requirement to be 'solely or mainly working, or last working in agriculture'.

In practice the policy is so detailed and potentially stringent that any development control officer prejudiced against LID, or nervous about what it might lead to, would have no problem in conjuring up reasons for rejecting the most faultless of applications. One Pembrokeshire smallholder facing planning difficulties told me that he was applying under the standard agricultural policy, because the low impact policy was too demanding. The first three applications under Policy 52, were all turned down. One, from a couple with 85 acres of woodland, took about 20 months to determine; a second was, yet again, Tony Wrench's roundhouse; and the third, the Lammas project, the most ambitious low impact development yet proposed in the UK, involving farmland subdivided into nine smallholdings plus a communal building for its first phase, with a second phase to come later.

There were mutterings that Pembrokeshire development control officers were systematically refusing every application, so that the Welsh Assembly's planning inspectors would take responsibility for any decision at appeal. But in September 2008, the National Park did allow a fourth application, this time a combined one for Tony Wrench's house, and Emma Orbach's incomparably low impact roundhouses,

Model of the communal hub building at Lammas. © Lammas.

also at Brithdir Mawr. They were given temporary permission for a trial period of three years, although they had already been lived in for periods of between five and eleven years.

However a second application from Lammas has been refused, and would be going to appeal were it not for the fact that the application has been ruled invalid on a technicality,[18] and so Lammas applied yet again. As is so often the case with non-retrospective applications,[19] it is the long-winded bureaucracy as much as the deliberate resistance from local authorities that threatens to wear out self-build projects.

Nonetheless, the Pembrokeshire policy has served to lift the profile of low impact development and to place it on the Welsh policy map. In July 2008 the Welsh Assembly issued a consultation document on affordable housing which invited comments, not on whether there should be an LID policy, but on what the criteria should be.[20] The most interesting aspect of this move is that the Assembly appears to be looking at LID, not only in regard to land-based agricultural and forestry holdings, but as one solution, amongst several, for the affordable housing problem. When Baker Associates were making soundings for their report on LID, I informed them that at least half the demand for LID came from people who either had marginal interest in land -based activities, or none at all, and mainly wanted to build their own low impact house. This was overlooked, and that goes a long way towards explaining why Policy 52 currently resembles an overcooked version of the standard agricultural dwelling policy. Hopefully the Welsh Assembly's consultation document will allow policies to evolve that meet the needs of all sections of the population.

The future

There is also an expectation that if an effective low impact policy does materialize in Wales, and doesn't result in the rape of the countryside, or a mass exodus of rats from the rat-race, that the English secretary of state will take note and start to recognize the existence of LID in England.

However it is not top down policies that engineer change, but popular demand. Throughout the early years of the millennium Scotland had some useful encouragement for 'low impact housing' in both its rural and and its housing planning guidances.[21] But this was never sufficiently taken up, and advice on low impact development is now limited to a brief reference in passing in the 2005 guidance on rural development, and no mention at all in the 2008 guidance on housing.[22]

The failure to use the policy probably reflects the land ownership pattern in Scotland which, thanks to the Highland clearances is very different from that in England and Wales. The biggest restraint upon rural development in the Highlands comes not from the planning system but from the concentration of much of the rural land in huge estates, and so land reform and community buy-outs are the main focus of people seeking access to land. Meanwhile the crofting areas offer opportunities for low impact lifestyles, for people who have some capital.

Nonetheless there are some significant LIDs in Scotland, including David Blair's wooden roundhouse and forestry holding in Argyll, and a recently established unlawful plotland development of 60 homes at Lunga, also in Argyll. The Scottish Government, unable to make up its mind either to allow or demolish the Lunga settlement, confirmed an enforcement notice on just one of the buildings, but then, in a classic example of what I call 'enforcement Inspector's fudge', gave a compliance period of five years. The plotholders at Lunga (on their land with a stay of execution of five years) are currently in a better position than those at Lammas (off their land and with an average five years wait for permission). When the planning system is subject to chronic paralysis, there seems to be more to be gained from moving on without permission, than from trying to conform to low impact policies.

However policies are necessary and desirable, not only to provide for people in need, but also to ensure that LIDs remain low impact. Policies will come in England when demand reaches a certain level: that is to say, when the number of tolerated illicit developments endangers the credibility of the planning system, or the scale of low impact settlement creates as many problems as gypsies and travellers were causing prior to the 2006 legislation.

Will this state of affairs ever be reached, or is LID going to continue indefinitely in a legal limbo? It is hard to say. Unlike travellers, who have no choice, only a minority of those who seek a low impact lifestyle are brazen enough to move on without permission, and the English government will probably continue to turn a blind eye to their their existence as long as it thinks it can get away with it. How long that may be probably depends upon the future course of the economy.

In the past, whenever capitalism has entered a crisis it has undergone a period of recession, and then bounced back. It is perhaps a safer bet that this is what will happen this time. Yet there are reasons why this particular crisis could turn out to be different. Whenever the economy has collapsed before, the problem has been purely financial, capable of resolution through a revival of confidence or a New Deal. But the current crisis is taking place under the shadow of two dark clouds: global warming and peak oil. In other words it is doubtful whether there is sufficient environmental space for the capitalist economy, which is dependent upon incessant growth, to expand into.

Under these circumstances, a logical response is to downsize, and for those who find themselves eased out of their home by economic circumstances, or who are worried about their future living space and lifestyle, downsizing often means some form of low impact development. The plotland settlers of the 1930s sought refuge from a distraught economy by staking out a simpler life, but their choice was not a response to perceived limits to human development. Low impact settlers of today are highly aware of their environmental footprint, and unless capitalism gets its act together, there will soon be many more of them. I look forward to that.

Fifteen Criteria for Developments Associated with Sustainable Land-based Rural Activities

These criteria were drawn up by the The Land Is Ours as a means of assessing the sustainability of projects in the countryside with an element of land-based use.

[1] The project has a management plan which demonstrates:

[a] how the site will contribute significantly towards the occupiers' livelihoods;

[b] how the objectives cited in items 2 to 14 below will be achieved and maintained.

[2] The project provides affordable access to land and/or housing to people in need.

[3] The project provides public access to the countryside, including temporary access such as open-days and educational visits.

[4] The project can demonstrate how it will be integrated into the local economy and community.

[5] The project can demonstrate that no activities pursued on the site shall cause undue nuisance to neighbours or the public.

[6] The project has prepared a strategy for the minimization of motor vehicle use.

[7] The development and any buildings associated with it are appropriately sited in relation to local landscape, natural resources and settlement patterns.

[8] New buildings and dwellings are not visually intrusive nor of a scale disproportionate to the site and the scale of the operation; and are constructed from materials with low embodied energy and environmental impact, and preferably from locally sourced materials, unless environmental considerations or the use of reclaimed materials determine otherwise. Reuse and conversion of existing buildings on the site is carried out as far as practicable in conformity with these criteria.

[9] The project is reversible, insofar as new buildings can be easily dismantled and the land easily restored to its former condition.

[10] The project plans to minimize the creation of waste and to reuse and recycle as much as possible on site.

[11] The project has a strategy for energy conservation and the reduction, over time, of dependence on non-renewable energy sources to a practical minimum.

[12] The project aims over time for the autonomous provision of water, energy and sewage disposal and where it is not already connected to the utilities, shall make no dstensibly, because these were more likely to be tolerated by the authorities) but many graduated into permanent settlements providing poor people with a retirement home or a dwelling close to work opportunities on the coast, or a smallholding or other smalstry standards or recognized permaculture principles.

[14] The project has strategies and programmes for the ecological management of the site, including :

[a] the sustainable management and improvement of soil structure;

[b] the conservation and, where appropriate, the enhancement of semi-natural habitat, taking into account biodiversity, indigenous species, and wildlife corridors;

[c] the efficient use and reuse of water, as well as increasing the water holding capacity of the site;

[d] the planting of trees and hedges, particularly in areas where the tree coverage is less than 20 per cent.

[15] The project can show that affordability and sustainability are secured, for example, by the involvement of a housing association, co-operative, trust or other social body whose continuing interest in the property will ensure control over subsequent changes of ownership and occupation.

From The Rural Planning Group of The Land Is Ours, Defining Rural Sustainability: 15 Criteria for Sustainable Developments in the Countryside together with Three Model Policies for Local Plans, TLIO, 1999, available from Chapter 7.

References

Introduction

1 The Town and Country Planning Association's admirable report *Planning for a Sustainable Environment*, edited by Andrew Blowers, Earthscan, 1993, fires most of its main recommendations over the heads of planning officers at various government departments, in particular the Treasury. *Sustainable Settlements*, by Hugh Barton, Geoff Davis and Richard Guise, University of the West of England, 1995, is a design manual, not on sale in bookshops.
2 See references for Chapter 3.
3 Thayer, R., *Gray World, Green Heart*, Wiley, 1994.

Chapter 1. Fifty Years of Rural Planning: Protecting the Environment

1 Gough, R., *The History of Myddle*, 1834 and Penguin 1986, p.151.
2 Moore, V., *A Practical Approach to Common Law*, Blackstone, 1994, p.1.
3 Batsford, H. and Fry, C., *The English Cottage*, Batsford, 1950, p.2.
4 Sharp, T., *Town and Countryside: Some Aspects of Urban and Rural Development*, Oxford University Press, 1932, p.69.
5 Batsford, H., and Fry, C., op cit, p.3.
6 Williams-Ellis, C., *England and the Octopus*, Portmeirion, 1975.
7 *Architects Journal*, 15 August 1928.
8 Cited in Newby, H., *Green and Pleasant Land*, Hutchinson, London, 1979.
9 Sharp, T., *Town and Countryside*, Oxford, 1932. For a discussion of Sharp's role, see Ward, C., 'Anarchy or Order', in *Talking Houses*, Freedom Press, 1990.
10 *Parliamentary Debates*, vol. 188, 12 May 1908, col. 949; cited in Cullingworth, J. and Nadin, V., *Town and Country Planning in Britain*, 1994, p.2.
11 Scott Report, *Report of the Committee on Land Utilization in Rural Areas*, HMSO, 1942.
12 White Paper, *Town and Country Planning Bill: Explanatory Memorandum*, Cmd 7006, 1947, p.5.
13 Ratcliffe, J., *An Introduction to Town and Country Planning*, UCL, 1981.
14 White Paper, *Rural England: A Nation Committed to a Living Countryside*, Cm 3016, HMSO, 1995.
15 CPRE, *The Lost Land*, 1992 and *The Regional Lost Land*, 1993. The Department of the Environment, in *Planning Policy Guidance 7*, paragraph 2.6, estimates the figure at 5,000 hectares.
16 Joseph Rowntree Foundation, *Inquiry into Planning for Housing*, 1994.
17 Bramley, G. and Watkins, C., *Circular Projections*, CPRE, 1995.
18 CPRE, *Rural White Paper: Submission by the CPRE*, February 1995.
19 Aslet, C., *Countryblast*, John Murray, 1991.
20 Dimbleby, J., *Continuity and Change*, CPRE, 1995.
21 Rackham, O., *The History of the Countryside*, Dent, 1986, pp.22 and 25.
22 Shoard, M., *This Land is Our Land*, Paladin, 1987, pp.518-524.
23 White Paper, op. cit. 9, p.131. The White Paper was first announced at a fringe meeting of the CLA at the Conservative Party Conference, October 1994.

24 Brundtland Commission, *Report of the World Commission on Environment and Development*, 1987.
25 Local Government Management Board (LGMB), *Local Agenda 21, Principles and Process: A Step by Step Guide*, 1994.
26 United Nations Conference on Environment and Development (UNCED), *Agenda 21*, Chapter 28, 1992.
27 LGMB, op. cit. 20.
28 Community Council of Devon, Designed Visions, and Devon County Council, *Developing Sustainable Communities: A Fieldworker's Manual, Part I*, 1995, p.20.
29 Borgstrom, N., *The Hungry Planet: The Modern World at the Edge of Famine*, Collier MacMillan, 1972. See also Goldsmith, E. and Hildyard, N., *Earth Report 3*, Mitchell Beazley, 1992, p.78.
30 UNCED, *Agenda 21*, 'Introduction to Overview', 1992.
31 *The Guardian, Section II*, p.5 (diagram), 24 January 1996.
32 'Planners Look Askance at Green Council Conversion', *Planning*, 22 September, 1995.

Chapter 2. Fifty Years of Rural Planning: Meeting People's Needs

1 White Paper, *The Land Commission*, Cmnd 2771, 1965.
2 Joseph Rowntree Foundation, *The Relationship between Land Supply and Housing Production*, Housing Research Findings No 121, August 1994.
3 Redwood, J., 'Betterment Makes Sense for Communities in the Firing Line', *Planning*, 1126, 7 July 1995.
4 Newby, H., *Green and Pleasant Land*, Hutchinson, London, 1979.
5 Estate agents consulted agreed that £25,000 was not an unreasonable guess for greenfield developments across the whole of Britain.
6 Redwood, J., op. cit. 3.
7 DoE, *Draft Revision of DoE Circular 16/91*, 1996.
8 Cullingworth, J. and Nadin, V., *Town and Country Planning in Britain*, Routledge, 1994, p.15.
9 Clunies-Ross, T. and Hildyard, N., *The Politics of Industrial Agriculture*, Earthscan, 1992, p.11.
10 See, for example, Clunies-Ross, T., ibid.
11 CSO, *Family Spending 1994-5*, HMSO, 1995, p.102. The rise in development land prices has been put forward as a partial explanation for the fact that few British manufacturing industries — with the exception of agriculture — are competitive on the world market; see Summers, W., *Loose Fit Positive Planning*, Planning Reform Group, 1991. The average price of agricultural land with planning permission in rural areas around Montpellier in the South of France is less than half that of similar land around Bristol in the west of England.
12 Body, R., *Agriculture: The Triumph and the Shame*, Temple Smith, London, 1982, p.5.
13 Pye-Smith, C. and Hall, C., *The Countryside We Want*, Green Books, 1987. Between 1953 and 1981, the number of farms in Britain fell from 454,000 to 242,000; Clunies-Ross, T., op. cit. 9, p.67.
14 Allaby, M., 'Must Britain Feed Itself?' in Girardet, H. (ed.), *Land for the People*, Crescent Books, 1976.
15 Cited in Country Landowners Association, *Towards a Rural Policy: A Vision for the 21st Century*, CLA, 1995, p.8.
16 'Councillors Call for Trickle Transfer Review', *Western Gazette*, 13 July 1995.
17 Pauncefoot, Z., *Communities at Risk in Wiltshire*, Wiltshire Community Foundation, 1993, p.60.
18 Monk et al., *Rural Labour Markets: a Literature Review. Final Report to the Department of the Environment*, Anglia University, December 1992, p.iii; cited in CPRE, *Submission to the Rural White Paper*, February 1995.
19 The environmental effects of horseyculture are dubious. Tony Crofts writes:

'Horseyculture is making a significant, and generally ugly, mark on the land ... To the pleasure pony keeper, the paddock is only a parking lot, and the animal's lax grazing habit rapidly allows it to deteriorate into an unkempt weedy mess.' (Crofts, T., *The Return of the Wild*, The Friendly Press, Waterford, Ireland, 1987, p.73). On the other hand horses require hay (as opposed to silage) and haymaking has a more beneficial effect upon grassland biodiversity than silage making.

20 CLA, op. cit. 15.
21 CPRE Herefordshire Branch, *Submission to the Rural White Paper*, June 1995.
22 Rural Development Commission (RDC), *Rural White Paper Submission*, 1995, p.3.
23 White Paper, *Rural England: A Summary*, HMSO, 1995. p.4.
24 RDC, op. cit. 22, p.2.
25 White Paper, op. cit. 23, p.4.
26 CPRE, op. cit. 18, p.v.
27 Monbiot, G., *A Charter for the Countryside*, The Land is Ours, 1995.
28 Neeson, J., *Commoners: Common Right, Enclosure and Social Change in England, 1700-1820*, Cambridge, 1993, p.65.
29 Ditchfield, P., *Old Village Life*, Methuen, 1920, p.216.
30 Neeson, op.cit. 28, p.65.
31 Ibid., p.311.
32 Slater, G., 'Historical Outline of Land Ownership in England', in *The Land: The Report of the Land Enquiry Committee, Vol I Rural*, Hodder and Stoughton, 1913.
33 Bourne, G., *Change in the Village*, 1912, Penguin, 1984, pp.77-78.
34 Collings, J., *Land Reform*, Longmans, Green and Co., 1908.
35 Elliott, D., 'Lessons of Land Settlement' in Girardet, op. cit. 14.
36 Shoard, M., *This Land is Our Land*, Paladin, 1987, p.144.
37 Somerset County Council notice, 1995.
38 White Paper, *Rural England*, HMSO,1995, p.26.
39 Hannis, M., *Kings Hill* Appeal, *Proof of Evidence*, 1995; see Appendix F.
40 *Tinker's Bubble* Appeal, *Proof of Evidence*, 1995, p.10; see Appendix F.
41 Shoard, op. cit. 36, p.161.
42 DoE., Circular 1/94.

Chapter 3. Tales of the Dispossessed

1   *Salisbury Journal*, 29 August 1991 and 19 September 1991.
2   The Town and Country Planning (General Permitted Development) Order 1995, Part 6. In Scotland the threshold is 0.4 hectares.
3   In this chapter, the names of those giving testimony have been altered or abbreviated, unless their names have already been published elsewhere. Unless otherwise stated, these testimonies were made in personal communications to the author.
4   'Demand for Second Homes', *Blackmore Vale Magazine*, 8 October 1993, p.100.
5   DoE and Welsh Office, *Planning Policy Guidance 7: The Countryside and the Rural Economy*, Annex E, HMSO, 1992.
6   Ward, D., "Brookside in Country" Gives Families a Chance', *The Guardian*, date unavailable.
7   Holt, G., 'Caravans and Registration', *Home Farm* (now *Country Garden and Smallholding*), August/September 1989.
8   Rural Resettlement Group, *Rural Resettlement Handbook*, Prism Alpha and Lighthouse Books, 1984.
9   Holt, G., op. cit. 7.
10 Smith, S., 'Tied in Rural Knots,' *Financial Times*, 15/16 July 1995.
11 Brown, A., 'Calm of the Countryside Ruffled by Planning Ruses and Wheezes', *Planning* 1143, 3 November, 1995.
12 DoE and Welsh Office, op.cit. 5, Annex E.18.
13 Telephone conversation with an employee of the company, February 1996.
14 DoE Planning Research Programme, *Planning Control over Agricultural and Forestry Development and Rural Building Conversions*, HMSO, 1995.

15 Ibid., pp.97, 115, 120, 233 and passim.
16 Ibid., p.168. The report recommends omitting the words 'last working in' from the agricultural tie clause — preventing the use of the building as a retirement home.
17 Ibid, p.161. The report does envisage tying agricultural buildings other than dwellings to their land, but, perversely when they are used for something other than agriculture (p.226).
18 Ibid., pp.80, 101, 170, and 235.
19 Ibid., p.233.
20 Rural Development Commission, *Meeting the Challenge of Agricultural Adjustment*, RDC, 1990.
21 Netting, R., *Farm Families and the Ecology of Intensive, Sustainable Agriculture*, Stanford University Press, California, 1993. See also, Seymour, J., *The Fat of the Land*, Faber, 1974.
22 DoE Planning Research Programme, op. cit. 14, pp.219 and 225.
23 Ibid., p.97.
24 Ibid., p.85.
25 White Paper, *Rural England*, Cm 3016, HMSO, 1995, p.131.
26 Brown, op. cit. 11.
27 Planning and Compensation Act 1991, Part I, Section 4.
28 *Low Impact News*, No. 2, 71 Dale Street, York, February 1996, p.18.
29 Crouch, D. and Ward, C., *The Allotment: Its Landscape and Culture*, Faber 1988 and Mushroom Bookshop, Nottingham, 1994, p.227. 'Home is our Potting Shed', *Southern Evening Echo*, Southampton, 4 March 1995; the Somerset case is known to the author.
30 *Nomad News*, FFT, Spring/Summer 1994.
31 Hannis, M., *Kings Hill* Appeal, oral evidence, November 1995.
32 Oubridge, B., 'A Tipi Dweller Writes …', *Built Environment Network* No. 4, Green Party, Winter 1993/4.
33 *June Buckley v UK, Report of the European Commission of Human Rights*, First Chamber, Application Number 20348/92, 11 January 1995,para.58.
34 Oubridge, op. cit. 32.
35 Hannis, M., *Kings Hill* Appeal, Proof of Evidence, November 1995, p.10; see Appendix F.
36 DoE and Welsh Office, op. cit. 5, Section 1.10.

Chapter 4. Low Impact Development: Creating a New Land Use

1 South Somerset District Council, *Draft South Somerset Local Plan*, Policy D/H12, 1995, pp.46-47. This policy may be dropped under pressure from the Department of the Environment.
2 Hannis, M., *Kings Hill* Appeal, Proof of Evidence, 1995, p.9; see Appendix F.
3 Wrench, T., 'Permaculture Land: Planning for a Creative Future', *Permaculture Magazine*, Spring, 1994.

Chapter 5. Nine Criteria for Low Impact

1 *Council Directive 85/337/EEC*, 1985.
2 *The Town and Country Planning (Assessment of Environmental Effects) Regulations 1988*, SI/1199, Schedule 3.
3 *The Town and Country Planning (General Permitted Development) Order 1995*, Part 4.
4 DoE and Welsh Office, PPG 7: *The Countryside and the Rural Economy*, HMSO, 1992, Annex E13.
5 DoE, *Circular 11/95*, HMSO, 1995, para 112. See also PPG 7, Annex E13.
6 See, for example, *Par* Appeal decision letter, in Appendix F.
7 South Somerset District Council, *Draft South Somerset Local Plan*, Policy D/H12, 1995, pp.46-47.
8 Letter to author from Helen Baczkowska, March 11 1996.
9 White Paper, *Rural England*, Cm3016, HMSO, 1995, p.35.
10 Crofts, T., *The Return of the Wild*, The Friendly Press, Waterford Ireland, 1987, p.152.

11 CPRE Herefordshire Branch, *Submission to the Rural White Paper*, June 1995, p.6.
12 For example at Tinker's Bubble, environmental objections to the development were dropped by the local authority after a management plan for conservation and wildlife was agreed upon by the appellants and the council, and became subject to a Section 106 agreement. *Tinker's Bubble* Appeal decision; see Appendix F.
13 Letter to the author from Sue Clifford, 8 August 1995.
14 Darley, G., 'Local Distinctiveness: An Architectural Conundrum', in *Local Distinctiveness: Place, Particularity and Identity*, Common Ground, 1993.
15 Skeuomorph: 'An object or feature copying the design of a similar artifact in another material'. Example: 'The transfer of thong-work from the flint axe where it was functional to the bronze celt where it was skeuomorphic'. *Oxford English Dictionary*.
16 Vale, B. and Vale, R. 'Building the Sustainable Environment', in Blowers (ed.) *Planning for a Sustainable Environment*, TCPA report, Earthscan, 1994.
17 Figures supplied by David Eliott, Druid Shore.
18 Thomson, T., letter to the Planning Inspectorate, 21 September 1995, in Hannis, M., *Kings Hill* Appeal, Proof of Evidence, 1995; see Appendix F.
19 *Annual Abstract of Statistics*, HMSO, 1995 p.140.
20 Among the examples cited in this book, Hockerton and the Lowland Crofting projects conducted by New Lives New Landscapes use reed beds; Kings Hill and Tinker's Bubble use dry compost toilets; and Tir Penrhos Isaf uses an intermediary system which is water-conducted, but from which compost can be harvested. None has encountered any problem with the health authorities.
21 White, P., 'Renewable Schemes Set to Founder on Policy Rock', *Planning*, 1148, 8 December 1995.
22 DoE and Welsh Office, *PPG 22, Renewable Energy*, Annexes on Wind Energy, and Active Solar Systems, HMSO, 1993,.
23 Letter to the author from David Olivier, 17 October 1995.
24 Vale, B. and Vale, R., *Planning Constraints for Autonomous Earth Sheltered Houses: The Hockerton Experience*, paper given at the Third National Earth Sheltering Conference, Coventry University, 22 September 1995.
25 Letter to the author from Tom Smerdon, 20 July 1995.
26 DoE, *Consultation Paper: Planning Policy Guidance on Transport*, Room C13/18, 2 Marsham Street, SW1, 20 April 1993, paras.2.7, 2.11.
27 Ibid., paras.2.12, 2..22(a).
28 DoE and DoT, *PPG 13: Transport*, HMSO, 1994, paras.3.2, 3.3, and 3.5.
29 Ibid., para.1.10.
30 Twenty per cent of rural households have no car, and in some areas it is as high as 36 per cent. Institute of Civil Engineers, *A Vision for Rural Transport*, ICE, 1996.
31 *Social Trends* 25, 1995, HMSO, p.202.
32 Royal Commission on Environmental Pollution, *Transport and the Environment*, Cm 2674, HMSO, 1994, para.9.22.
33 DoE and DoT, op. cit. 28, para.3.2.
34 South Somerset District Council, *Draft South Somerset Local Plan*, Policies D/H10 -12, 1995.
35 DoE and DoT, op. cit. 28, para.3.2.
36 CPRE Herefordshire Branch, op. cit. 11, p.9.
37 Illich, I., *Convivial Tools*, Fontana Collins, 1975, p.66.
38 At the *Tinker's Bubble* Appeal, the local planning authority agreed, under cross-examination, that the low input organic form of agriculture pursued generated less traffic, less pollution and less nuisance than a conventional method.
39 White Paper, op. cit. 9, p.35.

Chapter 6. Four Examples of Low Impact Development

1 West Lothian Planning, *The Lowland Crofting Handbook*, West Lothian DC., no date.
2 Cooper, A., *Lowland Crofting: Positive Planning in a Degraded Environment*, dissertation for degree in Land Economy, University of Aberdeen, April 1995, p.76.

3   Watt, M., *Crofting: A Model to Underpin Rural Planning Policy in Scotland*, dissertation for the Diploma in Town Planning, Edinburgh College of Art/Heriot Watt University, School of Planning and Housing, April 1995, p.94.

4   Ibid., p.94.

5   West Lothian Planning, op. cit. 1, pp.1 and 7.

6   Ibid., p.25.

7   Information from Peter Carpenter, British Earth Sheltering Association, Caer Llan Berm House, Lydart, Monmouth, Gwent.

8   *Wordsworth Trust* Appeal decision, Planning Inspectorate, Bristol, application number 7/90/5209, 27 February, 1991.

9   Dames and Moore, *Underground Space in Britain*, DoE, 1982; reviewed in *The Planner*, November 1982.

10 *Avoncliff Square* Appeal decision; see Appendix F.

11 Carpenter, P. *An Introduction to Earth Sheltered Development in England and Wales*, The School of the Built Environment, Coventry University, 1994.

12 *Avoncliff*, op.cit. 10.

13 Newark and Sherwood District Council, Planning Committee Meeting, 10 May 1994, Agenda Item D6, Application FUL/940113.

14 Nicholson Lord, 'Eco-Pioneers Go Underground to Help Family Life', *Independent on Sunday*, 8 January, 1995.

15 Newark and Sherwood District Council, op. cit. 13.

16 Interview with Nick Martin, 30 October 1995.

17 Mollison, B., *Permaculture: A Practical Guide for Sustainable Living*, Island Press, Washington DC, 1990.

18 Dixon, C., 'A Proposed Permaculture Project at Tir Penrhos Isaf' in *Tir Penrhos Isaf Planning Documents*; see Appendix F.

19 'If goods (for example materials or seeds) or services are required that cannot be produced on site, they are searched for first within the very local community. If not obtainable there the search then moves out to neighbouring communities. Next would be the wider [market town] area and only if proved unobtainable at this level would the buying in from other areas be considered. It is the action of searching that will generate the work locally which in turn keeps money and investment circulating at a local level'. Dixon, C., 'Draft Criteria for Assessing the Viability of Permaculture (Sustainable) Holdings', in *Tir Penrhos Planning Documents*, ibid.

20 Planning Officer's Report on Tir Penrhos Isaf, 1991.

21 Cited in Hopkins, R., *Permaculture: A New Approach for Rural Planning? An Investigation of the Reasons for the Success/Failure of UK Rural Permaculture Projects in Obtaining Panning Permission*, BSc Hons Environmental Quality and Resource Management, University of the West of England, 8 May 1996.

22 Dixon, C., interview with author, December 13 1995.

23 DoE and Welsh Office., *PPG. 7*, E.13, 1992.

24 *Hill House Road, Tinkers Bubble* and *Kings Hill*; see Appendix F.

25 *Town and and Country Planning Act 1990* para 183; amended in the *Planning and Compensation Act 1991*, see DoE, Circular 21/91, Annex 3.

26 DoE, *Circular 1/94*, 27.

27 *Higher Rockes* Appeal decision; see Appendix F.

28 In May 1996, the Welsh Secretary allowed that residential use was lawful on some of the land applied for, but not all of it. *Planning and Compensation Act 1991*, Part I, Sections 4 and 10; Oubridge, B., 'The Village: Part Two', *Built Environment Network* 5, Green Party, Spring 1994.

29 Gummer, J. Speech at Conservative Party Conference, October 1995.

30 Hannis, M., *Proof of Evidence, King's Hill* Appeal, 1995, p.1; see Appendix F.

31 Ibid., p.1.

32 Bower, K., 'Country Living with a Difference', *Fosse Way Magazine*, 27 October 1995.

33 Mendip District Council, Planning Committee Meeting, 2 August 1994.

34 Hannis, op. cit. 30, Appendix 11.

35 Ibid., p.10.

36 DoE, *Circular 1/94*, para.20.
37 *King's Hill* Appeal, Inspector's Report, pp.20-21; see Appendix F.

Chapter 7. Five Visions of Low Impact

1   Friends, Families and Travellers Support Group (FFT), *Draft Planning Policy: Sites for Nomadic People*, 1995, p.2.
2   Figures from Tony Thompson, Community Architecture Group, 33 North Road, Wells, Somerset.
3   Clements, L.,'Gypsies Face a New Age', *The Times*, 11 January, 1994.
4   Beale, A, and Geary, R., writing in *Solicitors Journal*, 11 Feb 1994; Clements, L., ibid.
5   *Criminal Justice and Public Order Act 1994*, Sections 77 to 80.
6   North Country Travellers Association, *Consultation — Planning Guidance on Gypsy Sites*, 1994.
7   Todd, D. and Clark, G., *Gypsy Site Provision and Policy*, DoE Research Report, 1991, HMSO, p.12.
8   Criminal Justice Bill, second reading in the House of Lords, 25 April 1994.
9   East Anglian Gypsy Council et.al., *Alternative Proposals for the Constructive Reform of the 1968 Caravan Sites Act*, Second Edition, 1994.
10 Elliott, D., 'Lessons of Land Settlement' in Girardet, H. (ed.) *Land for the People*, Crescent Books, 1976.
11 FFT., op. cit. 1.
12 Duncan, S. and Rowe, A., *Self Help: The World's Hidden Housing Arm*, Centre for Urban and Regional Research, Sussex University, August 1992.
13 Walter Segal Self-Build Trust, *Working with Self-Build Housing Groups: The Powers of Local Authorities*, 1995.
14 Bailey, R., *Homelessness: What Can be Done*, Jon Carpenter, 1994.
15 Walter Segal Self-Build Trust, *Out of the Woods: Ecological Designs for Timber Frame Housing*, 1994.
16 Letters to the author from Steve Walsh, 27 July 1995, and Mike Fisher, 17 July 1995.
17 Walter Segal Self-Build Trust, op. cit.13.
18 Ward, C., 'Self Help and Sustainability', *Town and Country Planning*, June 1994. See also Hardy, D., and Ward, C., *Arcadia for All: The Legacy of a Makeshift Landscape*, Mansell, 1984.
19 Letter to the author from Sue Clifford, 8 August 1995. For an appraisal of Scottish plotlands see Fielding, M., 'Hut Culture', *Reforesting Scotland* 14, Spring 1996.
20 Gunasena, M., and O'Connor, P., 'Holtsfield — A Community under Threat', *Squall* 11, Autumn 1995.
21 Kennedy, M., 'Time Running Out for "Arcadian" Woodland Chalet Community', *The Independent*, 30 August 1995.
22 Gunasena, M., and O'Connor, P., op. cit. 20.
23 *Perspectives on Architecture*, September 1995.
24 Kennedy, M., op. cit. 21.
25 DoE, *Circular 1/85: The Use of Conditions in Planning Permissions*, para.87. This has recently been revised and reissued as Circular 11/95, but the original paragraph on seasonal use (now para.115) remains unchanged. This paragraph also authorizes the absurd situation whereby high-impact caravan sites of 100 units or more are permitted to scar the countryside year round on the condition that they remain empty for eight months of the year.
26 Ward, C., *Talking Houses*, Chapter 1, Freedom Press, 1990.
27 Ward, C., op. cit. 18.
28 Letter of objection from A. Manning to the *Tinkers Bubble* Appeal, see Appendix F.
29 Prebble, J., *The Highland Clearances*, Penguin 1969.
30 Quoted in Hunter, J., *Skye: the Island*. Mainstream, Edinburgh, 1986, pp.115-116.
31 McIntosh, A., Wightman, A. and Morgan, D., 'Reclaiming The Scottish Highlands: Clearance, Conflict and Crofting', *The Ecologist*, Vol 24 No. 2, March/April 1994 p.68.
32 Watt, M., op. cit. Chapter 7 ref. 3, p.37; citing Hunter J., *The Claim of Crofting, the*

Scottish Highlands and Islands, 1930-1990, Mainstream Publishing, 1991.

33 Ross, D., 'Crofting Only a Little Earner', *The Scotsman*, 9 November 1989, cited in Watt, ibid.

34 West Lothian Planning, *Lowland Crofting Handbook*, West Lothian District Council, no date.

35 Scottish Green Party, *A Rural Manifesto for the Highlands: Creating the Second Great Wood of Caledonia*, 1989. pp.11 and 16.

36 McIntosh, A. et al., op. cit. 31.

37 Reforesting Scotland, Norway and Scotland; a Study in Land Use, 1994.

38 McIntosh, A. et al., op. cit. 31.

39 Hill, B., 'Our Friends at the Scottish Office', *Reforesting Scotland*, Spring 1996. *Forests and People in Rural Scotland*, Rural Framework, Rural Forum, 1995.

40 Clouston, E., 'Village to Run its Own Forest', *The Guardian*, 2 December, 1995. David Campbell interviewed by Oliver Tickell, December 1995.

41 Clouston, E., 'US Cash to Aid "Rebirth" of Thriving Highland Life', *The Guardian*, 30 December 1995.

42 White Paper, *Rural England*, Cm 3016, HMSO, 1995, p.119.

43 Ibid, Summary, p.14.

44 The Forestry Industry Committee of Great Britain, *The Forestry Industry Yearbook 1993-1994*, p.20.

45 Interview with Peter Wilson, 6 March 1996.

46 Pitts, J., 'Community Forest Cities of Tomorrow', *Town and Country Planning*, June 1991.

47 Kibblewhite, M., 'Green Woodwork?', *Marches Greenwood Network Newsletter*, February 1996.

48 Letter to the author from Hugh Ross, 14 September 1995.

49 *Sustainable Forestry: The UK Programme*, HMSO, 1994, p.11.

50 Barton, H., Davis, G., and Guise, R., *Sustainable Settlements: A Guide for Planners, Designers and Developers*, University of the West of England and the Local Government Management Board, 1995, p.96.

51 Letter to the author from Graham Bond, Stroud Sustainable Village Project, 4 October, 1995.

52 See, for example, Breheny, M., and Rookwood, R.,'Planning the Sustainable City Region', in Blowers, A. (ed.), *Planning for a Sustainable Environment*, TCPA report, Earthscan, 1993, pp.173-178.

53 Dauncey, G., 'Eco-Community Design', *In Context*, Canada, No 35, 1993. Updated 1995: Project Manager Scott Andrews, South Island Development Corporation, 749 Yates St, Victoria, BC, V8W 1L6, Canada.

54 'Countryside Campaign Hammers Home New Settlement Objection', *Planning* 1148, 8 December 1995, p.5.

55 McLaren, D., *Counter-Urbanization: How Do We Achieve a Trend Breach?*, Friends of the Earth Trust, no date.

56 Commission of the European Communities, *Green Paper on the Urban Environment*, Brussels, CEC, 1990.

57 McLaren, D., op. cit. 55.

58 Ward, C., 'The Do It Yourself New Town', in *Talking Houses: Ten Lectures*, Freedom Press, London, 1990.

59 *Planning* 1148, op. cit. 54.

60 Edwards, B., 'Going Dutch', *Planning Week*, 20 April 1995.

Chapter 8. The Tools for the Job

1 Cited in Carpenter, P. *An Introduction to Earth Sheltered Development in England and Wales*, The School of the Built Environment, Coventry University, 1994.

2 Moore, V., *A Practical Approach to Planning Law*, Blackstone, 1994.

3 *Tinker's Bubble* Appeal decision; see appendix F.

4 Carpenter, P., op. cit. 1, p.57.

5 *Poundstretcher Ltd, Harris Queensway PLC v Secretary of State for the Environment and*

Liverpool City Council, Queen's Bench Division, Mr. David Widdicombe QC (deputy judge), 10 June 1988.

6   Interview with Steve Briggs of South Somerset District Council, October 1995.

7   For example *Par* Appeal decision; see Appendix F.

8   DoE and Welsh Office, *PPG 7*, 1992, para.E.13.

9   DoE, *PPG 3 Housing*, 1992, para.43.

10 Letter to the author from James Clarke, 19 July 1995.

11 Eg. *Avoncliff* Appeal decision, Condition vii; see Appendix F.

12 DoE, *Circular 11/95*, paras.27 and B.6.

13 Ibid., paras.A.73-74.

14 Clouston, E., 'No Car Pledge for New Homes', *The Guardian*, 1 September 1995.

15 West Lothian Planning, *Lowland Crofting Handbook*, West Lothian DC, no date, p.33.

16 DoE, *Circular 11/95*, paras.B.9 and A.33.

17 Letter from Cllr Janet Repton to the Planning Inspectorate, 28 August 1994.

18 DoE, *Circular 16/91*, para.B.8.

19 Moore, V., op. cit. 2, p.266.

20 Eve, G., *Use of Planning Agreements*, DoE Research Report, HMSO, 1992.

21 DoE, *Planning Obligations: Draft Revision of DoE Circular 16/91*, January 1996, para.13.

22 Eve, G., op. cit. 20, Appendix G.

23 DoE, op. cit. 21, para.10.

24 DoE, *Circular 16/91*, para.B.8.

25 Section 50 Town and Country Planning (Scotland) Act 1972: Minute of Agreement between The West Lothian District Council and New Lives New Landscapes, no date.

26 Newark and Sherwood District Council, Planning Committee 10 May 1994, Agenda Item D6, Application FUL/940113.

27 *Tinker's Bubble* Appeal, Inspector's Recommendation, para.17; see Appendix F.

28 DoE, *Circular 28/92*, para.A.4.

29 Monbiot, G., *A Charter for the Countryside*, The Land is Ours, 1995, p.6.

30 Moore, V., op. cit. 2, p.33.

31 DoE and Welsh Office, *PPG 5: Simplified Planning Zones*, HMSO, 1992, paras.A.1 and A.5.

32 Cullingworth, J. and Nadin, V., *Town and Country Planning in Britain*, Routledge, 1994, p.73.

33 In June 1996, squatters occupying Gargoyle Wharf, a derelict site of 13 acres in Wandsworth, South London, made an applicationfor just such an SPZ. Copies of the application are available from The Land is Ours, East Oxford Community Centre, Princes Street, Oxford OX4 1DD.

34 The Community Council of Devon, Designed Visions and Devon County Council, *Developing Sustainable Communities: A Field Worker's Manual, Part One*, 1995, pp.33-34.

35 Hopkins, R., op.cit. Chapter 7, ref.21.

36 Tiffin, R., 'Weighing Anchor Roles in Town Centre Futures', *Planning*, 1160, 15 March 1966, p.22.

Chapter 9. The Legacy of a Makeshift Landscape

1   Quotes respectively from Geoffrey Moorhouse, *New Society*, 17 July 1969; Tyldesley Jones, South Down Preservation Bill Proceedings, House of Lords 1934; Thomas Sharp, *Town and Countryside*, 1932; Howard Marshal in *Britain and the Beast*, edited by Clough Williams Ellis, 1938; Ian Nairn and Nicholas Pevsner, *Sussex*, 1965; and S. B. Mais also in *Britain and the Beast*.

2   Darby, A. and Hamilton, G., *England Ugliness and Noise*, 1930; Mais, S. B., *op cit* 1; Abercrombie, P., *The Preservation of Rural England*, 1926; Dougill, W., *The English Coast: Its Development and Preservation*, CPRE, 1936.

3   Steers J,A., *Coastal Preservation and Planning*, 1944, public record office file HLG/92/80 and 81.

Chapter 10. Low Impact Development in the UK, 1996–2008

1 See pages 60 and 103.
2 See, for example, Woolley, T., *Natural Building: A Guide to Materials and Techniques*, The Crowood Press, 2006; or the photo collection at http://www.lammas.org.uk/lowimpact/gallery.htm
3 Rudofsky, B., *Architecture Without Architects*, University of New Mexico Press, 1964
4 Rosen, N., *How to Live Off Grid: Journeys Outside the System*, Doubleday 2007.
5 Weaver M, 'Planning System to be Fairer and Faster', in *Society Guardian*, December 12 2001, http://www.guardian.co.uk/society/2001/dec/12/communities.localgovernment
6 Chapter7 and the PPG7 Reform group, *Sustainable Homes and Livelihoods on the Countryside*, Chapter 7, 2003.
7 *Petter and Harris* v *Secretary of State and Chichester District Council*, 15 March 1999.
8 The Office of Fair Trading has recently highlighted the lack of opportunities for self-builders, observing that a third of all submissions to its consultation on the homebuilding industry were from people who wanted to see more self building. *Homebuilding Market Study*, Office of Fair Trading, September 2008/.
9 For more information on these policies, see Chapter 7 et al, op cit 6.
10 For example Ben Laws' first house in West Sussex, Pentiddy Wood in Cornwall, and both Tinker's Bubble and the Trading Post House in S Somerset.
11 Chapter 7, *DIY Planning Briefings*, Chapter 7, 3rd edition 2005, p 1.1.
12 Chapter 7 et al, op cit 6.
13 This judgment does not apply to Department of Transport public inquiries held in the 1980s and 1990s.
14 Op cit 7.
15 University of the West of England and Land Use Consultants, *Low Impact Development — Planning Policy and Practice*, Countryside Council for Wales, 2002. Available at www.tlio.org.uk
16 Ibid, paras 9.64 and 9.65.
17 Baker Associates, *Low Impact Development — Further Research*, Pembs Coast National Park, Feb 2004.
18 A ruling that appears to be peculiar to Wales, introduced in 2007,
19 I.e. applications that are made before moving onto the land.
20 *Planning Policy Changes to Support Sustainable Development in Rural Areas: Meeting Housing Needs*, Welsh Assembly consultation paper, July 2008.
21 *NPPG15 Rural Development*, Scottish Office 1999, and *NPPG 3 Planning for Housing*, Scottish Executive Development Department, 2002.
22 *SPP15, Planning For Rural Development*, Scottish Executive Development Department 2005; and *SPP3, Planning for Homes*, Scottish Government, 2008.

Index